Thailand's Crisis and the Fight for Democracy

Giles Ji Ungpakorn

Thailand's Crisis and the Fight for Democracy

Giles Ji Ungpakorn

ISBN 978-0-9565145-0-9

Published by WDPress
First edition 2010

The publication of this book was funded from individual donations made by Red Shirts in Germany, Australia, Britain, Sweden and Canada
To contact the author: ji.ungpakorn@gmail.com

Contents

Introduction

This book is my latest work concerning the on-going political crisis that has engulfed Thailand since the coup of 2006. It was written and assembled in Britain, where I am living in exile. A prominent academic who studies Thailand recently asked me if I ever regretted writing my previous book, *A Coup for the Rich*, which landed me with lèse majesté charges. I can say with all honesty that I do not regret standing up to the conservative anti-democratic forces which seek to put Thai society under dictatorship once again. It is only through writing a sharp critique of Thai politics in an open and honest manner that I can feel that I have lived up to my principles and that is important for my human dignity. Of course, such actions come at a personal cost. It was not easy to leave behind an academic career, a beautiful home and many good friends. One year before I wrote this introduction I was sitting in a warm sea on the East coast of Thailand, drinking a cold beer. Today, I look out on a foggy, cold December morning in Britain.

This book is a culmination of over twenty years of trying to apply a Marxist method to the study of Thai politics and history. What makes the Marxist dialectical method unique is the insistence on studying the whole picture of interactions between conflicting actors. Far too often Thai politics is merely explained by the actions of the elites or by stereotypical references to a monolithic "Thai Culture". The use of a class analysis is key to understanding the twists and turns of Thai politics and the development of a society under capitalism for the past century. It is a society of continuous conflict and it is important to identify the underlying fundamentals and the various detailed factors which then further shape and distort this conflict. Marxism also demands honesty. Without honesty we cannot change the World by the actions of the majority, we can only fool people and use coercion. When living in a repressive society like Thailand, it is often difficult to be brutally honest. One area which we all tried to avoid was an honest assessment of the Monarchy. This book does not avoid such an assessment since it was written from abroad.

Although I have tried to be factually correct and to use an objective analysis, I would never claim to be a neutral observer. Neutral observers either lie about their neutrality or write banal accounts. I am a socialist and a Red Shirt. I believe in Democracy and I want to see a republic in Thailand. I welcome debate and reasoned arguments against my views, which can only help to improve our understanding of the World.

This book analyses the nature of the deep political divisions between the "Red Shirts" and the royalist "Yellow Shirts", starting from the creation of the *Peoples Alliance for Democracy* (PAD), through the 2006 military coup and up to the present. It argues against the idea that the Red Shirts are merely tools of former Prime Minister Taksin and that somehow Taksin is anti-Monarchy and that this was the root cause of the 2006 coup. In trying to understand the political crisis, it must be seen in its entirety, including elite divisions and disputes, but also the roles of Civil Society activists, NGOs and the constantly developing social movements which are made up of ordinary people.

The first chapter argues that Taksin's pro-poor policies and repeated election victories threatened the entrenched interests of the conservative ruling elites, including the military, the civilian bureaucracy and the political establishment. Although Taksin was no socialist and had no plan to build his political party into an activist movement, his overthrow by the military in 2006 sparked the building of a self-organised Red Shirt movement. To some extent this movement has moved beyond Taksin's control, some sections becoming radical and republican.

The second chapter deals with the politics of the Peoples Movement and analyses how major sections of this movement, which include the NGOs, came to side with the royalist authoritarians against the majority of the poor and the democratic system as a whole. The explanation lies in the post-Cold War politics of the NGOs. The chapter also questions mainstream democratisation theory and critiques previous views about NGOs in the light of Thai events. This chapter discusses the extreme right-wing PAD movement which closed the international airports in late 2008. There is also a discussion of the labour movement.

The third chapter discusses the difficult issue of the Thai Monarchy. I have been struggling with an analysis of the Monarchy for many years and have held mistaken views in the past. Hopefully, this chapter will be a vast improvement on my previous writings. Unlike most academic commentators, I argue that the King is weak and lacking in character. His key role is ideological, the justification for elite rule and elite power. He symbolises the "legitimacy" of coups and anti-democratic actions, especially those carried out by the military. The 2006 coup and the King's old age and ill health have resulted in a crisis for the royalists. Once again there is a growing republican movement in Thailand today. The chapter also discusses the draconian lèse majesté law which the elites use against their political opponents.

The fourth chapter gives an historical background to Thai politics from the pre-capitalist era, through the turmoil of the 1930s and 1970s, up to the present day. This historical understanding is important in locating the dynamics of the ruling class and the changing politics of revolt from the time of the Communist Party through to the creation of the NGOs. The rise of Taksin's *Thai Rak Thai* cannot be understood without such an historical background.

The civil war in the Muslim Malay south is discussed in chapter 5. I argue that the fundamental issue is Thai state repression and until this is dealt with politically, there can be no long term peace. Yet mainstream policy in Thailand is still aimed at a military solution.

The final chapter deals with my personal political experiences and memories of my father, Dr Puey Ungpakorn. It might seem to be an egotistical self indulgence to write this personal note. I hope that it is not, and that the chapter helps people understand what shaped my political views and actions. This chapter has the English version of the *Red Siam Manifesto*, which I issued immediately after leaving Thailand in February 2009. It also contains an appendix with the 8 paragraphs from my previous book, *A Coup for the Rich*, which the Thai police deemed to be lèse majesté.

The spellings of Thai names in this book do not conform with spellings used in many other publications. This is so that readers will be able to make the correct pronunciations of Thai names. Mainstream spellings are based on a ridiculous system which writes names as though they were written in Sanskrit or written so that linguists would know the roots of the words. Under the official system the resort island of "Pu-ket" is written as "Phuket", often pronounced "Fuck it", much to the amusement of tourists, and the famous Thai beer "Sing" has a "ha" artificially attached to the end of the name. Similarly ex-Prime Minister Taksin is called "Thaksin", as in "Thatcher".

December 2009

Chapter 1
The Red-Yellow Class Struggle for Democracy

The political crisis and unrest which we have seen in Thailand since the 19th September 2006 military coup against the elected Taksin Government, represents a serious class war between the rich conservative elites (royalist "Yellow Shirts") and the urban and rural poor (pro-democracy "Red Shirts"). It is not a pure class war and those taking part have different aims and different concepts of Democracy. Due to a vacuum on the Left since the collapse of the *Communist Party of Thailand* (CPT), millionaire and populist politician, Taksin Shinawat and his *Thai Rak Thai Party* (TRT), managed to inspire millions of ordinary Thais and more recently have provided leadership to the Red Shirts. This class war has turned Thailand upside down and raised important political questions about the roles of many institutions. This period in Thai history represents a return to open social divisions which last appeared in the 1970s, when the mass of the population fought for Democracy against the military and the struggle became transformed into a fight for Social Justice under the leadership of the CPT[1].

---

[1] There are those in the academic world who fail to grasp the dimensions of this class struggle. Niti Eawsriwong argued in late 2009 that both sides were merely "nominees" of the divided ruling class. He called for people to reinvigorate anarchist style single-issue campaigning instead of getting involved with Reds or Yellows. *Matichon* 23/11/2009 (In Thai).

The underlying reasons for the conflict between the conservative royalists and Taksin

Despite the fact that many commentators try to explain the conflict that led to the 2006 military coup in terms of "the old feudal order" fighting back against "the modern capitalist class"[2], this is not what the conflict is really about.

Both Taksin and his conservative opponents are royalists. They are both royalists in modern terms, in that both sides seek to use the institution of the Monarchy in order to help support capitalist class rule. Feudalism was abolished in Thailand in the 1870s and since then Capitalism has dominated all aspects of society. This is no different from the fact that the modern capitalist ruling classes in Britain, Western Europe or Japan seek to use their Monarchies to stabilise the status quo. Taksin has always maintained his loyalty to the Throne. His TRT Government was just as enthusiastic as any other in its promotion of the King. Yet after the coup, he lost out to the conservatives in being able to claim the royalist mantle.

The real dispute between Taksin and his opponents was neither automatic nor inevitable. In the early years of his Government, he received wide spread support from all section of the elite. What gradually turned the conservatives against him was their fear that they would lose their privileges in the face of Taksin's widespread modernisation programme.

This modernisation programme involved such things as undermining local political mafia, illegal activities like gambling and the monopoly of the black market in the South by the armed forces. Taksin tried to upgrade the role of the police in providing Government security in the South. The power of Taksin's political machine came from the fact that TRT could win the hearts and minds of the electorate through genuine pro-poor policies. Taksin also built his popularity on the clever use of a combination of Government spending and the free market, in order to revive the economy at grass roots level after the 1997 recession. This political power was thus based upon the democratic process and backed up

[2] See Chapter 3.

by Taksin's wealth as a successful businessman. He used this power to try to consolidate the Prime Minister's control over the army and the bureaucracy. Despite cries of "nepotism" from some people, his attempt to control the army and the bureaucracy, as an elected Prime Minister, were quite legitimate in democratic terms. Local political bosses found that their use of gangsters, illegal activities and money politics was being undercut by TRT's direct links to the electorate through real policies. Many illegal underground activities were legalised and brought into the open. The Government waged a vicious war against small time drug dealers. Many politicians faced the choice of either joining TRT or sinking into electoral oblivion.

What frightened the conservatives was that Taksin had firm mass support from the electorate. Conservative ideas could not challenge this strong political base at the polls. That is why they eventually turned to using a military coup.

Previous to this, mainstream parties, including the *Democrats*, had not relied on any policies to win votes. Taksin was threatening the old networks of money politics, which had resulted in weak political parties, governing the country in corrupt and unstable coalition Governments. Taksin upset the apple cart by proving that the electorate were responsive to genuine pro-poor policies. Previously, politicians and the elites had just assumed that they could enrich themselves while ignoring the majority of citizens. Governments in the past had just "muddled along" making sure that they maintained the self-interests of the elites. Workers and farmers were simply regarded as the "ignorant poor". A good example was the policies pursued by the *New Aspirations* and *Democrat Party* Governments after the 1997 economic crisis. These Governments used massive amounts of public funds, raised by taxing the poor, to prop up the banks and finance companies. They turned their backs on the general population. The unemployed were told to "go back to their villages" and depend on their already poor relatives. Those in work were expected to take pay cuts. The elites had always behaved like that and assumed that they could carry on doing so. The elites had also ignored the crying need to develop

Thailand's chaotic transport and communications infrastructure and to improve health care and education for the majority. Taksin and TRT saw these tasks as central to improving the efficiency of the economy.

Taksin also saw the poor as stakeholders in society and partners in development, while the conservatives saw the poor as either people to be exploited or as a burden on society. Taksin was not a socialist. Nor was he a principled democrat or advocate of human rights. His vision was to build a modernised society where the state and big business could incorporate the majority of the population in development. He looked to countries like Singapore for inspiration. Taksin's model was not incompatible with being a royalist and maintaining the Monarchy. It just meant that the Monarchy would be used to protect and legitimise a modern, class divided, status quo.

Kevin Hewsion has shown that Taksin's initial aim in introducing pro-poor policies was to buy social peace in post crisis Thailand[3]. This explains why the majority of the business class backed Taksin in the early days. But six years on, when that social peace started to unravel with the mass protests led by the right-wing *Peoples Alliance for Democracy* (PAD), Taksin's business supporters dropped away. They were also unhappy that he seemed to have monopolised the rich business pickings and excluded many of them.

Class war

Neither the modern royalists, represented by Taksin and TRT, nor the conservative royalists, who organised and supported the coup, intended their dispute to turn into a class war. Taksin does not wish to lead a mass pro-democracy movement which is starting to question the entire elite structure, including the Monarchy. Instead, it is the arrogant attitude of the conservative royalists and the prolonged nature of the crisis, plus the self organisation of millions of Red Shirts at grass roots level, which has

[3] Kevin Hewison (2003) Crafting a new social contract: Domestic capitalist responses to the challenge of neoliberalism. In Ji Giles Ungpakorn (ed.) *Radicalising Thailand: new political perspectives*. Institute of Asian Studies, Chulalongkorn University.

transformed the crisis into a class war. This war is bringing about changes in political attitudes and putting all sections of society to the test.

Important changes in political attitudes

It was always an exaggeration to claim that "*all Thais revere the King*" or that "*the Monarchy has held the country together*". Statements like that glossed over the level of coercion surrounding public attitudes to the Monarchy and the serious lack of power, courage and character shown by this King throughout his reign. Never the less, there was a short period of 20 years after the collapse of the CPT in the mid 1980s when the Monarchy was very popular. This was more to do with the weakness of any opposition and the level of promotion that the institution received, rather than any "ancient or natural" love for the King among Thais. Yet, it was enough to convince most Thais that Monarchism was "deeply embedded in society".

The present crisis has shattered all these illusions. Since the coup, the royalists have been promoting the King's "Sufficiency Economy" ideology, which argues against redistribution of wealth. At the same time the majority of the population understand that the King is fabulously rich and that the Sufficiency Economy does not work for them.

Some commentators, who ought to know better, however, insisted on supporting illusions about the Monarchy. Benjamin Zawacki, South-east Asia researcher for *Amnesty International*, making a disgraceful comment on an 18 year jail sentence given to a Red Shirt activist for making a speech against the Monarchy, said that "*you have an institution here (the Monarchy) that has played an important role in the protection of human rights in Thailand. We can see why the monarchy needs to be protected*" (by the lèse majesté law)[4]. There is absolutely no evidence that the King has ever protected human rights. In fact, the opposite is true. Just look at what happened on 6th October 1976. The *Amnesty*

[4] Marwaan Macan-Markar (2009) THAILAND: lèse majesté Law Tests Mettle of Human Rights Groups. http://www.ipsnews.net/news.asp?idnews=48272 31/8/2009.

International office in Thailand was closely associated with the royalists. Annegret Meiners, the Laos / Thailand Coordinator for AI, also stated that those who are concerned with 'lèse majesté were "all supporters of former Prime Minister Taksin Shinawat". According to Ms Meiners, any demands for the abolition of lèse majesté and that the Thai King have the same constitutional status as the British or Japanese Monarchs, would pave the way for a return of Taksin.[5] This is just the tip of the ice burg when it comes to attitudes among Non Government Organisations (NGOs). The NGOs and most academics have lined up with the military and the conservative royalists against the people.

The actions by the conservative elites have forced millions of ordinary people to reject the mainstream ideas about loyalty to the Monarchy. The taboo about criticising the Palace and the King's advisors has been broken. Millions of Red Shirts have come to realise, if they did not before, that there is no justice or freedom of expression and that the conservative elites, who have run the country for decades, do not respect the rule of law or Democracy. The courts have been exposed as merely puppets of those in power and the mainstream media has openly taken the side of the elites. This is indeed a deep rooted social crisis, exposing the nature of the elites, the liberal academics and the NGO activists.

There has been a shift in attitudes among the elites as well. In the early 1990's, after the end of the Cold War, the elites, who originally supported an authoritarian "Security State" turned to ideas of a liberal parliamentary system[6]. Since 2006, they have stepped back and are now in favour of censorship, repression and political appointees rather than free elections.

The Red Shirt movement, starting out as passive voters, who supported Taksin and TRT, have now started to organise themselves into a grass roots pro-democracy movement. They have local groups in all communities and many run their own internet activities and community

---

[5] This was stated in an e-mail which was forwarded to me by a colleague in 2009.

[6] M. K. Connors (1999) Political reform and the state in Thailand. Journal of Contemporary Asia, 29(2), 202-225. M. K. Connors (2003) *Democracy and National Identity in Thailand*. Routledge Curzon.

radio stations. They represent the re-birth of a pro-democracy Civil Society, a movement of the poor and the oppressed. But the nature and ideology of the Red Shirts is complex and contradictory, as one would expect in any grass-roots mass movement which is in the process of struggle.

Brief background to the Thai political crisis

Under the elected Taksin Government, which first came to power in 2001, Thailand had a developing Democracy with freedom of expression, a relatively free press and an active Civil Society, where social movements campaigned to protect the interests of the poor. This was not, however the work of Taksin's TRT administration, since there were serious problems of human rights abuses. Taksin's Government used murderous repression in the Muslim Malay southern provinces and killed over 3000 people in the so-called "War on Drugs"[7]. His Government also sought to control the press through the threat to withhold advertising revenue and other means. Yet, this was an elected Government, street protests were tolerated and there was not blanket censorship like under the 2009 *Democrat Party* Government.

For the first time in decades, a political party (TRT) gained mass support from the poor because it believed that the poor were not a burden. They argued that the poor should be "stake-holders" rather than surfs. These "populist" policies were developed after the 1997 Asian economic crisis and were a result of widespread consultations in society[8]. This was no socialist party, but a party of big business committed to free-market policies at a Macro and Global level, and Keynesian policies at village or grass-roots level[9]. This was called the "dual track" economic policy. It was not some wild invention of a power-crazed leader, as claimed by those who refer to these economic policies as "Taksinomics". When the party

---

[7] See Jaran Cosananund (2003) Human rights and the war on drugs: problems of conception, consciousness and social responsibility. Thailand Human Rights Journal, 1, 59-87.

[8] Pasuk Phongpaichit & Chris Baker (2004) Taksin. *The business of politics in Thailand.* Silkworm Books.

[9] Kevin Hewison (2003) already quoted.

came to power in 2001, the banks had stopped lending and there was an urgent need to stimulate the economy. Pumping Government funds into village projects throughout the country made sense. So did universal health care and increased spending on education. It represented the modernising interests of an important faction of the capitalist class.

The present political crisis started with mass demonstrations led by the mis-named *Peoples Alliance for Democracy* (PAD) in late 2005. This was after TRT's landslide re-election earlier that year. The PAD began as an "alliance from hell" between disgruntled royalist media tycoon Sonti Limtongkul and a handful of NGO and social movement leaders. They attacked Taksin's Government for corruption. But they were never interested in criticising his human rights abuses or attacking the rampant corruption of other elites, including the military. Taksin responded to the growing crisis by dissolving parliament and calling fresh elections in April 2006. The opposition, including the *Democrat Party*, boycotted these elections because they knew that they were very unpopular with the electorate. "Liberal" academics "explained" that calling fresh elections was "undemocratic". The courts then annulled the election, using the bizarre excuse that the ballot boxes were the wrong way round in the polling booths. No evidence was presented that any serious electoral fraud had ever taken place.

Later the courts were used two more times, to dissolve TRT and then the party that was reformed under a new name (*Palang Prachachon Party* or Peoples Power Party, PPP). Rather than accepting that the electorate support for Taksin was because of the Government's first ever Universal Health Care Scheme and many other genuine pro-poor measures, Taksin's opponents claimed that the poor "did not understand Democracy". The *Democrat Party*, being extreme neo-liberals, spent most of the time attacking these pro-poor policies as being a waste of Government money and against "fiscal discipline". No wonder no ordinary Thai would want to vote for them! When the *Democrats* eventually formed a Government with military backing in December 2008, they cut the universal health budget by almost a third[10].

The NGO and social movement leaders of the PAD moved sharply to the right during the enfolding crisis, becoming fanatical royalists and calling on the King to use Section 7 of the Constitution to sack Taksin's elected Government in 2006. This, the King refused to do, but the PAD demands were seen as a green light for a military coup and the military obliged in September.

On the 19th September 2006, the Thai army staged a coup toppling the elected Government of Taksin Shinawat. Soldiers sported yellow royal ribbons and the military junta claimed that they were staging the coup to protect *"Democracy with the King as the Head of State"*. They certainly were not protecting Democracy, but most Thais believed that this was indeed a "Royal Coup", even if the real power of the Throne is in question[11]. PAD leaders and military junta leaders were later seen celebrating their victory at a New Year party in January 2007. At that time, the *Democrat Party* also welcomed the coup. According to deputy leader Korn Chatikavanij, who later became Finance Minister, *"there was no constitutional"* method of getting rid of Taksin. He also said that he *"respected"* the junta for trying to establish political "stability" [12].

After the coup, the PAD descended into a fascist type of organisation. It took on ultra-royalist and ultra-nationalist politics. Its supporters wore royalist yellow shirts. It nearly caused a war with Cambodia over an ancient hill-top ruin. It built up an armed guard who wore black jackets and openly carried and used fire-arms and other weapons on the streets of Bangkok. The PAD's media outlet, *Manager Group*, organised witch hunts and encouraged violence against academics and social activists who questioned the deterioration of Democracy and questioned the use of the lèse majesté law.

At first there was no mass response against the coup by the millions of citizens who had repeatedly voted for Taksin's TRT Government. TRT had not made any effort to build its electoral supporters into activists.

[10] http://www.prachatai.com/ 24/4/2009. (In Thai).

[11] See Chapter 3.

[12] Interviews with *ABC news* 20 September 2006, *International Herald Tribune* 29 September 2006 and with *Bangkok Business Day* 22 September 2006.

The party seemed to be paralysed by the coup. But a small group of left-wing activists, who called themselves *"the 19th September Network Against the Coup"*, did stage a protest and continued to organise repeated protests. I was one of those people who protested against the coup. But we were not supporters of Taksin's TRT and were critical of his human rights abuses in the South and in the War on Drugs.

After writing a new pro-military Constitution and using the courts to dissolve Taksin's TRT party, the junta held fresh elections in 2007. This was won by the *Peoples Power Party* (PPP), a new party set up by TRT politicians. Again the election results were ignored. The conservative courts, violent protests by the PAD, including the shutting down of the international airports, plus the behind scenes activity of the army, eventually resulted in an undemocratic Government with *Democrat Party* leader Abhisit Vejjajiva as the Prime Minister in December 2008.

In the period after the 2007 elections, the Red Shirts began to evolve under the leadership of three ex-TRT politicians who had run a television programme called "Truth Today". Mass meetings of ordinary people, numbering hundreds of thousands, were held in sports stadiums in Bangkok. The movement was initially built by former TRT politicians, but it quickly evolved into a grass-roots movement with branches in most communities throughout the country. Community radio stations, websites and educational meetings were set up in order to circumvent Government censorship and control of the media. The movement politicised and activated millions of citizens and many people became more radical than the initial leaders.

Thailand took further steps backwards under the *Democrat Party* regime in 2009. The Government introduced draconian censorship and rapidly increased the use of lèse majesté and computer laws against pro-democracy activists, all in the name of "national security". They also banned legitimate street protests by the Red Shirts and created an armed paramilitary gang called the "Blue Shirts". The Blue Shirts were thought to be soldiers out of uniform. They were controlled by Government politicians such as Newin Chitchorp, from *Pumjaitai Party*, and Sutep

Teuksuban, from the *Democrats*. The reason for the creation of the Blue Shirts was that the PAD was beyond the direct control of the Government and the army, and hence there were attempts to limit its power and even to assassinate PAD leader Sonti Limtongkul in 2009.

In response to the increasing polarisation of society, in September 2009, Government Minister Satit Wongnongtoey suggested a campaign of singing the National Anthem every night at 6pm in every province, "in order to build unity". Perhaps if Satit and his elite friends had learnt to respect the democratic wishes of the majority of citizens, there would not have been such divisions in the first place.

In April 2009, for the fourth time in forty years[13], troops opened fire on pro-democracy demonstrators in Bangkok. Some months later, a tape recording of a cabinet meeting was leaked to the public. Prime Minister Abhistit was caught on tape urging the military to create a situation in which they could shoot the Red Shirt protestors[14]. Each time the army have shot unarmed protestors the aim has been the same: to protect the interests of the conservative elites who have run Thailand for the past 70 years. This time, the protestors were Red Shirts, and at least two people died and hundreds more were injured, some seriously[15].

The 19th September 2006 military coup and the policies of the junta

The major forces behind the 19th September coup were conservative groups in the military and civilian elite, disgruntled business leaders and neo-liberal intellectuals and politicians. They make up a coalition of conservative royalists. The coup was openly supported by the Monarchy and also by the NGO movement. What all these groups had in common,

[13] Previously armed troops or police fired on pro-democracy demonstrators in Bangkok in October 1973, October 1976 and May 1992. See Giles Ji Ungpakorn (2007) *A Coup for the Rich*. WDPress. For free down loads go to: http://wdpress.blog.co.uk/.

[14] Abhisit claimed the tape was a "fake". No one denies that it had been edited. But the edits did not in anyway distort what Abhisit had actually said.

[15] See Nick Nostitz's eye witness account: http://rspas.anu.edu.au/rmap/newmandala/2009/04/20/the-crushing-of-the-red-shirts/

when supporting the coup, was contempt for the poor. They believed that "too much Democracy" gave "too much" power to the poor electorate and encouraged Governments to "over-spend" on welfare. The academics and NGO activists explained that Thailand was divided between the "enlightened middle-classes who understand Democracy" and the "ignorant rural and urban poor" who voted for the "wrong type of Government". In fact, the reverse is generally the case. It is the poor who are forced to understand Democracy and Social Justice, while the so-called middle-classes are determined to hang on to their privileges by any means possible.

The military junta called itself by the long rambling name of *"The Reform Committee in the Democratic System with the Monarchy as Head of State"*. The language of the military junta should remind us of George Orwell's 1984. "Democracy" means military dictatorship and "Reform" means tearing up the 1997 Constitution, abolishing parliament, independent bodies and declaring martial law. After the coup the media was tightly controlled by the military officers placed in all offices and the critical *Midnight University* website was shut down for a while; all in the name of "Democracy". The junta were so paranoid that they insisted that its full title (above) be read out each time the media made *any* reference to it in Thai. This was to reinforce the "fact" that it was a "Royal and Democratic Coup". Yet when the junta's name was mentioned in English by the foreign media, they were asked to cut out the words concerning the Monarchy, to avoid any foreign "misunderstanding" that it might be a Royal Coup. The BBC and other foreign TV broadcasts were censored, first by shutting down all local transmissions and later by substituting advertisements whenever they mentioned Taksin or showed his picture. In January 2007, the junta summoned media bosses to threaten them with harsh measures if the reported the views of Taksin or TRT politicians[16].

General Sonti Boonyaratgalin, head of the junta which destroyed Democracy, ripped up the 1997 Constitution and the man who failed to do his duty in protecting Democracy, gave an interview in late October where he said that: *"I suspect many Thais still lack a proper understanding of*

[16] *Bangkok Post* 11/1/2007.

Democracy. The people have to understand their rights and their duties. Some have yet to learn about discipline. I think it is important to educate the people about true democratic rule"[17]. Such arrogant stupidity is typical of most leaders of Thai coups, past and present. The statement is just a dusting-off of the tired old formula that the poor are not ready for Democracy. That lie has been used by the Thai elite since 1910. In December, General Sonti admitted that he and other junta members had spent 1 billion baht of public funds, located in the military's "secret fund", on the illegal coup[18]. Surely that counts as gross corruption and abuse of public money? In November 2009 General Sonti became head of the *Matupum Party* (Motherland Party). This is a party set up by Pak Nam mafia boss Watana Asawahame who fled the country just before being found guilty of corruption.

The junta promised to remain in office for only 2 weeks and to appoint a civilian Government. They achieved this by staying in power under the new name of *"the Council for National Security"* (CNS) and by appointing a retired army officer, General Surayud Chulanon, to be Prime Minister. This illegitimate Government was installed and could be dismissed at any time by the CNS. What is astounding is that the Thai junta believed that the international community would think it was "democratic". The junta's foreign Minister stated that they would encourage the Burmese generals to take steps towards Democracy. One can only imagine the conversation between the Thai and Burmese dictators on this issue!

The junta claimed that they had appointed a "civilian" Prime Minister. Commentators rushed to praise the new Prime Minister, General Surayud, by saying that he was a "good and moral man". In fact, Surayud, while he was serving in the armed forces in 1992, was partly responsible for the blood bath against unarmed pro-Democracy demonstrators[19]. He personally led a group of 16 soldiers into the Royal Hotel which was a temporary field hospital. Here, his soldiers beat and kicked people[20].

---

[17] *The Nation* 26/ 10/2006.

[18] *Bangkok Post* 20/12/2006.

[19] See Kevin Hewison (2006) "Genral Surayud Chulanon: a man and his contradictions". Carolina Asia Center, University of North Carolina at Chapel Hill.

[20] Surayud admitted this to Thai Post 22/6/2000.(In Thai).

News reports from the BBC and CNN at the time show soldiers walking on top of those who were made to lie on the floor. Three months after the 2006 coup, on the 4th December, the King praised Prime Minister Surayud in his annual birthday speech.

It may interest readers to know that passages such as the preceding paragraph, when originally published in the book *"A Coup for the Rich"* in 2007, resulted in my prosecution by the *Democrat* Government in 2009 for lèse majesté. This why I no longer live in Thailand. Apparently, just repeating the well known fact that the King praised Surayud is deemed to be lèse majesté!

Many overseas investors were initially worried by the junta's rhetoric on the "Sufficiency Economy". In fact, the new military appointed cabinet was stuffed full of neo-liberals. The first Finance Minister, Pridiyatorn Devakul, was a man who believed in "neo-liberal fiscal discipline". He was opposed to "too much spending" on public health. After the coup the Budget Bureau cut the budget for TRT's universal health care scheme by 23% while increasing military spending by 30%[21]. Pridiyatorn also threatened to axe many good mass transit projects which could solve Bangkok's traffic jams. The conservative elites do not care much for either public health care or public transport. They can pass through traffic jams with police escorts, unlike public ambulances responding to emergencies.

The Foreign and Commerce Ministers were supporters of un-popular Free Trade Agreements and the Energy Minister was a fanatical follower of Margaret Thatcher's privatisation policies. Apart from neo-liberals, the illegitimate dictatorship Government was staffed by ancient and conservative civil servants and self-serving scientists and technocrats without any integrity or democratic principles. This collection of autocrats ensured that they would not go hungry by paying themselves fat cat salaries[22], no doubt funded out of savings made by cutting the pro-poor policies of the previous Government. Military officers (cronies of

[21] Bangkok Post 19 & 20/12/2006.

[22] The Nation 8/11/2006.

the junta) were appointed to boards of state enterprises and received multiple full-time salaries, each of which were over 20 times the minimum wage rate. Trips to Europe were organised for these military officers and their families at public expense. There was even talk that Prime Minister Surayud himself was guilty of illegally obtaining a house in Kao Yai National Park. But those who had been vocal about "Taksin's corruption", now remained silent. Perhaps their mouths were full from the new feeding frenzy at the trough.

After appointing a Government, the junta then hand-picked a so-called "Parliament". One third of this appointed Parliament came from the military and police, and mixed in with these were liberal academics and some turn-coats who used to be part of the Peoples Movement. These "Tank Liberal" academics believed that Democracy could come about by staging military coups and tearing-up constitutions. The question was: would they now burn all their Comparative Politics books and scrap all courses on "democratisation" in favour of teaching military science or tank maintenance?

The members of the military appointed parliament received monthly salaries and benefits of almost 140,000 baht while workers on the minimum wage received under 5000 baht per month and many poor farmers in villages lived on even less. These parliamentarians also often drew on multiple salaries. The Government claimed to be following the King's philosophy of "Sufficiency" and the importance of not being greedy. Apparently everyone must be content with their own level of Sufficiency, but as Orwell might have put it, some are more "Sufficient" than others. For the Monarchy, "Sufficiency" meant owning a string of palaces and large capitalist conglomerates like the Siam Commercial Bank. For the military junta it meant receiving multiple fat cat salaries and for a poor farmer it meant scratching a living without modern investment in agriculture. In addition to all this, the junta closed the Taksin Government's Poverty Reduction Centre, transferring it to the office of the Internal Security Operations Command and transforming it into a rural development agency using Sufficiency Economics[23].

In December 2006, the junta, working hand in hand with state university bosses, who it had already appointed to the military legislative parliament, decided to push forward a bill to privatise state universities. The official title was "university autonomy", but the process involved the usual introduction of market forces, reduced state support and neo-liberal style management[24]. University privatisation is very unpopular among staff and students for good reasons. Student protests erupted and links were quickly made between privatisation, Neo-Liberalism and authoritarianism. Previous attempts at privatisation of universities and state enterprises by elected Governments had been stalled by opposition on campuses, workplaces and in the streets. This time the military Government and university authorities could ignore public opinion. The management of mainstream universities like *Chulalongkorn* gave orders that students "should not involve themselves in politics". This was where I taught political science and it was *Chulalongkorn University* that gave my book to the Special Branch Police so that they could charge me with lèse majesté.

The junta's version of immediate "political reform" was to tear up the 1997 Constitution and replace it with a "temporary constitution". The latter was a worthless piece of scrap paper which basically said that anything the junta decreed must be law. There were no guarantees of any basic rights. The military then started the process of hand-picking their cronies and toadies to form a so-called "Constitution Drafting Committee". The process of drafting a new military constitution was in stark contrast with the mass participation associated with the 1997 Constitution.

Despite being a good charter, some of the problems with the 1997 Constitution stemmed from a reliance on elitist liberal academics at the stage of writing. One such academic was Bawornsak Uwanno, who was

---

[23] *Bangkok Post* 4/1/2007.

[24] For an international perspective see Alex Callinicos (2006) *Universities in a neo-liberal world*. Bookmarks, London.

appointed to the junta's parliament after the coup. Previously, after having a hand in drawing up the 1997 Constitution, he went to work as a loyal servant of the Taksin Government. Later, as things did not look so well, he abandoned the sinking TRT ship and became a legal advisor to the junta. Middle-class intellectuals like Bawornsak certainly understand how to manipulate Democracy and survive!!

On the issue of the southern violence, given that the army and the police were the main cause of the problem, it was doubtful whether a military junta was in a position to bring peace and justice. The army and police have long been accused of extra-judicial killings and the Fourth Army was directly responsible for the massacres at *Krue-sa* in April 2004 and at *Takbai* in October 2004, during the Taksin Government. In November 2006 the Prime Minister, General Surayud, "apologised" for the actions of the previous Government and said that all charges *against the demonstrators* at *Takbai* would be dropped. However, he made no mention of bringing the army and police commanders to court on charges of murder!

The policies of the military junta can be summarised as "anti-Taksin, anti-democratic, pro-security, neo-liberal and royalist". But they soon found out that staging a coup was much easier than actually running the country and winning the hearts and minds of the population. The record of the Surayud military Government consisted of merely drawing up a military Constitution. There were no new policy initiatives and nothing else to show for their one year in power.

The new military sponsored Constitution of 2007

The military should never be put in charge of over-seeing the drafting of any Constitution. To promote such a role for the military is to support a greater social and political role for the army along the lines of the discredited *"dwifungsi"* (dual function) of the Indonesian Suharto dictatorship.

In January 2007 the junta's Constitutional Drafting Council was appointed. Nearly half the 100 members were Government officials or conservative politicians, 20% were business people and the rest were conservative academics and media people. There was not a single genuine representative from the social movements, trade unions or NGOs. Yet Suriyasai Katasila, from the PAD, was quoted in the *Bangkok Post* as being "optimistic" since various sections of society were "evenly represented" in the Council[25]. Obviously for the PAD, the working class and peasantry (80% of the population) are not an important part of society.

Later a referendum was held to approve this military Constitution. Many provinces were still under martial law at the time, campaigning for a "no" vote in the referendum was deemed to be illegal, and full page advertisements in the press urged people to vote "yes". The referendum result was extremely close, a small majority being in favour. Half the NGOs, the whole of the PAD, most academics, the main stream media and the *Democrat Party* all supported the new Constitution. Many sceptics voted to pass the Constitution, hoping that elections could be held quickly and that a future elected Government would amend or scrap the military Constitution.

Comparing the 1997 Constitution with the 2007 military Constitution

The 1997 Constitution was drawn up in a special process of mass popular participation. This was a result of the uprising against the military back in 1992. It was also a result of the political turmoil resulting from the 1997 economic crisis. Despite social movement and NGO involvement, the Constitution reflected mainstream liberal ideas due to the weakness of ideology among the Peoples Movement. Interesting features of the Constitution, some of which were progressive and some of which were regressive, included:

---

[25] *Bangkok Post* 3/1/2007.

1. The creation of so-called "Independent Bodies" such as the Human Rights Commission, the Electoral Commission and the National Counter-Corruption Commission. In one sense, this was a step forward, but it also sowed illusions in the idea that middle-class professionals who staffed these bodies could somehow be "independent".
2. The creation for the first time of a fully elected Senate, although political parties were banned from standing candidates and candidates were prevented from electioneering or talking about politics. The ludicrous idea was that the Senate would be populated by experienced, "non-political", worthies[26]. Yet this was also a step forward because it expanded the principle of elections for public bodies.
3. The introduction of a Party List voting system, along proportional representation lines, which gave more seats to big parties. The proportion system was designed to create stable Governments, not to increase representation of marginalised groups, like in other proportional voting systems.
4. Measures to impeach politicians. This was a step forward, but impossible to implement in practice.
5. Paper commitment to human rights, community rights and non-discriminatory practices for the first time. This was a step forward, if only by creating "standards" that people could quote in their struggles. Such rights were never voluntarily enforced or respected by Governments.
6. Elected local Government rather than central Government appointed local officers, which was a step forward.
7. A clause affirming the right of all citizens to resist a military coup! Impossible to enforce, but very symbolic.
8. Reactionary clauses stating that MPs/Senators must have

[26] My brother, Jon, who became an elected senator, was banned from wearing a red AIDS ribbon on his election poster. This was deemed to be "political". But the wearing military uniforms was not banned.

university degrees. The idea was that the educated middle-classes would make more honest politicians!! Apart from this, there was no change in the voters' lists, which meant that workers had to go back and vote in rural areas, despite the fact that they lived and worked in the city. This diluted the working class vote.

9. Free market policies were enshrined. This might have the effect of preventing any debate and democratic choice over economic policy, but it was never put to the test.

In contrast, the military Constitution of 2007 did not involve popular participation in its creation. The junta's constitution was born out of the barrel of a gun, from an illegitimate military coup and drawn up by a handful of people appointed by the junta. The 2007 constitution is a constitution of the military, the elites and big business, all of whom have no real belief in Democracy. Contrary to the claims by the PAD and important sections of the NGO movement, no significant improvement was made when compared to the 1997 Constitution. In fact, the opposite is the case. This can be seen by the content which includes:

1. A reduction in democratic space by increasing the role of the non-elected elites in public appointments. The junta created a corrupt crony system of mutual appointments by the elites: the judiciary and the so-called independent bodies appoint the Senate and the Senate appoints the independent bodies in a corrupt, unaccountable cycle.
2. The backward step of having half the Senate appointed by the military and the elites instead of being elected.
3. Continuation of the system of exclusion of the majority of the population from the Government and the Senate through age and educational criteria, despite scrapping the educational criteria for MPs.
4. Reduction in the role of political parties, which must face popular election, while increasing the role of the army, judiciary and the bureaucracy.

5. Clause 4 supports the idea of the "traditional Thai form of governance", which is another way of talking about non-democratic "Asian Values". The "traditional Thai form of governance" is about dictatorship, lack of Social Justice and economic inequality.
6. Clauses 82/83 combine the so-called King's "Sufficiency Economy" with the free market and Neo-Liberalism. The constitution supports big business, privatisation and restricts Government spending on social welfare under the neo-liberal phrase of "fiscal discipline". Governments are therefore supposed to adopt neo-liberal policies.
7. While the Government must restrict social spending on the poor, clause 76 stipulates that the military budget must be constantly increased without the need for fiscal discipline.
8. The increase in power and influence of the free-market and big business is not balanced by an increase in trade union rights and the bargaining power of workers or small-scale agriculturalists. There are no clauses about building a welfare state or collecting progressive taxes from the rich, a demand put forward by the 2006 Thai Social Forum.
9. There are no measures to prevent the military from intervening in politics, controlling the media or taking corrupt rich-pickings from board positions in State Enterprises. Clause 299 gives legitimacy to the 19th September coup. This only encourages further military intervention in politics. The right of citizens to oppose military coups, as stated in the 1997 Constitution, was scrapped.
10. The junta's constitution is full of ultra nationalism. There are no proposals for the possibility of self-governance and the respect for different cultures, religions and languages. There are no measures to build justice in society. This constitution will not help to bring peace to the South.
11. The junta's constitution does not expand or develop gender

rights, the rights of gays, lesbians, transgenders etc. There is still no right to choose abortion. No increase in rights for people of various ethnicities and no expansion of rights for the disabled.

12. Clause 32 maintains the barbarism of the death penalty. Death penalties, which were placed "on hold" for a brief period, were reinvigorated under the 2009 Democrat Party Government.
13. There are no provisions for compulsory referenda concerning issues like the signing of Free Trade Agreements.

Patron client systems

Pro-coup reactionaries complained that Taksin and TRT had built a so-called patron-client system, which "trapped the poor in a culture of dependency and prevented free voting". It is ironic that the most obvious and potentially destructive "patron-client system" in Thailand is the old crony network of the conservative royalist elites, which is constantly recreated. After the 19th September 2006 coup, there was a whirl-wind distribution of "jobs for the boys in uniform", with Fat Cat salaries, and positions on the various new committees and boards of state enterprises. This is the true "culture of dependence" on corruption and dictatorship among the elites.

More than ten years ago, Kraisak Choonhawan, son of elected Prime Minister Chartchai, who was deposed in the military coup of February 1991, explained that the civilian business politicians represented by his father's party were challenging the old vested interests of the military and top civil servants by using their new power-base among the electorate. The 1991 coup against the Chartchai Government did not achieve its mission to reinstate the absolute power of the old crony networks, since the military were soon overthrown in the bloody 1992 uprising. The power struggle between the military-bureaucrat cronies and the cronies of elected business politicians continued. Yet it is not a clear cut divide because there is much overlap and the different interest groups have on many occasions come to mutually beneficial deals. People swap sides too. It is an argument among the elite about the road to power and wealth: elections or coups.

The "Tale of Two Democratic Cities" ?

Liberal academics in Thailand believe that Taksin cheated in elections by "tricking or buying the ignorant rural poor". For them the rural poor were trapped in a patron-client system. The person who mapped out this view most clearly was Anek Laotamatat in his 1995 book: *"The Tale of Two Democratic Cities"*.

Anek Laotamatat's book attempted to claim that the major divide in Thai democratic society was between the rural and urban areas. These were the "two democratic cities" of Thai politics. According to Anek, the divide was not just geographical but it was an issue of class too. In his view, the rural electorate were mainly small farmers and the urban electorate were "middle-class".

It was the overwhelming dominance of the rural electorate in various constituencies that meant that they had the voting power to elect Governments. These Governments were mainly corrupt and deeply involved in money politics. In Anek's view, the rural people voted for these politicians because they were "patrons" of the poor who had to prove themselves by their work record of helping local communities. Vote buying was a ceremonial part of this "patron-client" relationship and not seen as "wrong" by the rural voters. Anek believed that rural people did not vote by using "independent thought" about political policies, but were bound by ties of obligation to their patrons.

For Anek, the urban middle-classes were well educated and chose their Governments and politicians using independent thought and a strong sense of "political morality". They cast their votes after carefully considering the policies of various parties, and when the Governments which were chosen by the rural poor turned out to be corrupt and immoral, they took part in street demonstrations to bring those Governments down.

This was an inaccurate and patronising view of Thai political society. It provided the justification for the 2006 coup. Yet, Anek's solution to this bad state of affairs was interesting. He suggested that in order to break down the barriers between the two halves of Thai society, the state had to increase rural development projects so that these areas became more urban-like and linked into the capitalist market through technological advances. Equally important was the need for political parties to develop clear policies and propose new solutions. Together, such measures would weaken the patron-client system and reduce vote-buying. Examples from Britain, and even Thailand in the 1970s, seem to support his view by indicating that vote-buying was reduced by increasing the importance of policy choice at election times.

If we ignore many dubious claims in this book, for example, that all urban people are middle class, or that the patron-client system is deeply rooted in the countryside because it can be traced back to the pre-capitalist *"Sakdina"* system etc., the book raises some important issues. What is interesting about this book is that it was written before TRT was ever established. More than this, it appears that TRT followed closely all the major points put forward in the book for developing Thai politics. Not only was TRT the only party for over two decades to take the issue of party policies seriously, the party took a keen interest in winning votes from the rural and urban poor on the basis of such policies. The 30 baht Universal Health Care Scheme was typical. The Taksin Government then proceeded to actually honour its election promises and use state funds to develop rural areas so that they could be linked to the world market. The Village Funds and *"One Tambon One Product"* (O.T.O.P.) are a good examples. In short, Taksin and TRT followed Anek's prescriptions to the letter and therefore the rural voters started to vote for clear pro-poor policies, while reducing their personal attachment to local political patrons or bosses.

Yet during the PAD mass campaign against Taksin, liberal academics and some social activists often quoted Anek's book to "prove" that the rural poor were too stupid to understand Democracy and that they were tied into Taksin's new "patron-client system" via TRT's populist policies. This was reinforced by Anek himself, who claimed, in a later book that TRT had built a new patron-client system and that this showed that Thailand could never have fully functioning Democracy[27].

The very concept of a "patron-client system" is not about a political party which offers populist policies to the entire national electorate, carries them out and then gets overwhelmingly re-elected on a national ballot. Political patron-client systems are about individual relationships between a local political boss and the boss's constituents. The relationship results in preferential treatment for some. It is pure nonsense to state that TRT was building a new strong patron-client system in the countryside on a national level. For those who genuinely believe in Democracy, Governments and political parties *ought* to carry out policies which the people want. Of course if you are a "Tank Liberal"[28] who thinks that the poor are too stupid to have the right to vote and that state spending on improving the lives of the poor is creating a "culture of dependence" and destroying "fiscal discipline", you will disagree.

The conservative royalist alliance

1. The military

Despite the fact that millions of Thais believe that the centre of power among the conservative elites is the Monarchy or the Privy Council, the real centre of power, lurking behind the Throne, is the military. The military has intervened in politics and society since the 1932 revolution against the absolute Monarchy. At important moments in history, the power of the military has been significantly reduced or kept at bay by social movements and popular uprisings. The post 1973[29] and 1992 periods are good

---

27 Anek (2006) *Taksina-Populism*. Matichon Press, (in Thai).

28 See criticisms of *Thai Rak Thai* Populism made by the *Democrat Party* (*Bangkok Post* 17/06/06) and neo-liberals such as Tirayut Boonmi and Ammar Siamwalla (*Nation* 6/01/03, 28/07/03, *Matichon daily* 25/12/2002 - In Thai, Tirayut Boonmi "Taksinomics" in Jermsak Bintong (ed) *Keeping up with Taksin*, 2004 -In Thai).

29 This is why the Boarder Patrol Police and the semi-fascist gangs were used against the students and the Left in 1976.

examples. It would be more accurate to state that the military is an important centre of power among many. Other elite centres include big business, political bosses[30] and high ranking bureaucrats. What is unique about the army, however, is its weaponry and decisive ability to topple Governments through coup d'états. The military has a monopoly on the means of violent coercion and it has been prepared in the past to gun-down protestors in the streets. Never the less, there are three factors which limit the power of the military: (1) the power of social movements, (2) the power of other sections of the elite which hold economic and political power, and (3) the fact that the military is divided by factionalism.

The military never had absolute power, even in the 1950s and 1960s and always had to take into account the views of social movements, technocrats, powerful politicians and big business. This is even more the case today after decades of economic development and social movement struggles. The 2006 coup could never have been successful if the PAD and most of the NGOs had not given the green light to such actions. The lack of organisation among TRT supporters also helped. There was no Red Shirt movement at the time of the coup. When the Red Shirts were actually formed, the military had to use behind the scenes actions to get rid of the PPP Government. One important thing which the military did in 2008 was to refuse orders from the elected PPP Government to re-open the international airports which had been blockaded by the PAD.

The military is split into squabbling factions which are often a law unto themselves. Those who engage in military watching are often over-obsessed by the various factions and their leaders, forgetting the actions of other societal players. The military factions are purely about self-interest. They are also linked to various retired soldiers, businessmen and politicians. No one is allowed to hold on to top military positions for long. For historical reasons, the army is the most powerful section of the armed forces. The navy sided with factions of the elite that were on the

---

[30] Political bosses are mafia like politicians with local influence, especially in areas outside Bangkok. For a study of political bosses in the Philippines see John T. Sidel (1999) *Capital coercion and crime. Bossism in the Philippines*. Stanford University Press.

losing side, for example, siding with Pridi Panomyong, and the air force has been under developed. The police were powerful for a brief period under Police General Pao Siyanon in the 1950s, but they were soon despatched to forth rank in the uniformed pecking order. The Supreme Commander of the Armed Forces is a purely ceremonial position. Real power lies in the hands of the army chief. The position of chief of the army is rotated to ensure an equal distribution of opportunities. Since the death of Field Marshal Sarit, there has been no single military strong man. Generals must take their turn at the feeding trough. The military has lucrative commercial interests in the media and in the state enterprises.

Violent coercion is never enough to maintain political power. Legitimacy must also be built through socialisation and the use of ideology. "Democracy" as an ideology is extremely powerful in Thai society and has been so for decades. That is why past military dictatorships have never been able to claim that they were "good dictatorships". They always tried to say that they were "democratic" or "temporary regimes in the process of developing Democracy". Despite the high number of coups in Thai history, there has not been a stable and long lasting military junta since 1973. The Democracy Monument, in the centre of Bangkok, built by an anti-Monarchy military dictator in the 1930s, has come to symbolise the popular ideology of Democracy and it means that the army could never pull it down, even in the 1960s and 1970s.

The military has always had a problem with trying to legitimise its actions by quoting "Democracy". Therefore, it has relied heavily upon using the Monarchy to shore-up its legitimacy. The military always claim that they are "protecting the Monarchy" and that "they are the servants of the King". We see the generals in photo poses, supposedly taking orders from royalty. Yet it is the generals who are really in charge. Claiming legitimacy from the Monarchy is a way to make the population afraid of criticising the army and the draconian lèse majesté law is in place to back this up.

"Nation, Religion and Monarchy" are the three pillars of the elite's conservative ideology. Since the 1992 uprising against the military, they have sometimes reluctantly added "the People" as a forth afterthought[31]. However, the most important element in the three pillars ideology, as far as the army is concerned, is the Monarchy. "Religion" is difficult to use as a coercive force due to the fact that not all Thais are Buddhist and the version of Buddhism, designed by the elites in the past, does not give any political power to the clergy. "Nation" might seem to be a powerful symbol, and it is. Yet, ever since the 1930s there has been an underlying tension between "Nation" and "Monarchy" because the former implies a more collective idea, with collective interests, where as the latter is concentrated in one single individual. "Nation", in a more egalitarian concept, was also the ideology of the Peoples Party in 1932, the Maoist Communist Party and many of the social movements. That is why "Monarchy" best serves the narrow and elitist interests of the army.

2. The courts and lack of justice or "rule of law"

The courts in Thailand have never been independent or just. This is because of the legacy of elitist rule. The general experience of ordinary people is that there is no justice or human dignity through the court system. Trade unionists know that labour courts side with the bosses and the Government. In many provincial courts, judges sit in a room above the actual court and defendants have to communicate with judges through a CCTV system. Poor people know that they will never be treated with respect and that the rich can commit crimes with impunity. Prisoners are brought to court in shackles and treated as sub-human. The police and courts are riddled with corruption.

To support this system of injustice, the courts have their own version of the lèse majesté law. No one is allowed to discuss or criticise any court decisions. The courts claim to "answer only to the Monarchy" and anyone criticising the courts will be charged with "contempt of court". There is no public accountability or transparency of the court system and therefore no justice. There is no belief in the rights of prisoners, no

[31] See signs outside military camps.

attempts at creating humane prison conditions and no public participation in the criminal justice system because there are no juries.

During Taksin's Premiership, the courts were very favourable to him, acquitting him of any wrong-doing by hiding his assets just before his first election victory. By 2006, the tide of political power turned and the judges quickly adapted themselves.

In 2006, just before the military coup, the King urged the courts to act against "political wrong-doing" in the country. This alternative strategy to a direct coup d'état, was used later in 2008 to topple the elected PPP Government. In addition to this, after the 2006 coup, the military used the courts to dissolve the TRT on the supposed grounds that some executive members of the party had engaged in bribery. These executives were found guilty of paying a group of people to stand against TRT in the April 2006 elections. The boycott of the elections by the *Democrat Party* and other opposition parties, which could have been deemed to have broken the election laws, meant that according to the 1997 Constitution, TRT would have to have won over 25% of the possible vote in each constituency where it was unopposed in order to send an MP to parliament. The Constitution also stipulated that parliament could not be convened unless all constituencies had sitting MPs. This legal trap meant that Taksin's attempt to call for a democratic mandate from the people in April 2006, was thoroughly frustrated by the conservatives, who laid the ground for the coup. The actions of TRT executives was immoral, but hardly "election fraud" and it was no more immoral than the election boycott by the opposition. There is no question that TRT commanded an overall majority of the popular votes. Yet TRT was singled out to be dissolved and its entire executive committee banned from politics, thus punishing the entire party and the majority of the electorate.

When elections were held again in late 2007, they were won by PPP. This was a reconstituted TRT party. So the courts were used for a second time to dissolve this party on the grounds that Executive members had engaged in vote-buying. The *Democrat Party* and other parties had also handed out money, as is the tradition in Thai elections, yet the

Democrat Party was not punished by courts because there was a plan by the military to manoeuvre it into Government. Earlier, the courts had sacked PPP Prime Minister Samak Sundaravej for appearing on a TV cooking programme, which was deemed to be "engaging in business". Many Democrat Party politicians and Government ministers have held business interests, but the party has not been dissolved. It is clear that the aim was to cripple the most popular party and never to allow it to form a stable Government.

The irony was that TRT or PPP won votes because of their policies. This was decreasing the importance of vote-buying in Thai elections. In contrast, parties like the *Democrat Party* or *Chart Thai Party* had always won seats, outside Bangkok, through patronage and vote-buying. None of what I have written above should be seen as a justification for bribery, vote-buying and corruption carried out by any politician or political party, including TRT or PPP or *Peua Thai Party* (PTP), the party which emerged from the wreck of PPP. What is important is to have a proper standard of justice and an understanding about how vote-buying can be eliminated. The most affective way to eliminate money politics is to have political parties which propose serious and differing policies in an atmosphere of Democracy and total freedom of expression.

At the same time that the courts were being used to destroy TRT and PPP, the PAD launched their deliberate "campaign of chaos" in order to achieve their "New Order" brand of authoritarianism. They violently took over Government House, wrecking the interior. In October 2008, they staged violent actions to try to prevent an elected parliament from opening. They were armed with guns, clubs and home-made bombs. The police responded with tear gas. It is likely that one PAD member was killed by the police because a tear gas canister was fired directly at the crowd. Other PAD members died because their own explosives blew up. The PAD was caught on film deliberately driving a pick-up truck over a policeman. Yet, it was remarkable how all the mainstream media, the academics and the NGOs were united in their one-sided condemnation of the police. The Faculty of Economics at *Chulalongkorn University* mounted an official exhibition board praising the PAD and attacking the police. Finally in December, the PAD seized the two international airports with the support of the military and the *Democrat Party*, thus shutting down the country and destroying the tourist industry.

At time of writing, no one from the PAD has been punished for any of these criminal acts and some cases have been dismissed by the courts. Remaining court cases for royalists are painfully slow, while a number of Red Shirts have been quickly thrown into prison, purely for expressing their views. The police have also been found guilty of using excess violence in 2008. Yet there is no mention, by the justice system, of the army's role in killing people in April 2009, or the illegal act of staging a coup in 2006. These are all blatant examples of double standards in the justice system and a total lack of the rule of law.

3. The Monarchy and the Privy Council

More detail about the nature of the Thai Monarchy appears in Chapter 3 of this book. So this section will be brief.

As has already been explained, the conservative elites have a long history of legitimising their anti-democratic actions by referring to the Monarchy. Many Thais and some foreign observers, including Paul Handley[32], believe that the King is the most powerful political figure in Thailand. In Chapter 3, I will argue that this is a mistaken point of view. The King is weak, unprincipled and lacking in vision. He has always been this way, not just in his old age. Yet the elites, especially the military, have promoted an illusion about his power, which is contrary to the Constitution. This illusion serves the purpose of protecting the whole of the elites against popular challenges. The illusion creates a climate of fear and coerced loyalty.

There are three main elements to the power of the conservative elites in Thailand: (1) coercion through violent means, which is carried out by the military and paramilitary gangs, (2) economic power achieved by

[32] Paul Handley (2006) *The King Never Smiles*. Yale University Press.

controlling the commanding heights of the economy and (3) legitimacy provided by the ideology of the Monarchy.

As a "stabilising force", the Monarchy has only helped to stabilise the interests of the elite. The King has never had the courage to defend Democracy or oppose military violence and he has never built unity in times of crisis.

Taksin has been accused of wanting to usurp the Monarchy and become President. There is absolutely no evidence for this. In fact, throughout the period when Taksin was Prime Minister, he promoted and was seen to be servile to the King, just like the conservative generals who are his rivals. His Government paved the way for and participated in the lavish royal celebrations on the 60th anniversary of the King's accession to the throne in 2006. His Government also introduced the "Yellow Shirt Mania", where we were all "asked" to wear yellow royal shirts every Monday.

Because of the 2006 coup, the conservative elites are fully in power again. They never totally lost power to an elected Government. However, the interesting factor is that by losing power, Taksin lost the fight to legitimise himself by using the Monarchy and thus became a target for those who wanted to brand him as a republican.

Some Thais see the "wicked figure" of General Prem Tinsulanon, ex-PM and head of the Privy Council, as being behind the 2006 coup. Some extremists even claim that Prem wants to become the next King! All this is very unlikely. Often people refer to Prem instead of talking directly about the King, because they are justifiably afraid of lèse majesté. Prem is an important coordinator between the army, the civilian elites, political bosses, businessmen and the Palace, but he merely remains as a coordinator. Many people forget that Prem was pushed out of Government office by various generals and politicians in the late 1980s and kicked upstairs into the Privy Council.

4. The semi-fascist *"Peoples Alliance for Democracy"* (PAD) and the NGO royalists

Chapter 2 in this book details the nature of the Thai Peoples Movement, the NGOs and the PAD. All that will be stated here is that the PAD was neither a "Peoples Alliance" nor was it for "Democracy". Rather, it was a middle-class based, ultra-right wing organisation, which was prepared to use violence and intimidation to destroy Democracy. The involvement of some NGO leaders, was one factor, among many, which allowed the NGOs to be pulled to the extreme Right after the 2006 coup. The majority of the NGOs are firmly in the camp of the conservative elites against the majority of the poor.

In late 2009, the PAD established a political party called *"The New Politics Party"* in order to promote their New Order authoritarianism. This party would be in direct competition with the royalist *Democrat Party* and would split the anti-Taksin vote. Some people have argued that the PAD is in decline. It is perhaps too early to make such a judgement in 2009.

5. The "Tank Liberal" academics

Today in Thailand we have the phenomenon of "Tank Liberals". These are people who for years have claimed to be "liberal democrats", in favour of Democracy. Yet when put to the test during the post-coup crisis in 2006, they sided with the military and the PAD, rather than siding with Democracy. They justified this by saying that only a coup could get rid of Taksin. As the Left has shown in its public opposition to the coup, whether it be actions by the *"19th September Network against the Coup"* or the progressive movements in the 2006 *Thai Social Forum*, it was possible to oppose Taksin and oppose the coup. But liberal academics claimed that Taksin had built a "parliamentary dictatorship" which had to be ousted by a military coup.

For decades most Thai academics have shunned political debate, preferring personal squabbles to principled arguments. No one is ever forced to justify or argue for their beliefs. On the occasion when academic papers are written, they are descriptive and ignore work by those who pose awkward, alternative, explanations. Surveying various points of view in the academic literature and citing other works is not what most Thai academics do. They also tend to copy fashions and schools of thought from abroad and repackage them as their own ideas, without proper acknowledgements. This leads to a climate of arrogance, a lack of debate and poor academic standards in social sciences. In general, Thai students are not encouraged or taught to write argumentative essays in the social sciences. Those, like myself and a handful of other academics, who have campaigned for such methods of education, have faced stiff resistance from colleagues.

When these liberal academics defended their middle-class interests and supported the 2006 coup, they saw no need for a serious explanation other than to say that the poor "did not understand Democracy". Many were also supporters of the free-market. The list of liberal collaborators with the junta in the military's appointed parliament is a list of shame. Rubbing shoulders with army and police officers and top business people were the following notables: Ammar Siamwalla, Pratumporn Wucharasatien, Kotom Ariya, Sopon Supapong, Chai-anan Samudwanij, Bawornsak Uwanno, Wutipong Priapjeerawat, Sungsit Piriyarungsan, Sujit Boonbongkarn and Surichai Wankeaw[33]. Also of note are Chaiyan Chaiyaporn, Surapong Jaiyarnarm, Surat Horakul and Panitan Wattanayakorn[34] from the Faculty of Political Science at *Chulalongkorn University*, where I used to work. My university banned my book, which criticised the 2006 coup, from the bookshop[35]. In 2007, my faculty also had the audacity to set up a well-funded unit called "Democracy Watch". One would be forgiven for thinking that its aim was to "watch out for any signs of Democracy in order to destroy it"!

---

[33] Surichai had previously built a reputation for being an "NGO-academic".

[34] Panitan took up a political position in the military-backed *Democrat Party* government in 2008. http://thaipoliticalprisoners.wordpress.com/, 8/9/2009, aptly described him as "one of the academics-for-hire architects of the draconian Internal Security Act." In September 2009 he suggested that the government would continue to spy on citizens engaged in legal political activities.

[35] Giles Ji Ungpakorn (2007) already quoted.

Other liberal academics and intellectuals like Anek Laotamatat, Tirayut Boonmi and Anan Panyarachun (former Prime Minister under the 1991 junta) started to promote the idea of Asia Values in their attempt to justify the coup. For them Thai-style Democracy was the order of the day. Anek argued that Thailand needed a "mixed" system where elected Governments share power with the King and *Thai Rak Thai* Populism was replaced by "Third Way" social welfare. Anek is an ardent admirer of Anthony Giddens[36].

The lessons about liberalism from the 19th September 2006 coup are clear. It took a military coup to reverse the popular Keynesian and social welfare policies of the TRT Government. Liberalism and the free-market therefore go hand in hand with militarism and dictatorship. As Arundhati Roy wrote: *"What the free market undermines is not national sovereignty, but Democracy. As the disparity between the rich and poor grows, the hidden fist has its work cut out for it....Today corporate globalization needs an international confederation of loyal, corrupt, authoritarian Governments in poorer countries to push through unpopular reforms and quell mutinies."* [37]

Liberalism has always claimed to be the protector of Democracy, yet when one looks at the evidence it becomes clear that there has always been an issue about the right to vote among the poor majority. That right has only been won in many countries by mass struggle from below[38]. Liberals have constantly argued that the poor are not ready for Democracy because they may use Democracy to challenge the interests of the rich.

Not all Thai academics took up an elite position. Honourable exceptions include the *Midnight University* in Chiang Mai, a group of progressive law lecturers at *Tammasart University*, Sutachai Yimprasert from *Chulalongkorn University*, Wipa Daomanee and Pichit Likitkitsomboon from *Tammasart University*, Somchai Pataratananun from

[36] Anek Laotamatat (2006) already quoted.

[37] Arundhati Roy (2004) *The ordinary person's guide to Empire*. Harper Perennial.

[38] See Paul Foot (2005) *The Vote. How it was won and how it was undermined.* Penguin/ Viking.

Mahasarakam University and Tanet Choroenmuang and Chaiyan Rajakool from *Chiang Mai University.*

The Taksin Government

Taksin Shinawat, a mobile phone and media tycoon, founded TRT after the economic crisis of 1997. He had previously held Government positions through the *Palang Tum Party* in the 1990s. TRT was unique in recent Thai political history in that it actually spent considerable time developing policies[39]. They held meetings with different social groups and came up with real policies at the time of their first election victory in 2001. TRT was a "populist" party which offered pro-poor policies and village level Keynesian economic stimuli, by pumping state money into local projects. The aim was to modernise and create social peace after the crisis so that the Government could increase Thailand's economic competitiveness[40]. At the same time, this party of big business also pursued neo-liberal policies such as privatisation and the support for free trade agreements (FTAs). This was what TRT called its "dual track" policy. The overall aim was to modernise Thai society for the benefit of big business, while at the same time making the majority of poor citizens "stake holders". This formula ensured that the party gained overwhelming electoral support by 2005.

The poor, who form the vast majority of the Thai electorate, voted enthusiastically for the two flagship policies of the party. These were a Universal Health Care Scheme (the first ever in Thailand) and a 1 million baht fund loaned to each village to encourage small businesses. TRT won a second term of office with an overall majority in parliament in 2005. It is easy to see why. The main opposition party, the *Democrats*, spent the whole four years attacking the health care system and other social benefits. They said that it contravened neoliberal "fiscal discipline". Academics Tirayut Boonmi and Ammar Siamwalla echoed Margaret Thatcher in talking about

[39] For more details see Pasuk Phongpaichit & Chris Baker (2004) already quoted.
[40] Kevin Hewison (2003) already quoted.

"a climate of dependency" built up by "too much" welfare. Previously the Democrat Government, which came to power immediately after the 1997 economic crisis, had used taxes paid by the poor to prop up the financial system. The banks were in crisis due to wild speculation by the rich which resulted in non-performing loans.

In the initial years of TRT there was much enthusiasm for the various new policies among many social activists, especially the ex-student activists from the 1970s who are known as the "October Generation". One prominent NGO activist, Pumtam Wechayachai, who became a senior figure in TRT, boasted that, unlike in the old days of the Communist Party, they had now "seized state power" without living the hardships of the jungle *("without eating cassava and sweet potatoes")*.

Taksin often complained about the red tape and rivalries among civil servants from different Ministries and proposed a "CEO type" Government management structure in the provinces. The autonomous power and influence of local politicians and mafias was reduced because politicians became dependent on TRT political policies in order to win elections. Large scale mega-project infrastructural developments were planned and the Government attempted to raise the technological capabilities of school students in various ways. Some times the projects were rushed and Taksin could be too boastful about what he was going to achieve in a short period of time. His claim that he would rapidly eradicate poverty was a good example. Often the pro-poor policies were underfunded or undercut by free-market policies. Refusing to produce cheap drugs in Thailand in the face of opposition from the global drug companies, or the introduction of internal markets within the health care system were two examples. However, TRT brought about many improvements to the lives of Thai people, especially through the Universal Health Care Scheme. The party was also starting to destroy the influence of the old patron-client networks by providing progressive political policies which the electorate could eagerly support.

It is often wrongly assumed that TRT pro-poor policies were targeted only at rural areas. In fact the Universal Health Care Scheme and the 1 million baht Village Funds had a beneficial impact on urban workers. Previously they had carried the burden of sending part of their poverty-level wages back to support their relatives in rural areas. By raising living standards in rural areas, TRT also raised standards for the urban working class.

There was of course a very nasty side to the Taksin Government. During their first term of office they waged a so-called "war on drugs" in which over 3000 people were shot without ever coming to trial. Unfortunately, this was extremely popular among the electorate and most of the elites because of weak opposition by human rights activists. Many Buddhist priests also supported this policy. In the three southern-most provinces the TRT Government waged a campaign of violence against the Muslim Malay-speaking population. The Government was also responsible for the murder, by the police, of defence lawyer Somchai Nilapaichit, who was defending people from the south.

In addition to gross abuses of human rights, Taksin and his cronies avoided paying tax, just like all the other elites. Together, Taksin and his associates, netted 70 billion baht from the sale of their mobile phone company and did not pay a single baht in tax on this sale. This was totally legal, but many quite rightly found it to be immoral.

Before the political crisis in early 2006, the Taksin Government had a huge majority in parliament and this allowed the *Thai Rak Thai* party to dominate political society. Taksin's business corporation could also buy shares in the media and put pressure on the media to support the Government through threatening to withdraw advertising revenue. However, the claims that this was a "parliamentary dictatorship" or that there was no Democracy under Taksin, are without foundation. His power ultimately rested on the number of votes his party could win from the electorate. This is in stark contrast to the power base of military-backed Governments.

The authoritarian Government led by the *Democrat Party*

At the end of 2008, after the repeated use of the courts to destroy TRT and PPP, the army bullied and bribed some of the worst, corrupt elements in Taksin's party to change sides and support the *Democrats*. Foremost among them was Newin Chitchorp, named after the former Burmese military dictator. Abhisit Vejjajiva became the Prime Minister. His name sums it all up. It means "privilege". He was educated at Oxford and Eton.

Despite the attempts to create an image that the *Democrat Party* Government was "clean" and different from the "corrupt" Taksin Government, a corruption scandal over medical purchases soon emerged concerning members of parliament belonging to the main Government coalition parties[41]. Other corruption scandals also implicated people working on the King's projects and the Government's *"Thai Kem Kaeng"* campaign[42].

By 2009, the Thai Government, and their elite supporters, were once again using the language of the Cold War and from the era of past military dictatorships, in order to throttle free speech and Democracy. They were branding the opposition as "Communists" and "enemies and destroyers of Thailand". There was total Government control of the mainstream media and widespread censorship of alternative websites and community radio stations. All official TV and radio channels are owned, either by the Army, or by the Government and the print media tycoons were Government supporters.

As soon as the *Democrats* came to power, they announced that their priority would be to crack down on people who were deemed to have "insulted" the King[43]. Lèse majesté cases increased dramatically. Two thousand three hundred websites were closed down by the ICT Ministry and a further 200 were being reviewed. The ICT Ministry was given a

---

[41] http://www.bangkokpost.com/news/politics/25208/five-coalition-mps-named-in-medical-scam 08/10/2009.

[42] http://thaipoliticalprisoners.wordpress.com/ 27/09/2009.

[43] This applied exclusively to those who opposed the 2006 military coup, myself included.

budget of 80 million baht to help its campaign of censorship[44]. After the unrest in April 2009, when the army, with Government support, shot pro-democracy demonstrators, 66 Red Shirt websites were closed for ten days under an Emergency Decree. The police went around various community radio stations to put them off the air[45]. When the ICT unblocked some of these sites, they threatened to use "other laws" to close them again if they stepped out of line. The Government also channelled funds into spying activities against their opponents.

The Government staged witch-hunts against pro-democracy journalists and academics. In September 2009, the TV journalist, Jom Petpradap, was forced out of his job for daring to interview ex-Prime Minister Taksin in an attempt to present a balanced view in the media. Prominent among Jom's critics was Government Minister and *Democrat Party* MP Satit Wongnongtoey, who took a prominent role in promoting censorship and the use of lèse majesté. Supporting this criticism were many military appointed senators and also the elected senator for Bangkok, Rosana Tositrakul, known as an "NGO Senator". Rosana stated that she *"saw no benefit in allowing an exchange of arguments and accusations on air."* [46]

In November 2009, four people were arrested and charged under the computer crimes act for "spreading rumours which caused the Bangkok stock market to fall". In fact the stock market fall was prompted by real fears about the health of the aged King who was in hospital for a prolonged period. Because of the lack of transparency about the Palace and continuous obtuse announcements made about the King's "improving health", there were rumours that he was dead or dying. This is what caused the fall on the stock market. Yet the level of paranoia and deceit in Government circles was such that a web of lies was created to explain that "an international conspiracy" had been hatched in order to destabilise the country by spreading "false rumours".

---

[44] http://www.prachatai.com/ 13/1/2009 (In Thai). The manager of this alternative newspaper was also arrested. See http://thaipoliticalprisoners.wordpress.com

[45] http://www.prachatai.com/ 16 & 17/4/2009 (In Thai).

[46] http://thaipoliticalprisoners.wordpress.com/ 7/9/2009.

No evidence was found of any such conspiracy or any unusual profit-taking as a result of the crash and the people who were arrested were merely posting explanations on various websites about why the stock market had crashed. Yet Panitan Wattanayagorn, ex-*Chulalongkorn University* academic and Government spokesman, claimed that the use of the computer crime law in this case was "necessary in order to protect national security"[47]. Korn Chatikavanij, 2006 coup supporter and Finance Minister, justified the arrests "because the accused had posted comments on anti-Government websites"[48]. What the royalist Government and the army were really frightened about, was not any rumours, but how they could continue to justify their undemocratic actions after the King died.

Abhisit himself has a history of constantly telling lies. At St John's College in Oxford, in March 2009, he said that a number of specific cases of lèse majesté had "been abandoned". Yet many months later they were clearly being pursued by the courts. He also lied that his Government would not obstruct the Red Shirt petition to the King in August 2009, seeking a pardon for Taksin. In fact his Government was busy denouncing the campaign and trying to organise a counter petition. Then in late November 2009 Abhisit, along with fellow Democrat Sutep Teuksuban, lied that the Red Shirts were forcing migrant workers from neighbouring countries to take part in Red Shirt demonstrations[49]. Abhisit likes to project the image of a young, modern and honest politician. In fact he is a cold, calculating and ambitious member of the elite who is prepared to do and say anything to stay in office. He is of the old mould of Thai politicians, prepared to work closely with the military in the destruction of Democracy.

As has already been mentioned, the Government created the armed paramilitary gang called the "Blue Shirts", controlled by Government politicians such as Newin Chitchorp, from *Pumjaitai Party*, and Sutep Teuksuban, from the *Democrats*. The Blue Shirts were used for violent

---

[47] *Wall Street Journal* 03/11/2009.

[48] *Matichon on line* 02/11/2009 http://www.matichon.co.th news detail.php?newsid=1257138216&grpid=00&catid=

[49] http://www.prachatai.com/ 24/11/2009. (In Thai).

confrontations with Red Shirt protestors in April 2009 and to also protect Abhisit and other Government politicians on their trips to the provinces. These politicians needed constant protection since they nearly always encountered enraged locals whose democratic rights had been trampled underfoot.

In September 2009, Abhisit's Government declared what amounts to "Martial Law" in Bangkok, under the Internal Security Act, around the 3rd anniversary of the 2006 coup. This was in order to try to prevent a pro-democracy demonstration by Red Shirts. No such actions were ever taken by the Taksin Government against PAD protests. In the event, the Bangkok protest was peaceful.

On the same day another demonstration was organised by PAD fascist thugs on the Cambodian border. Their aim was to attack Cambodian villagers living and working around the ancient Kao Prawiharn (Preah Vihear) temple. The temple is inside Cambodia, but the area surrounding it is disputed territory. For over a year, the PAD had been trying to whip-up extreme nationalist sentiment against Cambodia, thus risking a war. They claim that the temple should belong to Thailand. In fact, Preah Vihear was built by the ancient Khmers and clearly belongs to Cambodia, both from a legal and historical point of view[50]. On the 19th September the PAD went to the border armed, as usual, with guns, bombs and clubs. They attacked the police and then a group of local villagers who were opposed to them. One villager was shot in the leg and seriously wounded. Local villagers on both sides of the border have traditionally held joint religious ceremonies together at the temple on this day. This had not happened since the PAD forced the closure of the temple. Two months later the Justice Minister Pirapan Salirathavibhaga took a group of foreign journalists to the border and claimed that the temple belonged to Thailand[51].

Teptai Senpong, personal spokesman for Prime Minister Abhisit, earlier stated that there was no reason to declare a State of Emergency in the border area, unlike in Bangkok, *"since the PAD were defending Thai*

[50] World Court ruling in 1962.

[51] Chris Blake, AP writer, 19/11/2009.

national interests". Abhisit himself re-affirmed that the aims of the PAD were the same as the Government on this issue[52]. Suriyasai Katasila, PAD spokesperson, said that the PAD leadership supported Wira Somkwamkit, who headed the violent raid on the border. Not surprisingly, no one was punished for this violence. In November, the Cambodian Prime Minsiter Hun Sen responded to all this by appointing Taksin as a political advisor to his Government.

It is interesting to compare other activities which took place on 19th September 2009. They help to illuminate the fault lines in Thai society. In the northern city of Chiang Mai, the progressive *Midnight University* held a seminar to discuss the problems which arose from the coup in 2006. In the north-eastern town of *Ubon Rajatanee*, the group called *Chak Tong Rop*, an *Ubon*-based Red Shirt group, protested at the fact that the Rector and another key academic at the local university had come out in support of the PAD actions at Preah Vihear[53]. At *Mahasarakam*, *Khon Kan* and *Ubon Rajatanee* universities, the North-eastern Students Federation held anti-coup meetings.

But in another meeting in *Khon Kan University*, NGOs organised a joint seminar with the law faculty to discuss issues of "Human Rights". What gave this seminar a strange and unreal feeling was that the 19th September coup and the destruction of Democracy were never mentioned. Neither was the problem of the lèse majesté law and draconian censorship. Among the main speakers were the Chairperson of NGO-COD, Pairote Ponpet, and also the PAD member of the discredited National Human Rights Commission, Dr Niran Pitakwatchara[54]. They discussed issues of villagers' local rights and problems arising from mining as though they had nothing to do with the political turmoil going on in Thai society.[55]

---

[52] http://www.prachatai.com/journal/2009/09/25901 posted 21/9/2009 (In Thai).

[53] Ubon Rajatanee University is unusual in that most academics lean towards the Red Shirts and are in favour of Democracy.

[54] Niran called for the King to sack elected PM Taksin just before the coup and has tried to stop Red Shirt meetings at Ubon Rajatanee University.

[55] http://www.prachatai.com/journal/2009/09/25899 posted 21/9/2009 (In Thai).

Elitist democratisation

Political Science in Thailand, up to the early 1990s, was dominated by right wing ideas from the USA. Most mainstream academics agreed with the Structural Functionalist School of democratization[56]. The main ideas were about building "stability" and "social norms" within democratic societies. The ideal model was the USA or Britain. Academics taught about the "systems approach" with "inputs" and "outputs", as though Democracy was like a machine. Added to this were the ideas that countries with "Protestant democratic cultures" were more likely to be fully functioning Democracies. Modernisation theory helped explain why it was not a problem for the USA to align itself with Thai military dictatorships as part of the "Free World". This was because it was a priority to develop and modernise the economy and after that Democracy would automatically grow[57]. The emphasis was on crafting Democracy from above by enlightened academics. The "people" had to be "educated" to understand Democracy. Organisations like the *King Prachatipok Institute*, named after Thailand's last absolutist king, took it upon themselves to craft Thai Democracy and educate the people.

The name of the *King Prachatipok Institute* was not the only ironic contradiction. The vast majority of Structural Functionalist academics served various military dictatorships in the 1960s and 1970s. The fact that three decades later so many Thai academics supported the September 2006 coup and collaborated with the conservative royalists, raises serious questions about the ability or the will to craft Democracy by any of these "professional intellectuals".

---

[56] Gabriel Almond & Bingham Powell (1966) *Comparative Politics: a Developmental Approach*. Little Brown, Boston. Gabriel Almond & Sidney Verba (1963) *The Civic Culture: Political Attitudes and Democracy in Five Nations*. Princeton University Press. Lucian Pye & Sidney Verba (1965) *Political Culture and Political Development*. Princeton University Press.

[57] See Fred Riggs (1966) *Thailand. The modernisation of a Bureaucratic Polity*. East West Press. U.S.A.

By the mid 1980s, the Civil Society School of democratisation had come to dominate Thai mainstream academia. Despite the fact that this school emphasised mass movements in building Democracy, those who merely saw Civil Society as movements of the middle classes, ended up with similarly elitist views to the Structural Functionalists. There are also serious problems with looking at Civil Society from a non-class perspective, for it does not enable us to understand the important class dynamics which underpin all social movements, however distorted they may be. In some cases, such as Haiti or Eastern Europe, organisations with clear business links or funding from the U.S. Government have masqueraded as "Civil Society Organisations"[58]. In authoritarian countries like Singapore so-called "Civil Society" groups are actually established by the Government[59].

The belief that Civil Society is concentrated among the intellectual middle-classes or NGOs[60], overlooks the possible anti-democratic nature of the middle classes and intellectuals, who often benefit from unequal societies and authoritarian states[61]. Somchai Pataratananun has described how influential people like Prawase Wasi and Chai-anan Samudwanij have been advocating the idea of "Elite Civil Society" in Thailand[62]. This involves an unequal partnership with the state, where the state dominates

[58] Peter Hallward (2007) *Damming the Flood. Haiti, Aristide, and the Politics of Containment*. Verso.

[59] Garry Rodan (1997) Civil Society and other political possibilities in Southeast Asia. Journal of Contemporary Asia 27(2),156-178.

[60] J.L. Cohen & A. Arato, A. (1997) *Civil Society and political theory*. M.I.T. Press, U.S.A. A. Touraine (2001) [Translated by D. Macey] *Beyond Neoliberalism*. Polity Press, Cambridge, U.K. J. Keane (1998) *Civil Society. Old images, new vision*. Polity Press, Cambridge, U.K. R. Robison & D.S.G. Goodman (1996) (eds) *The New Rich in Asia*. Routledge, UK. Kevin Hewison (1996) Emerging social forces in Thailand. New political and economic roles. In: Robison, R. & Goodman, D. S. G. (eds) *The new rich in Asia*. Routledge, UK.

[61] Garry Rodan (1997) already quoted. Victor T. King, Phuong An Nguyen & Nguyen Huu Minh (2008) Professional Middle Class Youth in Post-Reform Vietnam: Identity, Continuity and Change. Modern Asian Studies 42(4), 783-813. J. Pearce (1997) Civil society, the market and democracy in Latin America. Democratisation, 4 (2), 57-83.

[62] Somchai Pataratananun (Phatharathananunth) (2006) *Civil Society and Democratization. Social Movements in Northeast Thailand*. NIAS press. p. 84.

Civil Society. It means that the threat to "Democracy" is seen as coming from the uneducated masses. This neatly encapsulates the ideology of the royalist Yellow Shirts. In such a mainstream or elite vision of Civil Society, there is no place for the Red Shirts who are made up of primary school educated small farmers, urban taxi-drivers, street vendors or factory workers.

The urban and rural poor, who form the Red Shirts want the right to choose their own democratically elected Government. They started out as passive supporters of Taksin's TRT Government. But they have now formed a new citizens' movement for what they call "Real Democracy". For them, "Real Democracy" means an end to the long-accepted "quiet dictatorship" of the conservatives.

Most of those in the Red Shirt movement support Taksin for good reasons. His Government put in place many modern pro-poor policies, including Thailand's first ever Universal Health Care System. Yet the Red Shirts are not merely Taksin puppets. There is a dialectical relationship between Taksin and the Red Shirts. His leadership provides encouragement and confidence to fight. Yet by 2009, the Red Shirts were self-organised in community groups and some were showing frustration with Taksin's lack of progressive leadership, especially over his insistence that they continue to be "loyal" to the Crown. Old- style TRT politicians had to run to keep up with the movement. By 2009, a republican movement was growing, but a significant proportion of Red Shirts still loved both Taksin and the King[63].

Many middle class observers will feel uncomfortable that the Red Shirts are a movement of ordinary citizens and not the educated middle class. The Red Shirts are not "refined folk" with experience of activism. But they are rapidly developing organisational, media and internet skills. In a situation where the NGOs and the middle class intellectuals have turned their backs on Democracy and Social Justice, this is what is really required to build a democratic movement. This is what "People Empowerment" looks like. But one important weakness of the Red Shirts is that they have

[63] See Andrew Walker & Nicholas Farrelly (2009) *Thailand's Royal Sub-plot*. http://inside.org.au, 14/4/2009.

not so far made serious attempts to organise among the trade unions. They also need to move away from the influence of populist capitalist politicians like Taksin.

The class struggle and the movement for Democracy

What we have been seeing in Thailand since late 2005, is a growing class war between the poor and the conservative elites. Those who started this class war, only intended it to be an inter-elite dispute in order to get rid of Taksin, but they have succeeded in unleashing major class forces. The elites are now seen by the Red Shirts as an autocracy *(Ummart)*, existing outside the formal confines of the Constitution, or as Jakrapop Pencare calls it: a "state within a state".

It is of course not a pure class war. Due to a vacuum on the Left, millionaire and populist politicians like Taksin Shinawat managed to provide leadership to the poor. For the last 80 years there have been many movements of the poor and oppressed, throughout the World, who have fought the ruling classes using different ideologies and organisational forms. This does not mean that class is not the fundamental underlying issue. Hamas, Hezbollah, the Bolivarian Movement, various national liberation movements in Asia and Africa or pro-democracy movements in Eastern Europe, may not look like the Bolsheviks of 1917, but they are, never the less, movements of oppressed classes. It is only sectarian purists on the Left who would turn their backs on such movements.

We need to cut down the military's influence in society, reform the judiciary and the police and to expand freedom and Democracy from this grass-roots movement. And we need to abolish the Monarchy too. For in the minds of millions, it has now become an obstacle to freedom and human dignity. Thais need to create a culture of citizenship rather than being merely "royal subjects".

The Redshirts have learnt through struggle since the 19th September 2006 coup, that "Real Democracy" will not just be achieved by mass demonstrations or by winning repeated elections. Demonstrations have been put down by bloody repression and election results have been repeatedly overturned by unconstitutional means. The pro-democracy movement has come to realise that our aims are being blocked by powerful and entrenched interests. It isn't any single person or institution among the elites.

The debate among Redshirts in 2009 was about reform or revolution as a road to Democracy. It was not about whether or not to overthrow Capitalism. The full power of the elites is now plain for all to see. The question is how to deal with it. The stakes are very high. Only a revolutionary movement can overthrow the power of the conservative elites. But many Red Shirt leaders want compromise. Any compromise has the risk of instability because it will satisfy almost no one. The old elites might want to do a deal with Taksin to stop the Red Shirts from becoming totally republican or socialist. But whatever happens, Thai society cannot go back to the old days. The Red Shirts represent millions of Thais who are sick and tired of intervention in politics by the conservatives. At the very least they will want a non-political Constitutional Monarchy.

Taksin and the 3 political leaders of the *Kwam Jing Wan Nee* (Truth Today) programme [64] are in the reform camp. They feel that the task of overthrowing the elites is too big, too risky and counter-productive. They want a peaceful road with compromise. They are prepared to keep the Monarchy like it is today with minor changes. Many Redshirts would agree with them because they fear violence and upheaval. Revolution risks a bloody crack-down and long jail sentences. It is a difficult task. But the reform road risks capitulating to the conservative elites. The 2009 petition to the King to pardon Taksin, which was supported by this faction, and organised by millions of grass-roots Red Shirts, carried many dangers. It risked perpetuating an image which justifies the power of the King in an undemocratic fashion. But equally, it was used to expose the King and the royalists for being against the people. It caused a real head-ache for the conservatives.

---

[64] These are three ex-TRT politicians: Wira Musikapong, Jatuporn Prompan and Natawut Saikua.

Jakrapop Pencare and I are for revolution. But we may disagree on many issues. Jakrapop is clear that the Monarchy must be reformed. My view is that it is too late to wish for a reformed Constitutional Monarchy in Thailand in the same model as Britain or Japan. The army generals and the conservative elites have shown that at any time they are prepared to use the Monarchy to destroy Democracy and rip up the Constitution. Therefore we must abolish the Monarchy and cut down the size and power of the army. Thai history teaches us from the 1970s and 1990s that such significant changes in society only come about through mass struggle. Actions by small groups or by a so-called "liberation army"[65] cannot achieve the necessary thorough-going changes. It would mean denying the role of millions of Red Shirts.

As a socialist, I would hope that during the revolutionary struggle for Democracy, many people will come to realise that parliamentary Democracy is not enough. We need Social Justice and equality. We need to build a democratic space from where we can move forward to fighting for Socialism and that means also building a socialist party among the Red Shirts. We need economic Democracy where the people decide on investment and production. This is the true Democracy of Socialism. It is a million miles from the Stalinist dictatorships of North Korea, China, Laos, Vietnam or Cuba.

There is no guarantee of success for the revolutionary road in Thailand. It will be a long hard struggle. But I believe that there is no longer any room for reform in order to achieve Democracy. The behaviour of the elites since the 2006 coup has once again proved this. But in the real world there are no cast-iron guarantees. As Gramsci once said..... the best way to try to predict the future is to get involved in the struggle.

---

[65] Advocated by Surachai Sa-Darn.

Chapter 2
The Disgrace of NGOs, the Semi-Fascist PAD, and the Tragedy of Civil Society

It is in times of crisis that activists face difficult tests and choices. Political positions that previously seemed to be roughly in line with Democracy and Social Justice can, in times like this, be put to the test and be found wanting. No social activist operates in a vacuum of theory, even if they declare that they are only practical people, uninterested in theory. The importance of political theory has been proved by events in Thailand since the 2006 military coup and the position taken by most Thai Non-Government Organisation (NGOs). Activists who set up or joined NGOs because they were committed to Social Justice and democratic rights have now ended up siding with a military coup and the conservative elites against the poor. This behaviour by the NGOs cannot be explained in terms of personal failings or "lack of character". It is about politics.

Five years ago, Thailand, under the elected Taksin Government, had an active Civil Society, where social movements campaigned to protect the interests of the poor. This activity was not particularly encouraged by Taksin's *Thai Rak Thai Party* (TRT), despite the fact that this big business party argued that the poor should be "stake-holders" in society. The vibrancy of Civil Society was therefore due to the activities of social movements, NGOs and various activists.

The problems started in late 2005 when mass anti-Government demonstrations led by the mis-named *"Peoples Alliance for Democracy"* (PAD) hit the streets of Bangkok. The PAD began as a strange cross-class alliance between disgruntled royalist media tycoon Sonti Limtongkul and a handful of NGO and social movement leaders. Rather than accepting that the electorate support for Taksin was because of the Government's first ever Universal Health Care Scheme and many other pro-poor measures, Taksin's opponents, including most of the NGOs, claimed that the poor did not understand Democracy. Many NGO leaders and activists claimed that the poor "lacked political information" and therefore the voting system, which was dominated by the poor, was somehow flawed.

The NGO and social movement leaders of the PAD got pulled sharply to the Right by Sonti Limtongkul and donned royal yellow shirts. They also called on the King to sack Taksin's elected Government. This, the King refused to do, but the PAD demands were seen as a green light for the military coup in September. After the 2006 coup, the PAD descended into a fascist type of organisation. It took on ultra-Royalist and ultra-Nationalist politics. It nearly caused a war with Cambodia over an ancient hill-top ruin. It built up a black jacketed armed guard who openly carried and used fire-arms and other weapons on the streets of Bangkok. The PAD's media outlet, *Manager Group*, launched witch-hunts and encouraging violence against academics and social activists on the Left.

The politics of the PAD

The Peoples Alliance for Democracy was a popular front movement against the Taksin Government, comprising 23 so-called "Peoples Organisations" in alliance with royalist businessman Sonti Limtongkul and conservative Buddhist Chamlong Simuang . The bulk of its mass base was among the Bangkok middle classes and it organised large rallies against the Taksin Government in the period February to April 2006. The largest of these rallies was attended by more than 100,000 people.

The PAD had 5 leaders:

1. Sonti Limtongkul: Conservative royalist media tycoon and owner of the Manager Group media company.
2. Chamlong Simuang: Ex-*Palang Tum Party* leader, leading light in the Buddhist *Santi Asoke* movement, extreme anti-abortionist, and one of the leaders of the May 1992 Democracy protest.
3. Somsak Kosaisuk: Retired leader of the Railway Workers Union, organiser of the *Thai Labour Solidarity Committee* and one of the leaders of the May 1992 Democracy movement.
4. Pipop Tongchai: Advisor to the *Campaign for Popular Democracy*, education reform activist and "NGO elder"[1].
5. Somkiat Pongpaiboon: Lecturer at Korat Rajpat Institute and activist working with teachers' groups and farmers.

The PAD spokesperson was Suriyasai Takasila, ex-student activist and head of the *Campaign for Popular Democracy*.

Crudely speaking, businessman Sonti Limtongkul provided the funds and used his media empire to publicise the movement, while the other four leaders helped to draw activist supporters to the rallies. This was a case of a top-down "cross-class popular front" often favoured by the Stalinist and Maoist Left in the past, including the now defunct *Communist Party of Thailand* (CPT). Ex-Maoists in the PAD argued that they needed to build an alliance with royalists against big business "agents of neo-liberal imperialism" like Taksin[2]. Both Somsak Kosaisuk and Somkiat Pongpaiboon have been directly influenced by Maoist ideas originating from the CPT. The irony of the Maoist "cross-class alliance" legacy in Thailand is that there were also ex-CPT activists on the opposite side, inside Taksin's TRT. They were busy building a mirror image cross-class alliance with

[1] The seniority system is a strong component of local Thai NGOs.

[2] This strategy was first suggested by Pipop Tongchai at an NGO "Peoples Assembly" meeting on 23rd January 2005, although Pipop himself was never a supporter of the CPT. However, CPT politics has influenced most social movement activists.

"progressive capitalists" against the "feudalists". Some comparisons can be made with the Philippines in the case of the anti-Arroyo movement in the same period. The Maoist *Communist Party of the Philippines* chose to build a top down alliance with the so-called "progressive bourgeoisie", rather than build an independent working class and peasant movement against Arroyo as advocated by *Laban ng Masa*[3].

A major debate between the Stalinist / Maoist Left and the Trotskyist Left had always been about the issue of forming cross-class alliances or popular fronts. This emerged very seriously in the debates around the tactics of the Chinese Communist Party in the mid 1920s and the Spanish Communist Party in the 1930s[4]. The major criticism of the popular front strategy, which also applies to the case of the PAD in Thailand in 2006, is that the interests of the working class and peasantry are sacrificed in such an alliance and the leadership is handed over to the elites and the middle-classes. Without doing this, the elites and conservative middles classes would not join the alliance in the first place.

In the case of the PAD, major sections from the Peoples Movement and NGOs joined up with Sonti because they believed that the Peoples Movement was "too weak" to mobilise against Taksin on an independent class basis. Many activists also believed that it was a wise tactic to team up with Sonti who had a large media outlet and lots of funds[5]. They also believed that by using the language of the royalists that they would gain mass support. This explains why Sonti had real control of all PAD policies. It also explains why the PAD ignored all issues which affected the working

---

[3] *Laban ng Masa* (Struggle of the Masses) is an anti-Maoist left-wing coalition made up of people who split from the Communist Party.

[4] See Nigel Harris (1978) *The Mandate of Heaven. Marx and Mao in Modern China. Quartet Books*. And Ian Birchall (1974) *Workers against the monolith. The Communist Parties since 1943*. Pluto Press.

[5] The information in this section on the politics of the PAD comes out of interviews of 31 Peoples Movement activists, carried out by the author's research team in early to mid 2006, together with surveys of media reports and declarations. The full results have been published in Thai in the book: Ji Ungpakorn et al. (2006) *Social Movements in Thailand*. Workers Democracy Publishers.

class and peasantry, concentrating on "defending the Monarchy" and accusing Taksin of corruption.

By November 2009 Pipop Tongchai could make a speech at a PAD rally about the need to sacrifice ones life for Nation, Religion and Monarchy. "Nation Religion and Monarchy" have always been the key pillars of reactionary ideology. Whether he personally was prepared to sacrifice his own life, was not clear. Perhaps he meant the lives of young soldiers, from poor families, on the border with Cambodia. Pipop also argued that Thailand was "indivisible", taking up the extreme nationalism of the ruling class. The logical conclusion would be to rule out any autonomy or independence for the southern Muslim provinces. Somkiat Pongpaiboon, at the same rally, descended into superstition, claiming that Thailand would always be safe from its enemies because there was a royal angel protecting the country. Presumably Thailand's enemies are in fact the majority of the population who are Red Shirts.

Before joining the PAD in late 2005, NGO and Peoples Movement activists had great illusions in Taksin's TRT after its first landslide victory at the polls in 2001. Some NGO activists even joined Taksin's inner circle.

The view that the Peoples Movement was too weak to act independently has some truth, given the way that the movement was and still is fragmented by single issue campaigning and an anarchistic refusal to build any unified political theory or political party. Yet it is also a gross exaggeration which overlooks the realities of class struggle on the ground, especially during the Taksin era. One important aspect of the problem of seeing the movement as weak in 2005, stems from the fact that the Peoples Movement representatives in the PAD lacked a genuine mass base. Somsak, Pipop and Somkiat are good examples. They are figure heads of the movement who rely on others to mobilise people.

Somsak was unsuccessful in mobilising significant numbers of workers to PAD rallies, despite the fact that he was an important leader in the *Thai Labour Solidarity Committee* and a retired leader of the Railway Workers Union. While he led the Railway Workers Union, he failed to lead any strikes against privatisation or to stem the spread of casualisation on the railways. Instead he built relationships with senior management and politicians. Another reason for Somsak's weakness in attracting workers to the PAD was very much related to the fact that the PAD campaigned solely around the middle-class and business class issue of Taksin's corruption, rather than talking about issues directly relevant to the labour movement and the poor. Of course corruption is an important issue for poor people, but they rightly see that all politicians, military men and business elites are corrupt. In the past, the working class and peasantry had been successfully mobilised on issues such as human rights, Democracy, land rights and opposition to privatisation and Free Trade Agreements. Yet the PAD hardly mentioned any of these issues and only once mentioned the problem of violence and human rights abuses in the South.

The issue of Taksin's corruption and the conflicts of interest became real issues for those business people who were missing out on the rich pickings which were being taken by those in the Taksin loop. It is this fact which turned Sonti Limtongkul against Taksin, since they used to be friends. The lack of sincererity over this issue could be seen by the fact that ex-TRT M.P. and corrupt politician Sanoh Tientong was welcomed like a hero on to the stage at a PAD rally. The fuss about Taksin's domination of so-called "independent bodies", such as the various bodies over-seeing privatised industries or the media, was not about the fact that these bodies were not representative of the population as a whole (ie. the working class and peasantry), but more about the fact that Taksin was shutting out rival capitalist interests. The censorship and domination of all official bodies by the army and their allies since the 2006 coup has not been criticised by the PAD at all.

Pipop Tongchai, although a senior figure in the NGO movement, had no real mass base in the NGO movement either. Even the *Campaign for Popular Democracy*, which was a large campaigning organisation against military rule back in the early 1990s was an empty shell ten years later. Pipop relied on asking people in the various NGO networks to do him "a favour" by mobilising people to the rallies. However, they were not that successful in mobilising villagers who were the main constituency of

NGOs. This is because most villagers voted for TRT. In fact Somkiat Pongpaiboon had long complained that ever since the Taksin Government came to power he had been unable to mobilise any rural villagers to protest events.

The tragedy of the cross-class alliance strategy, used by the NGOs, was that by handing over the political leadership to Sonti, they came to rely more and more on the reactionary urban middle classes to make up the movement. Despite claiming that they would be able to "tone-down" Sonti's royalist rhetoric, as part of the justification for linking up with him, this never happened[6]. The entire PAD leadership supported the demand for the King to appoint a Government, over the heads of the wishes of the poor, by using Section 7 of the 1997 Constitution[7]. The *Assembly of the Poor* and a number of trade unions and rural activists were extremely unhappy with this demand to use section 7 and they refused to support PAD rallies.

Worse than this, the PAD leadership positioned itself in opposition to the poor by accusing them of voting for Taksin out of a "lack of information" ie. stupidity. Taksin's pro-poor policies were portrayed as "bad for the nation's finances" in classical neo-liberal fashion, and the poor people who came to Bangkok to support Taksin in the *Caravan of the Poor* were slandered as being merely "rent a mob". It may well be the case that TRT helped pay the travel expenses of these poor villagers, but Sonti also paid for the demonstration expenses of the PAD. In neither case did it mean that the participants were not genuine volunteers with genuine beliefs.

Eventually the final act of the cross-class alliance was played out. The 19th September coup leaders would never have had the confidence to stage the coup if the NGOs had had a clear anti-dictatorship position from the very beginning. But that would have meant respecting the poor and trying to pull them away from TRT to a left-wing party, with better pro-poor policies.

---

6 Nitirat Supsomboon from FOP was one among many who used this excuse.

7 Somsak maintains that he always opposed the use of Section 7, but had to bow to the wishes of the majority.

The position of those NGOs most closely associated with the PAD was clear when they showed no interest what so ever in building or taking part in the Thai Social Forum (TSF) in October 2006, despite the fact that Pipop was invited to take part in a plenary debate. Similarly, Somsak's *Thai Labour Solidarity Committee* played no part in the Social Forum either, but did try to mobilise some days earlier to meet the military junta in order to make futile suggestions as to who should be the new Minister of Labour.

Added to the problem of the cross-class alliance was the fact that the PAD leadership was entirely middle-aged and male. This reflected the most backward ideas that respect Male Seniority. The PAD leadership is even more backward in the light of the fact that it is very rare today to find any social movement or NGO in Thailand without significant involvement and leadership by women activists. During the anti-Taksin campaigns by the PAD, a group of women activists, varying in age, made a serious approach to be included in the leadership[8]. However this was angrily dismissed by Sonti and seen as a bit of a "joke" by the other male leaders of the PAD.

In response to some accusations that the PAD leadership acted in an undemocratic manner, the PAD leadership complained that the various representatives of the 23 Peoples Organisations never bothered to turn up to meetings. This is probably true. However, the question is why was this so? Was it because they had already been excluded from any real decision-making process, or was it because these organisations were mere "ghost organisation", shells without mass membership? Both are probably true.

How the NGOs sided with the conservative royalists

It is shocking that almost the entire Thai NGO movement lined up with the conservative elites against the pro-democracy poor. It is shocking because NGO activists started out by being on the side of the poor and the

[8] The chairwoman of NGO-COD Rawadee Parsertjaroensuk was part of this delegation.

oppressed in society. This reactionary position needs to be explained in a political and historical context, rather than in terms of any personal failings by NGO leaders.

Unlike the business community who turned against Taksin at the last moment, the Peoples Movement was not dormant in its criticism of the Taksin Government after the honey-moon period in the early days. The largest movement mounted by the working class against the Taksin Government was the action against electricity privatisation by 200,000 workers in 2004. It helped to delay privatisation plans and energised the labour movement. Despite the protests against the Government's human rights abuses, against gas pipelines, against privatisation or the huge rally against Free Trade Agreements by the social movements, the Government retained strong support among the poor because there was no credible left-wing party that could mount an electoral challenge. The right-wing mainstream parties obviously had no appeal to the poor. This weakness in political representation is a symptom of the autonomist and right-wing reformist policies of the social movements and their NGO advisors who opposed the building of a left-wing party.

At the start of the anti-Taksin protests, many NGOs joined the PAD demonstrators. They joined this cross-class alliance without any pre-conditions. It was legitimate to protest against the excesses of the Government, but it was highly questionable whether the NGOs should have joined forces with conservative royalist businessmen like Sonti Limtongkul. Soon NGO involvement with the PAD, and then with the military junta, after the coup of 2006, went far beyond anything that can be classified as a genuine support for freedom and Democracy.

After the 2006 coup, some Thai NGO leaders, such as Rawadee Parsertjaroensuk (*NGO-Coordinating Committee* NGO-COD), Nimit Tienudom *(AIDS network)*, Banjong Nasa *(Southern Fisher Folk network)*, Witoon Permpongsajaroen *(Ecology movement)* and Sayamon Kaiyurawong *(Thai Volunteer Service)* etc. put themselves forward in the hope that the military would select them as appointed Senators. They were to be disappointed. Earlier, long standing social activists such as Chop Yodkeaw,

Tuenjai Deetate and Wiboon Kemchalerm were appointed to the junta's parliamentary assembly. NGO activists such as Rawadee Parsertjaroensuk and Nimit Tienudom attended PAD rallies. Nimit claimed at a rally on 23rd March 2006, that most Taksin supporters "did not know the truth" about his Government[9]. This is extremely patronising to the poor. Many NGO leaders such as Nimit, also told their members not to protest against the military junta at the closing ceremony of the Thai Social Forum in October 2006, although the leadership of the NGO-Coordinating Committee did support this protest. Immediately after the coup, even the Thai staff of *Focus on Global South* supported the coup[10], although Walden Bello maintained a principled opposition to dictatorship.

While some NGO activists became Government appointees under the military junta, most also had illusions that the military would clean up Thai politics with their new constitution. During the Social Forum, large Thai NGOs like *Raks Thai Foundation* brought yellow-shirted villagers along. This NGO receives a large amount of money from the Thai State. The World Social Forum movement was initially founded on the concept of being totally independent from the state, yet The Thai Social Forum received funds from state organisations such as the "Office of the Thai Health Promotion Fund"[11].

It is interesting to compare a number of statements made by NGO-COD about the violent PAD protests throughout 2008, with the statements made in April 2009 about Red Shirt protests. The substance of the difference is in the emphasis. In May, June and September 2008, Pairot Polpet, as NGO-COD chairperson issued statements calling for the pro-Taksin Government to respect the right of the PAD to "peaceful protest". In June 2008, NGO-COD called on the pro-Taksin Government to resign. Elected PAD and NGO Senator Rosana Tositrakul stated that the Government had no right to disperse the PAD protestors who had seized

---

[9] http://www.prachatai.com/ 23/3/2006 (In Thai).

[10] http://focusweb.org/the-thai-coup-democracy-and-wearing-yellow-on- mondays.html?Itemid=93 by Chanida Chanyapate and Alec Bamford.

[11] www.thaihealth.or.th

Government House. It is important to note that the pro-Taksin Government did not use the army or live ammunition on the PAD. Police mis-use of tear-gas, may however have caused one PAD death outside parliament in October 2008. Other PAD deaths were accidents caused by the PAD's home made bombs.

Later, after the *Democrats* had been manoeuvred into power by the Army and PAD, in April 2009, NGO-COD called on the Red Shirts to stop "violent protests" against the new Government. They later praised the voluntary ending of Red Shirt protests as a way to build peace. They called on the *Democrat* Government to "only use legal means to disperse protestors". One day later, the army and the Government used live ammunition to disperse the Red Shirts, killing and injuring many. An NGO-COD statement a week later did not call on the Government to resign[12]. *The Consumers' Association, AIDS networks and Slum Dwellers group*, under the leadership of Nimit Tienudom and Saree Ongsomwang, went further and denounced the Red Shirt protests on 13th April, but not the actions of the Government. A month later, on 8th May 2009, the northern section of NGO-COD issued a statement about the Thai political crisis. This statement claimed that the root cause of the crisis was the way that "politicians had been able to manipulate the system for their own benefit". There was not one single mention of the role of the army in destroying Democracy[13].

Four days earlier, the chairperson of NGO-COD joined a military sponsored event in front of the statue of King Rama 6th, called "Stop Harming Thailand"[14]. Despite its claim to be about "peace" the event was aimed at opposing further mass protests by Red Shirts. No such activity had ever been organised at the time when armed PAD thugs roamed the streets and shut down the two international airports. In response to this military sponsored event, Niti Eawsriwong, a prominent social critic, pointed to the fact that "Thailand was harming the people" by marginalising

[12] http://www.prachatai.com/ May,June, September 2008, 13,15 & 23 April 2009 (In Thai).

[13] http://www.prachatai.com/ 12/5/2009 (In Thai).

[14] *Matichon* on line 5/5/2009 www.matichon.co.th (In Thai).

the majority from politics and creating great social injustices. Under such circumstances, he asked, "why should Thailand be safe from the protest of the people?[15]

In the 1980s Thai NGOs worked under the slogan "the answer is in the villages", reflecting a respect for ordinary villagers. Today they seem to be working under the new slogan "build Democracy by military coups, the answer is with the army". Despite their initial well-meaning aims, the politics or lack of politics in the NGO movement, and also their own lack of Democracy and accountability has let them down and they have been increasingly drawn to reactionary right-wing politics.

The historical and political context of the NGO position

Like most countries throughout the World, Thailand went through a process of mass radicalisation in the late 1960s and early 1970s. The high point was when a mass movement of students and urban workers overthrew the military dictatorship in October 1973[16]. The Maoist CPT was the organisation which gained most from this radicalisation, especially after the ruling elites fought back with a blood bath in October 1976. However, the Maoist strategy failed because the CPT mainly ignored workers struggles in urban areas, they were shocked by the growing friendship between "Maoist" China and the Thai military Government in the late 1970s, and the student activists became disillusioned with the Party's authoritarian nature. By the mid 1980s, the Party had collapsed. Into this vacuum on the Left, stepped the NGOs. Many of the founding members of Thai NGOs came from the ruins of the CPT.

---

[15] *Matichon* on line 11/5/2009 www.matichon.co.th Niti Eawsiwong "Thailand Stop Harming the People". (In Thai).

[16] Ji Giles Ungpakorn (2007) *A Coup for the Rich.* WD Press. Ji Giles Ungpakorn (2003) contributing editor, *Radicalising Thailand: new political perspectives.* Giles Ungpakorn (2001) "The political economy of class struggle in modern Thailand." Historical Materialism 8, Summer , 153-183.

The legacy of the Communist Party

All during the two decades of the 1960s and 1970s the CPT, with its Stalinist-Maoist politics, was the dominant influence on the Peoples Movement. Like their sisters and brothers around the world, Thai activists reacted to the collapse of Communist Party both in terms of its failure and its authoritarian nature. The negative legacy of the CPT meant that there was a dominance of Autonomism, Post-Modernism and right-wing Reformism among the Thai Peoples Movement. These are all political theories which lead to an acceptance of the free market and liberalism, either because they reject "theories" and "Grand Narratives" or because they see no alternative to free-market Capitalism since the movement from below is "doomed to failure". CPT Maoism was also a "de-politicising" ideology, given that it did not discuss many important issues such as the free market, gender politics and class issues while promoting nationalism[17].

The overall result was a movement which was de-politicised and concentrated on single issue problem solving. The rejection of the need for an independent theory, or theories, of the Peoples Movement goes hand in hand with the rejection, by many, of the need to build a political party of the working class and peasantry. It is this vacuum of theory in the Thai Peoples Movement which allowed the liberals to dominate. Examples of this can be seen in support for the free-market as a mechanism to bring about "accountability" and the total acceptance of liberal political ideas about "independent bodies" which were created in the 1997 Constitution[18]. In Europe, the Left sees "independent bodies", such as the European Central Bank, as being the result of neoliberal mechanisms.

---

[17] See Ji Giles Ungpakorn (2003) Challenges to the Thai N.G.O. movement from the dawn of a new opposition to global capital. In Ji Giles Ungpakorn (ed.) Already quoted. Also Giles Ji Ungpakorn (2006) "The impact of the Thai "Sixties" on the Peoples Movement today. *Inter-Asia Cultural Studies*, 7 (4). Published by Routledge.

[18] See Michael Kelly Connors (2003) *Democracy and National Identity in Thailand.* RoutledgeCurzon, and Ji Giles Ungpakorn (2002) From Tragedy to Comedy: Political Reform in Thailand. Journal of Contemporary Asia 32 (2), 191-205.

Never the less, the recent Thai Social Forum and the massive protests against electricity privatisation and against the Free Trade Agreement with the United States, show that there was a deepening concern about the market and Neo-Liberalism among the Peoples Movement which could have been developed into a principled class position. After the Social Forum, many statements were made about the need for a welfare state. But the NGOs soon reverted back to their old ways, re-adopting "Community Economics" or even the King's "Sufficiency Economics".

NGO politics after the collapse of the CPT

After the "collapse of Communism" the NGO movement turned its back on "politics" and the primacy of mass movements and political parties in the 1980s[19]. Instead they embraced "lobby politics" [20] and/or Community Anarchism[21]. Despite the apparent contradiction between lobby politics, which leads NGOs to cooperate with the state, and state-rejecting Community Anarchism, the two go together. This is because they reject any confrontation or competition with the state. Lobbyists cooperate with the state, while Community Anarchists hope to ignore it. They both reject building a big picture political analysis[22]. Instead of building mass movements or political parties, the NGOs concentrated on single-issue campaigns as part of their attempt to avoid confrontation with the state. This method of working also dove-tailed with grant applications to international funding bodies. It led to a de-politicisation of the movement. Thus, NGOs cooperated with both military and elected Governments in

---

[19] Ji Giles Ungpakorn (2003) Already quoted.

[20] A lack of power among NGO bureaucrats leads to lobby politics. Ana Margarida Esteves, Sara Motta & Laurence Cox (2009) "Civil society versus social movements" (editorial) *Interface: a journal for and about social movements* 1 (2): 1 - 21 (November 2009).

[21] See Chattip Nartsupa et al., (1998) Agricultural Community Economics in Thailand. Wititat Poompanya 7. (In Thai).

[22] Somchai Pataratananun (2006) *Civil Society and Democratization. Social Movements in Northeast Thailand.* NIAS press. p.84.

Thailand since the early 1980s. In 1989 they were invited to be part of the state's 7th National Economic and Social Development Plan and by 1992 NGOs were receiving budget allocations from the Ministry of Health. The Social Welfare department and the department of Environment also provided funds[23]. This raises the issue of "GNGOs" ie., Government funded NGOs. Can they really be called NGOs?

The NGOs also oppose Representative Democracy, along Anarchist lines, because they believe it only leads to dirty Money Politics. But the Direct Democracy in village communities, which they advocate, is powerless in the face of the all powerful state. It also glorifies traditional and conservative village leaders who are not subject to any democratic mandate. Eventually, the idea goes together with a failure to defend Parliamentary Democracy. Their anarchistic rejection of representative politics, allowed them to see "no difference" between an elected parliament controlled by TRT and a military coup. Instead of bothering to carefully analyse the political situation, the distrust of elections, votes[24] and Representative Democracy allowed NGOs to align themselves with reactionaries like the PAD and the military, who advocate more appointed public positions.

Initially, in 2001, the NGOs loved-up to Taksin's TRT Government. They believed that it was open to NGO lobbying, which it was. TRT took on board the idea of a Universal Health Care System from progressive doctors and health-related NGOs. But then, the NGOs were wrong-footed by the Government's raft of other pro-poor policies that seemed to prove to villagers that the NGOs had only been "playing" at development. What is more, the increased use of the state to provide welfare and benefits by the TRT Government went against the Anarchist-inspired NGO idea that communities should organise their own welfare. After their about-face in

---

[23] Shinichi Shigetomi, Kasian Tejapira & Apichart Thongyou, Contributing editors (2004) *The NGO way: Perspectives and Experiences from Thailand.* Institute of Developing Economies, Japan External Trade Organization, Chiba, Japan. p.49

[24] NGOs are opposed to taking votes in meetings, preferring "consensus". Ji Ungpakorn (2006) *Social Movements in Thailand.* Already quoted, p.64, (In Thai). Chris Nineham (2006) Anti-capitalism, social forums and the return of politics. *International Socialism* 109, U.K.

attitude to TRT, the NGOs turned towards the conservative royalists and the army.

The link between the ideas of conservative royalists and the NGOs had been forged even earlier in the late 1990s, when NGOs started to take up the Kings theory of the "Sufficiency Economy", claiming that it was the same as their Anarchist ideas of Community Self-Sufficiency, which argued for a separation from market Capitalism[25]. Thus, both NGO-COD and the *Thai Volunteer Service* enthusiastically promoted the Sufficiency Economy. Later, Yuk Si-Araya, an ex-CPT activist turned right-wing nationalist and supporter of the PAD, argued for the Sufficiency Economy on the same basis[26]. He also argued that "Western-style" democracy was incompatible with Thai culture. Finally, the conservative royalist and medical doctor, Prawase Wasi, provided the bridge between the NGOs and the conservatives in the state[27].

Again, despite the apparent contradiction between the conservative elite's idea of "Sufficiency Economy", which is really a reactionary ideology aimed at keeping the poor "happy" in their poverty, and the Anarchist Community Self-Sufficiency, which is more about villagers becoming independent from the state, the two ideas fit together. Both reject state welfare and the use of the state as an instrument to redistribute wealth. Both also fail to challenge the power and authority of the ruling elites and the state. Both Community Self-Sufficiency and Sufficiency Economy claim to oppose the modern capitalist market, yet the military junta managed to write Sufficiency Economy into their 2007 Constitution alongside extreme neoliberal free-market policies. The utopian nature of both sufficiency theories allows them to be very flexible and detached from reality.

---

[25] Yukti Mukdawichit (2005) *Reading Community Culture*. Fa Deaw Kan Press, In Thai.

[26] Yuk Si-Araya or Tienchai Wongchaisuwan (2007) http://www.thaioctober.com/forum/index.php?topic=198.30

[27] Chanida Chitbundid, Chaithawat Thulathon & Thanapol Eawsakul (2004) The Thai Monarchy and NGOs. In Shinichi Shigetomi,Kasian Tejapira & Apichart Thongyou, Contributing editors (2004) *The NGO way: Perspectives and Experiences from Thailand*. Institute of Developing Economies, Japan External Trade Organization, Chiba, Japan. pp.131-137.

The Anarchistic distrust of state-organised welfare, helped the NGOs to oppose the Taksin Government. For many NGOs, welfare should be organised by communities. But this anti-state position opened the door to accepting a neo-liberal concept of a small state, a view shared by the conservative royalists.

Just because Anarchism can fit together with lobby politics and conservative royalist ideas, it does not mean that all Anarchist organisations automatically link up with conservative elites. The *Assembly of the Poor* (AOP), a mass movement of poor farmers, which was led by some NGO activists, never supported the 2006 coup and never supported the PAD. However, it was one of the honourable exceptions. The key point about the *Assembly of the Poor* is that it was a social movement with mass involvement of the poor, unlike most NGOs or NGO networks. Many AOP activists remain extremely hostile to military coups and the strong hand of the state. AOP tactics emphasised mass protests rather than trying to get positions on state-sponsored committees, although they have also adopted lobby tactics as well[28].

The political situation, before and just after the coup, was extremely messy and difficult. There was not much to choose from between the two elite sides, except for the important fact that TRT held power through the electoral process. In this situation the NGOs should have remained neutral and with the poor and they should have opposed the coup. But they were angry that TRT had won over their supporters and were distrustful of TRT's use of the state to build welfare programmes and stimulate the economy.

Because Community Self-Sufficiency, separated from state and market, are extremely utopian ideas which are not particularly popular with rural people, there was a danger that NGOs which advocate such ideas could become elitist in outlook, seeing villagers as hopelessly misguided. Since

---

[28] For a good account of the *Assembly of the Poor*, see Bruce Missingham (2003) *The Assembly of the Poor in Thailand.* Silkworm Books. It has a sharper analysis than Prapart Pintoptang (1998) *Street Politics: 99 days of the Assembly of the Poor*. Krerg University, Bangkok.(In Thai).

the poor voted on mass for TRT, the NGOs became viciously patronising towards villagers, claiming that they "lack the right information" to make political decisions. In fact, there was always a patronising element to their practical work. Many Thai NGO leaders are self-appointed middle class activists who shun elections and believe that NGOs should "nanny[29]" peasants and workers. They have become bureaucratised. They are now fearful and contemptuous of the Red Shirt movement, which is starting a process of self-empowerment of the poor. Of course, the Red Shirts are not angels, but in today's crisis, they represent the poor and the thirst for freedom and Democracy.

The Thai NGO experience

In general terms, what we can say about the Thai experience is that the NGO movement is now lined up with the elite against the mass of the population[30]. It is no longer possible for progressive people to work with them[31]. Unless serious splits and changes occur, they cannot be regarded as part of any Civil Society movement for Thai Democracy.

International issues concerning NGOs

What are the international lessons for NGO activists? What we can generalise from Thailand is that NGOs run the risk of taking the wrong side in any serious social conflict. There are four major reasons which might cause such mistakes.

1. **Funding pressures.** NGOs increasingly receive money from local Governments and imperialist organisations like the World Bank. They are "GNGOs" and can become reluctant to oppose

[29] In Thai they refer to themselves as *Pi-Liang*.

[30] One honourable exception is the *Thai Labour Campaign*, which has consistently opposed the coup and any destruction of Democracy. http://www.thailabour.org

[31] As I used to believe when I wrote: "NGOs: Enemies or Allies?" *International Socialism Journal 104* Autumn 2004, U.K.

the elites. NGOs in northern Vietnam are a good example [32]. In some cases, NGOs funded by the U.S. Government, mainstream U.S. political parties or local businessmen, have masqueraded as "Civil Society Organisations" and taken an anti-democratic stance. A good example is the support for the coup against the elected Aristide government in Haiti in 2004 [33]. Such support even came from organisations like *Christian Aid.* In the case of some Eastern European revolutions against authoritarian regimes, NGOs funded by the U.S. Government have worked to promote the free-market and a friendly orientation towards the West, rather than concentrating on issues of social equality. However, in Thailand, because of the historical strength of the Peoples Movement and Civil Society, the NGOs have not been political tools of Western Imperialism, but have been more home-grown organisations. Never the less, they have come under the influence of the elites in Government.

2. **Lobby politics** mean there is always a tendency to be opportunistic, being prepared to work with authoritarian Governments. NGOs need to commit to building mass movements, rather than relying only on "professional" lobby politics and "nannying" the poor. It is mass social movements which build Democracy and help to establish basic rights. The serious pitfalls of lobby politics in South-east Asia were revealed at the ASEAN [34] summit in Thailand in October 2009, when various NGOs in the region lobbied to get a collection of repressive and undemocratic Governments [35] to set up a Human Rights Commission which then acted as a powerless fig-leaf to hide anti-democratic policies.

---

[32] Joerg Wischermann (2003) Vietnam in the era of Doi Moi. Issue-oriented Organisations and their relationship to the government. *Asian Survey* 43(6) 867-889.

[33] Peter Hallward (2007) *Damming the Flood. Haiti, Aristide, and the Politics of Containment.* Verso.

[34] ASEAN: The Association of South-east Asian Nations.

[35] Burma, Thailand, Vietnam, Laos, Cambodia and Singapore are authoritarian regimes.

3. **Rejection of politics**, especially class politics, and a rejection of debate. This lack of politics and debate means that in difficult and messy situations NGOs do not have the necessary theory to be able to choose the side of the poor or Democracy. What is needed is more political theorising and more open debate. The consensus politics of NGOs works against this.
4. **Adoption of utopian Anarchist ideas** about traditional rural communities and small states, can lead NGOs to take up conservative and elitist ideas or align themselves with neo-liberal free-market ideology.

What the above four issues all have in common is that they are dangers which arise from the bureaucratisation or professionalisation of powerless NGOs such that they find themselves in a middle position between genuine social movements and the ruling elites. As with trade union bureaucrats the NGOs will value their lobby and funding links with the elites and try to keep at bay the radical demands of social movements[36]. This means that they may oscillate between siding with reactionary elites against the movements of the poor and trying to lead social movement struggles when the elites fail to take them seriously.

NGOs, trade unions and "new" social movements in South-East Asia

Apart from the problem of NGOs supporting the destruction of Democracy, in countries like Thailand and Haiti, or giving legitimacy to authoritarian regimes through their lobby politics, there is also the issue of NGOs and their relationship with mass social movements, especially the trade unions.

NGOs are like small businesses. They are not mass organisations like trade unions and they do not have any democratic tradition of electing leaders and representatives or of seeking decisions through the balloting of

[36] Ana Margarida Esteves, Sara Motta & Laurence Cox (2009) Already quoted.

members. NGOs are also geared to giving poor people advice rather than building networks of political activists who can lead themselves at grass-roots level[37].

Although there are commonalities among all NGOs working with trade unions, there are also important differences. NGOs affiliated to or funded by Western Governments, such as the *American Center for International Labour Solidarity* (ACILS) or the German Social Democratic Party funded *Friedrich-Ebert-Stiftung* (FES) encourage non-combative trade unions which engage in "good labour relations exercises" and stick to labour laws irrespective of the nature of regimes. The ACILS was funded by the CIA in the Cold War and the FES has worked with Government sponsored trade unions in Vietnam and under the Suharto regime in Indonesia. They do not encourage strike action, preferring lobby politics.

Local grass roots labour NGOs do encourage strikes and often support illegal independent trade unions under repressive regimes. A good example is the support given to the Indonesian independent unions *Serikat Buruh Merdeka Setiakawan* (SBM), *Serikat Buruh Sejahtera Indonesia* (SBSI), *Pusat Perjuangan Buruh Indonesia (PPBI)*[38]. In Thailand, the Thai Labour Campaign supports militant action by trade unionists and opposed the 2006 coup. However, these labour NGOs also tend to concentrate on welfare work for sacked workers or trade unions which have already been defeated. They provide advisors to the unions rather than build militant workplace activists. This welfare work is useful and justified, but it fails to build the strength of the trade unions because such strength requires victories which can be copied and generalised throughout society.

The strength of the trade union movement is inversely proportional to the dominance of NGOs. In countries with a weak union movement, like Thailand or Cambodia, NGOs are important in supporting workers. However, in South Korea, where unions like the KCTU are very strong, campaigning NGOs often seek help from the unions.

---

[37] Deborah Eade & Alan Leather (eds), *Development NGOs and Labor Unions: Terms of Engagement*. Kumarian Press, Bloomfield, CY.

[38] Vedi Hadiz (1997) *Workers and the state in New Order Indonesia*. Routledge.

Another problem with the approach of labour NGOs is their belief that the working class is in decline and that trade unions are therefore less relevant. These NGOs advocate "new forms of labour organisation", which emphasise communities rather than workplaces[39]. This is similar to Autonomist ideas about the importance of "The Multitude" instead of the working class, put forward by people like Hardt and Negri[40]. Yet local communities lack the economic power needed to balance the power of capital precisely because they are not located in workplaces. In Indonesia, communities were unable to negotiate wage increases or stop job losses in the economic crisis of 1996[41]. Despite this, one would have to be pretty stupid to say that trade unions did not need solidarity and support from working class communities, especially in areas with large concentrations of workers. Such areas can be found in the huge industrial areas surrounding Bangkok or Jakarta.

After the end of the Cold War, many mainstream academics started to talk about the "new" social movements. These were single-issue movements which were supposed to be a better alternative to the "old" socialist organisations. "New" social movements, according to these academics, rejected the struggle for state power or the building of political parties and concentrated on life-style politics rather than class issues[42]. This celebration of single-issue campaigning coincides with the project proposals which NGOs write up in order to obtain funding. The consequences are that "politics" becomes much less important in these movements. In Indonesia, like Thailand, many NGOs reject the building of political parties or political movements[43]. Yet Sidney Tarrow has argued

[39] See Angela Hale (2005) Beyond the barriers. New forms of labor organizations. In: Deborah Eade & Alan Leather (eds) Already quoted.

[40] Michael Hardt & Antonio Negri (2000) *Empire*. Harvard University Press.

[41] Michele Ford (2003) Labour NGO as Outside Intellectual: A History of Non-Governmental Organisations' Role in the Indonesian Labour Movement, Unpublished PhD thesis, University of Wollongong. See also Vedi Hadiz (1997), Already quoted.

[42] A. Touraine (2001) Translated by D. Macey *Beyond Neoliberalism*. Polity Press, Cambridge, U.K. J. Keane (1998) *Civil Society. Old images, new vision*. Polity Press, Cambridge, U.K.

[43] Paige Johnson Tan (2002) Anti-party reaction in Indonesia. Causes and implications. *Contemporary Southeast Asia*. 24 (3), 484-508.

against the idea that present day movements fit the model of classless "New" social movements[44]. In 1906 the Marxist Rosa Luxemburg, in her book *"The Mass Strike"*, showed that strikes over single "bread and butter" issues always had links with general class politics. Marxist theory also locates gender or race oppression as integral parts of the repression found in class societies. The struggles to defend life styles are therefore part and parcel of the class struggle against Capitalism.

Funding and the adoption of post-Cold War politics are not the only reasons why NGOs turn their backs on politics. In semi-authoritarian countries like Malaysia, NGOs are faced with a hard choice of having either to work in the restrictive legal space offered by the state or to work outside repressive laws. The radical organisation *"Sisters in Islam"* faces such a problem in trying to campaign on general political issues which affect women[45]. The organisation takes up issues such as repression due to the conservative interpretation of Shari'ah Laws. It also opposes the Internal Security Act. But in Singapore, where the democratic space is non-existent, women's organisations remain "non-political".

The working class

Throughout the recent development of Capitalism in Thailand there has been a steady decline in the peasantry and a corresponding increase in the modern working class. This is a phenomenon found in all developing countries, especially those in South-East Asia[46]. Since the mid 1990s, less than half the Thai population is now engaged in rice farming or horticulture[47]. The truth is that the working class is rapidly becoming the largest class in Thai society.

[44] Sidney Tarrow (1999) *Power in movement. Social movements and contentious politics.* Cambridge University Press, U.K.

[45] Norani Othman, Zainah Anwar & Zaitun Mohamed Kasim (2005) Malaysia: Islamization, Muslim politics and state authoritarianism. In: Norani Othman (ed.) *Muslim Women and the Challenge of Islamic Extremism.* Published by Sisters In Islam. (This is a banned book in Malaysia).

[46] R.E. Elson (1997) *The end of the peasantry in southeast Asia.* Macmillan & A.N.U., UK & Australia.

[47] "Workforce statistics 1997" Department of Welfare and Labour protection.

Before going any further, it is important to state clearly who we are actually talking about when we refer to the "working class". Much has been made of the "new middle class" in Thailand, especially in the context of the 1992 uprising[48]. In fact the majority of people who have been classified as "middle class" are part of the white-collar working class. The Marxist definition of class, used by this author, is based on the relationship to the means of production. It explains why white collar workers, despite the fact that they may regard themselves as middle class, behave just like factory workers when it comes to forming trade unions and taking part in class struggle. In Thailand, white collar workers have a long tradition of classical working class activity. The first strike by white collar workers occurred at the Siam Electricity Company in 1931 and white collar bank employees have been organising trade unions for decades. Apart from this, the bulk of state enterprise workers, who have a tradition of activism in the labour movement, are either white collar or service workers.

"Stinking Water Trade Union Leaders" or grass-roots activists?

The power of the working class depends very much on its level of organisation into trade unions and political parties. At present there are no political parties of the working class, but what is the state of the trade unions? In 1998 trade union membership stood at 270,000 in the private sector and 160,000 in the state sector. This was a mere 3% of the workforce. Not much has changed since. However, such an average figure can be misleading. Most state enterprises and large factories in the private sector are fully unionised or at least dominated by unions. This includes some offices, especially the banks. Apart from this, unionised workers are mainly concentrated in Bangkok and the surrounding provinces of the central region. Such concentrations of working class organisations allow for more influence than would be supposed from just looking at the national figures for unionisation. But what is the state of the unions themselves?

[48] Richard Robison & David Goodman (1996) (eds) *The new rich in Asia*. Routledge.

Anyone who is familiar with the back streets of Bangkok and the problem of sewage drainage will understand instantly what is meant by the term "Stinking Water Trade Union Leader". In Thailand there are three general types; (a) Gangster trade union leaders, who set up trade unions in order to extract protection money from employers by threatening strikes, (b) Stooges of the security forces and (c) Fat Cat Bureaucrats (or *"Fat Pig"* Bureaucrats in Thai). The latter are trade union leaders who start out with the intention of representing their members' best interests but gradually become used to the good life of the bosses. Such characteristics among the trade union bureaucracy have long been recognised in the West[49].

In Thailand, these trade union bureaucrats enjoy a better standard of living than their members through funding from union subscriptions, inflated payments for "travel expenses" when dealing with a particular group of workers' problems, grants from foreign foundations, and occasionally money from state security bodies. Thus there may at times be overlap between the second and third type of trade union leader. For these leaders, workers' struggles are to be avoided at all costs, since they threaten to disrupt the smooth business of the labour congress. They do not see themselves as leading struggles, their role is to "sort out problems" and "get people back to work".

All these union officials seek to rub shoulders with those in the corridors of power, but in reality they have little industrial muscle, since they have no long-term interest in building grass roots activity. If the strength of the Thai working class were to be measured purely on the record of these leaders, and their peak organisations, as many authors have done[50], it would indeed be in a very pitiful state.

---

[49] S. Webb & B. Webb (1920) *A History of Trade Unionism*. London. Leon Trotsky (1969) *On Trade Unions*. Pathfinder Press. U.S.A. James Hinton & Richard Hyman (1975) *Trade Unions and Revolution: the industrial politics of the early British Communist Party*. Pluto Press, London. Tony Cliff & Donny Gluckstein (1986) *Marxism and Trade Union Struggle. The Great Strike of 1926*. Bookmarks, London. Alex Callinicos (1995) *Socialists in the Trade Unions*. Bookmarks, London.

[50] Andrew Brown & Stephen Frenkel (1993) "Union Unevenness and Insecurity in Thailand". In: S. Frenkel (Ed) *Organized Labor in the Asia-Pacific Region*. ILR Press, Ithaca, NY. Kevin Hewison & Andrew Brown, (1994) "Labour and Unions in an Industrialising Thailand". *Journal of Contemporary Asia*. 244, 483-514.

Fortunately, this is not the entire picture. Networks of unofficial rank and file activists, independent of top leaders, exist in *"Area Groups"* and *"Coordinating Committees"*. Even official groupings, such as the *Federation of Textile, Garment and Leather Workers' Unions,* are able to group together different unions at rank and file level, independent of the various peak bodies and congresses. However, these more class-conscious union groupings still form a minority of the labour movement.

The main type of unofficial union grouping, which brings together rank and file representatives from different enterprise unions, is the geographical *"Area Group"* or *"Klum Yarn"*. *Area Groups* exist in many industrial areas in and around Bangkok, for example, in *Rungsit, Nawanakorn, Saraburi, Ayuttaya, Prapadaeng* and *Omnoi-Omyai* and also in the industrial estates of the Eastern Seaboard. These area groupings are considerably more democratic and unofficial than the peak bodies or congresses. The entire committee of the group is usually elected every year and made up of men and women lay-representatives covering different workplaces and industries. *Area Groups* were initially established in the mid 1970s by activists from the CPT and later, by NGO workers.

Rank and file union groupings are a way in which "enterprise unions" can build solidarity with one another. There is a mis-conception among many academics that Thai trade union law forces workers to form individual and atomised unions in each enterprise and that this results in unions under the control of management. This is not the case. Firstly, the law allows for the setting up of "industrial unions", although these only seem to have appeared in metal working. The main reason for the domination of enterprise unions may have something to do with advice given to workers by "stinking water trade union leaders" who stand to gain from setting up lots of little enterprise unions, because of the nature of the voting system to elect members of tripartite committees. Secondly, the existence of enterprise unions is not all negative, in terms of the strength of the movement. Enterprise unions, by their very nature, are run by rank and file elected leaders who work on the shop floor. Thus the system of enterprise unions may help to prevent bureaucratisation of trade union representatives and can even help to reduce the influence of "stinking water trade union leaders".

Apart from the organisational weaknesses of unions, there is also an ideological factor which has held back the working class. This is due to the fact that the CPT, which originally organised urban workers in the 1940s and 1950s, took a Maoist turn away from the working class, towards the peasantry, in the 1960s. For this reason there has been a lack of left-wing activists willing to agitate among workers for the past 30 years. Unlike South Korea, where student activists had a long tradition of going to work in urban settings with the aim of strengthening trade unions, Thai student activists headed for the countryside after graduation. Later, the field was therefore left open for NGOs and reformist academics to school worker-activists in "good industrial relations" and respect for biased labour laws.

The working class is fast becoming the majority class in Thai society. Despite the fact that it has serious organisational weaknesses, an important source of its strength, which is constantly overlooked, is the role of rank and file union leaders and their unofficial networks. For this reason, the working class should not be regarded as passive subjects of repression and exploitation, but potential agents of change.

The growth of the working class and the decline of the peasantry and many traditional life styles, is a direct consequence of the expansion of Capitalism in Thailand. This has had a contradictory effect on the well-being of ordinary Thais. On the one hand, the development of the economy has been of benefit to everyone, in terms of standards of living. It simply is not true that development has made the poor poorer. But development has not been used to its full potential for the benefit of the majority of the population. This is because capitalist development in pursuit of profit results in great inequalities and is beyond democratic control. In other areas of human life, the effect has also been contradictory. Capitalism tears up traditional ways of living, rips apart the environment and concentrates enormous economic power in the hands of an elite few. Yet at the same time, it creates a modern working class that is more literate and more potentially powerful than the peasantry. Changes through struggle, such as the struggle for democratic rights, have occurred in new urban areas. The role of women has also changed. The experience of factory work for young women whose sisters and mothers are peasants, has actually been liberating in many ways, with women becoming more independent and self-confident[51]. This is not to deny that women and men workers need to struggle hard in the future to improve their earnings, their social benefits and their conditions of work.

Yellow Shirt led unions

The majority of the population, including the majority of the working class, voted for Taksin's TRT. For workers, the Universal Health Care Scheme did not affect them directly because they were already covered by the Social Insurance Scheme. However, it benefitted all urban workers because their relatives and family members were now covered by TRT's health care scheme. This took an enormous burden off their shoulders. The village funds also benefitted their rural relatives. It is therefore reasonable to say that the majority of workers support the Red Shirts.

However, because the Red Shirt Movement was initiated by TRT politicians, it lacked a strategy for building the movement among the trade unions. Instead, the PAD, because of the presence of Somsak Kosaisuk, has gained some influence in the trade union movement, although this is severely limited to sections of the state enterprise workers and some sections the trade unions from the Eastern Seaboard.

The specific nature of sections of the labour movement who went in with PAD were as follows.

---

[51] Mary Beth Mills (1998) *Thai women in the global labour force*. Rutgers University Press. Goretti Horgan (2001) "How does globalisation affect women?" *International Socialism* 92 Autumn 2001, London. Giles Ji Ungpakorn (1999) Thailand: *Class struggle in an era of economic crisis*. Asia Monitor Resource Center, HongKong & Workers' Democracy Book Club, Bangkok.

1. They had personal connections with Somsak Kosaisuk and his allies in organisations like *"Friends of the People"* (FOP). Somsak and his allies organised educational groups for these trade unionists. But it was a "top down" form of education where people were not encouraged to question or debate with people like Somsak. Self leadership and self analysis were not encouraged. This is the only way that trade unionists could be drawn to support a conservative royalist agenda which had no practical benefits for workers.
2. There was a tendency for pro-PAD trade unionists to be full time union activists or NGO-sponsored activists, distant from rank and file workers. If they were close to the rank and file, they would have felt pressure from Red Shirt ideas at grass roots levels because ordinary members benefitted from TRT policies.
3. The "state enterprise union mentality" of putting more faith in talking to "sympathetic" management or elites, rather than organising and building a mass base drew some trade unionists towards the PAD. The EGAT[52] union failed to take seriously the task of building shop stewards during their long campaign against privatisation, instead concentrating on building alliances with sections of management. Despite this, the EGAT union could pull people out on work stoppages and demonstrations against privatisation. However, active support by EGAT union members for the PAD was much smaller.

When genuine action was taken by PAD unions, there was a tendency to ignore the importance of solidarity from other workers because the leaders were too confident that they had "powerful backers". A good example was the Ford Mazda strike over bonus payments in late 2008. The factory was on the Eastern Sea Board. Another example was the railway union which was "brave enough" to strike once for PAD in 2008, because it knew that management would not punish anyone. Before that,

[52] Electricity Generating Authority of Thailand.

the union failed to fight against the increased use of low paid casual workers on the railways who have been suffering for years. Later, in 2009, however, they did manage a genuine strike over railway safety in the south. Because of the railway union's association with the PAD, there was much hostility from Red Shirts to this genuine strike.

Even in most state enterprise unions, support for the PAD was limited. There was a huge argument in the Thai Airways union about supporting the PAD when some of the leaders wanted to organise a pro-PAD strike and the EGAT union response to supporting the PAD was very patchy.

Among private sector unions support for the PAD did not exist. The *Thai Labour Solidarity Committee*, which was made up of Wilaiwan Sa-Tia's factory workers in *Omm Noi*, in alliance with Somsak, pulled out of supporting the PAD in the 2nd half of 2008. Their members were horrified with what the PAD was doing. *Ranksit Area Group* of industrial workers never supported the PAD nor the coup. Neither did the *Triumph* underwear workers. The *Eastern Sea Board Area Group* leadership was split between Red and Yellow. There were also some splits between pro-PAD leaders and their rank & file Red Shirt members in this area.

In 2004 the labour movement was showing signs of regeneration with more independence and militancy. But by 2009, in the midst of another economic crisis, that militancy and independence had subsided. The trade unionists and NGO activists who supported the PAD are greatly to blame for this. The lack of interest in the labour movement among Red Shirt strategists is also a factor.

The student movement today

There is much evidence that there has been interest in politics and social issues among students and young people over the last ten years. This can be seen in the flowering of new critical magazines produced by small independent student societies. Student groups spontaneously organised protests against Government violence in the South and there were large student protests against privatisation (or corporatisation) of universities at

Chulalongkorn, Pranakorn Nua, Kasetsart, Mahasarakarm, Burapa, and Pattani Universities.

Today the *Student Federation of Thailand* and its *"Pi-Liang"* from the older generation of Peoples Movement activists, is extremely weak. In the 1970s the *Student Federation of Thailand* was an important coordinating body, but today it has withered at the vine and become a bureaucracy without a mass movement. After the 2006 coup the leadership refused to take a position on university privatisation while thousands of students in a number of universities were organising protests. It was scared to link university privatisation with the issue of state enterprise privatisation, out of fear that the protests would "get out of hand". The leadership also admitted that they were extremely lacking in political theory and analysis and that was why they shied away from debates with small left-wing student groups. More recently, despite not joining the PAD, the Federation refused to take a clear stand and support the Red Shirt movement for Democracy, claiming neutrality in the political crisis. On 19th September 2009, three years after the coup, a tiny handful of *Federation* leaders held a symbolic protest at the Democracy Monument while tens of thousands of Red Shirts rallied for Democracy at the royal plaza.

The *Student Federation* was the training ground for office holders in organisations like the *Campaign for Popular Democracy*. Ex-student leaders in the Peoples Movement then became "advisors" to new generations of *Federation* leaders. Meetings of the *Student Federation* took the usual form found in many Peoples Movement meetings. Political debate and voting were discouraged in favour of "consensus". Funding was obtained from NGOs or outside organisations, rather than from the student body itself. This led to a culture of dependency and a seniority system.

The various student clubs and political parties at *Ramkamhaeng Open University* have been an important site for student activity against military dictatorships, especially in the 1970s and around May 1992. Some present day politicians first became active as student leaders in this university[53].

[53] The Red Shirt Jatuporn Prompan is a good example.

Outside the traditional movement: GLBT and disabled activists

One effect of Maoism on the Peoples Movement is that most traditional NGO activists ignore gender and issues affecting disabled people. Despite the fact that half NGO activists are women, NGO attitudes towards sexual matters are extremely conservative. The only area where "abortion on demand" has been raised is inside sections of the trade union movement. The brand of Feminism inside the NGOs and most social movements is the mainstream Feminism of middle-class women. There is no critique of conservative family and sexual values and Thai society is also only just waking up to the issue of disabled rights.

Many people see Thai society and culture as being liberal and tolerant towards alternative sexual life styles. Yet, a deeper study of the experiences of Gays, Lesbians and *Katoeys* shows the real need for a Gay, Lesbian, Bisexual and Transgender (GLBT) Movement[54]. Such a movement began to emerge in the late 1980s as a result of AIDS. The reason why a Gay or Lesbian Liberation movement never arose in Thailand in the early 1970s, like it did in many other countries, is mainly explained by the fact that the Maoist CPT, which had ideological domination over the Peoples Movement, never supported Gays or Lesbians.

The CPT, like most Maoist organisations, had a very conservative and moralistic attitude to sex, matching the conservative attitudes of the ruling class[55]. The Maoists upheld the sanctity of marriage and the family, ignoring the classical Marxist analysis of women's oppression in the works of

---

[54] See Peter A. Jackson (1999) Tolerant but unaccepting: the myth of a Thai "Gay Paradise". In Peter A. Jackson & Nerida M. Cook (eds) *Genders & Sexualities in Modern Thailand.* Silkworm Books. Megan Sinnott (2000) Masculinity and "Tom" identity in Thailand. In Peter A. Jackson & Gerard Sullivan (eds) *Lady Boys, Tom Boys and Rent Boys.* Silkworm Books.

[55] Wipa Daomanee (Comrade "Sung") (2003) Looking back to when I first wanted to be a Communist. In Ji Giles Ungpakorn (ed.) Already quoted. See also, the attitude of the Communist Party of the Philippines, which only adopted a more liberal attitude to gays and lesbians in 1998. Patricio N. Abinales (2004) *Love, Sex and the Filipino Communist.* Anvil.

Engels or Kollontai. Party members had to ask permission of their party superiors before they could form relationships with the opposite sex. There was no tolerance of same sex love. Jit Pumisak, a leading CPT intellectual, in his book about the Thai *Sakdina* system, wrote about the "abnormalities of homosexuality" arising among women in the harems of the royal palace[56]. Such "abnormalities" would presumably cease to exist under Communism.

It was not always like this in the Thai movements. In the early 1930s, before and after the revolution against the Monarchy, women's movements existed which aligned themselves with the trade unions and the movement against the King. *Ying Thai* (Thai Women) was a radical journal edited by Nuanchawee Tepwan. Because of its radicalism it faced constant repression from the state. Closely associated with *Ying Thai* was the *Siam Association of Women*, which had its offices in the Tram Workers Union office[57]. Kularp Saipradit, a leading male socialist intellectual in the 1930s and 40s, translated Engel's *Origin of the Family* and wrote about the struggle for women's rights. In the 1970s many women students became radicalised by the women's liberation struggles in the West. These earlier movements had a much more libertarian attitude to sexuality.

Because the "1968" wave of international struggle failed to ignite a GLBT movement in Thailand in the 1970s, it was not until the spread of AIDS that a GLBT movement began to emerge, especially among gay men. Examples of Gay and *Katoey* organisations today are *Fa Sri Rung* (Rainbow Sky) and *Bangkok Rainbow*, established in 2000 and 2002, respectively. *Anjaree* and *Sapaan* (Bridge) are examples of Lesbian movements set up in the same period, but these Lesbian organisations were established as Lesbian web-sites[58]. These GLBT movements, which gradually emerged throughout the 1990s, exhibit the usual problems and contradictions of identity politics after the international defeats of the 1980s. Identity politics in that era, especially among GLBT movements, often

[56] Jit Pumisak *(Somsmai SriSootrapan)* (1996) reprint of *Chome Na Sakdina Thai*. Nok Hook Press, p. 376.

[57] Numnual Yapparat (2006) The political development of the Thai women's movement. In: Ji Ungpakorn et al. (2006) Already quoted. (In Thai).

[58] *Anjaree* has now folded. The main remaining political Lesbian web-site being *Sapaan*.

emphasised building spaces for consumption and entertainment. While politics was reduced, the influence of Pink Businesses increased. Another issue was the "Virtual Struggle" emphasising the use of the internet and web-sites instead of mass movements.

Some people in the GLBT scene claim that *Fa Sri Rung* is less Pink Business orientated than *Bangkok Rainbow* because it is dominated by health professionals and NGO activists rather than business people. This may be true to some extent, but *Bangkok Rainbow* is more political if you consider the fact that it organises seminars and political discussions and backed a gay candidate for the Senate elections in 2006. The business-backed people who established the *Anjaree* web-site for lesbians were also more overtly political than the rather conservative health professionals working in *Fa Sri Rung*. However, a social movement cannot be built solely round a web-site or seminars. Without a real supporting membership, *Anjaree* collapsed. In contrast, the educational advice and welfare provided by *Fa Sri Rung* has resulted in a real membership or mass base. These members have exerted pressure on the leaderships of the organisation to push them into becoming more political. Today any blatant homophobic acts or public policies, such as barring gays from teacher training colleges or the media, are immediately countered by the GLBT movement. Recently there were complaints against an obnoxious advertisement showing a "straight" man slapping a *katoey*.

Despite these positive developments, the CPT past still haunts the Peoples Movement on the issue of gender. GLBT organisations are still not regarded by the traditional Peoples Movement as a normal part of the movement. Peoples Assemblies and Peoples Movement publications do not raise the GLBT issue or any radical gender issues. But there is an indication that a new generation of social activists, some of whom are gays, lesbians or socialists, will force a liberalisation of attitudes among the traditional movement. Evidence of this was seen in the fact that the Thai Social Forum (TSF) included GLBT organisations.

What was even more impressive about the 2006 TSF was the participation by disabled activists. This was the first time that the Peoples

Movement as a whole had joined forces with disabled organisations and the highlight of the event was when militant activists in wheel chairs led the TSF anti-coup demonstration in the centre of Bangkok in October 2006.

It is not only the traditional Peoples Movement which has ignored gender and the PAD is not the only sexist organisation. A Red Shirts group in the northern city of Chiang Mai expressed openly anti-gay attitudes when it tried to oppose a Gay Pride march. Red Shirts also often attack Privy Council Chairman Prem Tinsulanon for being gay.

Moving away from single issue activism is a complex process. The politics of the movement has to develop through a process where trade unions and peasant organisations actively taking up each other's issues and fight for all the oppressed in society. But equally, gender rights and GLBT activists as well as disabled organisations need to take up the issues of the wider movement. A political party can act as a bridge to connect struggles and build solidarity.

The legacy of the CPT is not the only obstacle to fighting for gender rights in the Peoples Movement. Autonomist Localism *(Chumchon-nyom)* both rejects universal political theories and places "local wisdom" above all else, irrespective of the nature of that local wisdom. A recent debate over signs barring women from golden Buddhist pagodas in the north is a prime example. Northern localists, such as Tanet Charoenmuang, argued against socialists and feminists who want the signs removed. Tanet's argument was that the feminists and socialists were "outsiders" who should learn to respect Northern local wisdom, which he claimed did not oppress women. This is despite the fact that most religious experts admit that the barring of women from pagodas, is done on the basis of the belief that women are "unclean" due to their menstrual cycles. However, Niti Eawsriwong, who is also a localist and founder of the *Midnight University*, argued that it was pointless to say this local belief did not oppress women. For Niti, the way to change such local beliefs was for northerners to argue for change from within, not to rely on forces from the outside[59].

---

[59] The debates around this issue are collected in a book edited by Supakorn Apawatcharut (2004) *Women and Prathat*. Urban Development Institute Foundation. (In Thai).

The way forward

Because of the appalling political position taken by NGO and Peoples Movement activists, the Red Shirts represent the hope for the future in terms of building a vibrant pro-democracy Civil Society. Yet unless they break out of their own brand of single-issue struggles and take up issues that affect workers, small farmers, women, GLBT people, the disabled and marginalised ethnic groups, they cannot be successful in building a new Democracy with Social Justice.

Chapter 3
The Thai Monarchy: Myth or Reality?

Like the story of "the Emperor's New Clothes", the conservative elites have relied on telling the Thai population (and maybe even the King), a pack of lies in order to promote their own agenda. *The King is a God! The King is a genius in all fields! The King is all powerful! We are willing to die to serve the King! The King has guaranteed peace and happiness for the people!*. The lèse majesté law, and other authoritarian measures, are used to back up these lies. But the little boy in the story has already spoken! Most people in Thailand can see that the Emperor has no clothes! The King didn't "hold together Thai society". He didn't created justice and equality and he sided in public with the military and the anti-democrats throughout his reign. People are sick and tired of the elite's privileges and arrogance. All traffic is stopped for the Royals to pass in Bangkok, while emergency ambulances are stuck in traffic jams. Citizens are forced to crawl on the ground like animals and use special royal language when in the company of or referring to the Royal Family. Hospital bulletins on the King's health have had to be regularly "translated" into plain Thai so that the public understands them!

The process of destroying the corrupt, privileged and authoritarian network which includes the present Monarchy will take time. People like

Suwicha Thakor, Da torpido, Boonyuen Prasertying and many others are suffering in jail because of the lèse majesté law. The Red Shirts will have to continue to mobilise and organise on a long-term basis. Meanwhile, politicians like Taksin, and many others, are still clinging to royalist ideas, claiming to be "loyal subjects" of the King and his heir. Many Red Shirts are restless and want to go much further in order to build "Real Democracy" and Social Justice.

If we are to understand the role of the King in Thai society, we have to understand the double act performed by the military and the King. For ruling classes to achieve hegemony in most modern societies, they require both coercion and legitimacy. The military and their bureaucratic allies have their armed might to stage coups and manipulate political society. The King symbolises the conservative ideology which gives legitimacy to the authoritarian actions of the military and their allies. It is a double act of "power" and "ideological legitimacy". In this double act the weak-willed King has no real power, but he is a willing participant.

There are a number of myths about the Thai Monarchy which have been constantly reproduced in schools, public arenas, and in the media, by the Thai conservative elites and most foreign observers. As with most political myths, they contain differing degrees of truth and untruth. Four of the main myths are outlined below.

1. The King has a special place in the hearts of all Thai people.
2. King Bhumibol created stability and held the country together.
3. The King tried to promote Social Justice with his royal projects.
4. The King is very powerful.

Let us consider these issues in more detail.

1. Does the King have a special place in the hearts of all Thai people?

It is undoubtedly true that millions of Thai people have a high regard for King Bhumibol. It is also true that millions more hate and despise his son. Millions are also turning against the Monarchy system because of what has been done in the King's name, starting with the 2006 military coup. For those who love the King there is the important question about whether it is a love for the individual or for the Monarchy as an institution. This King allowed his supporters to proclaim that he is "the father of the nation," and yet his own son is not respected by anyone in Thai society! This destroys the myth that all Thais have a special historical regard for the Monarchy system. Yet, even most foreign observers are reluctant to spell this fact out clearly. This is because journalists and academics who write about Thailand face a tough lèse majesté law when they set foot in the country. One honourable exception to this generalisation is Paul Handley[1]. But Handley can never set foot in Thailand again until we have true Democracy. In recent years the outspoken *Economist* magazine has shown some courage in writing about the Monarchy, but many issues have been banned in Thailand.

Since 2006, the Thai conservative elites played a dangerous game with the Monarchy. Since the collapse of the Communist Party in the mid 1980s, they had achieved political hegemony for royalist ideas in society. They wrecked all this by starting a civil war with millions of people who are represented by the Red Shirts. In 2006 they decided that they would use a military coup and other extra-Constitutional means to get rid of a popular elected Government. They did this in the name of King. In 2008 the Queen openly supported the Yellow Shirt PAD by attending the funeral of a PAD protestor. This instantly turned her into an "enemy of the people" in the eyes of millions of Red Shirts. The result of all this is the revival of a significant republican movement in Thailand, on a level not seen since the mid 1970s. Even staunch establishment royalists such as Chai-anan Samudwanij concede that this is the case[2]. It would be true to say that by 2009, most Red Shirts were at best lukewarm about the Monarchy, if not out and out republicans. For those who were not republicans, the majority wished the ageing Bhumibol a peaceful life. They may even have had some

---

[1] Paul Handley (2006) *The King Never Smiles*. Yale University Press.

[2] http://www.manager.co.th/Daily/ViewNews.aspx?NewsID=9520000087280 02/08/2009 (In Thai).

respect for him, but they are not at all enthusiastic about continuing with the Monarchy after Bhumibol.

With hindsight we might think that the military and the conservatives ought to have left the King out of the 2006 coup and all their anti-democratic actions which followed. Yet did they have any choice? If they were to stop and overthrow Taksin, they could not use democratic means. Just talking about corruption was not enough because corruption charges could be leveled at the military and the conservatives as well. They had to continue with their double act and use the Monarchy as a legitimising excuse. Apart from their fear that Taksin would end their long-held privileges, they were scared that Taksin would use his power to influence the next king, thus cutting them out. They were afraid of the Taksin-Wachiralongkorn double act. Bhumibol was getting old and sick and Taksin is known to have helped Crown Prince Wachiralongkorn pay off his gambling debts. So we see another dimension to the political crisis. It was also a tussle between Taksin, as a royalist, and the conservative royalists. The aim was to gain the right to use the Monarchy to legitimise their interests.

This is not the first time that there has been a republican mood in Thai society. The Monarchy was in disrepute ever since the later years of King Chulalongkorn (Rama 5th). The monopoly of power held by the Royal Family was causing friction between them and the newly created military and civilian bureaucracy. By the time King Rama 6th came to the throne, the Absolute Monarchy was doomed. Rama 6th was lacking in much political ability and spent most of his time writing plays and spending the nation's wealth. This led to an unsuccessful rebellion. Rama 7th added to the republican mood by making the population pay for the 1930s economic crisis. This was the last straw and resulted in the Monarchy's eventual overthrow in 1932[3]. Yet the leaders of the 1932 revolution were forced to make compromises with the conservatives and retained the Monarchy in a Constitutional form. This was because their *Peoples Party* lacked a strong enough mass base.

---

[3] Kullada Kesboonchoo Mead (2004) *The rise and decline of Thai absolutism*. Routledge.

King Bhumibol was not in direct line to the throne and only became king after his brother, Anand, died in a gun incident involving Bhumibol. Three innocent Palace staff were executed. To begin with Bhumibol was very nervous and had a low profile under the military dictator Field Marshal Pibun Songkram, who had republican leanings. Pibun was one of the leaders of the 1932 revolution. Later, in the late 1950s, after Pibun was overthrown in a coup, Bhumibol grew in stature under the promotion of corrupt military dictator Field Marshal Sarit Tanarat[4]. Royal promotion continued under the joint dictatorship of Tanom kitikajorn and Prapart Jarusatien after Sarit's death. In this post-Pibun period, loyalty to "Nation, Religion and King" was enforced by the military dictatorship by various means, including the use of lèse majesté. The need for such enforced loyalty should alert any investigative mind to question the idea that "the King has always had a special place in the hearts of every Thai".

In the last century there have been three historical periods when there was republican sentiment among significant sections of the Thai population: around the 1932 revolution, during the rise of the Communist Party in the mid 1970s, and today. Before the 1950s, many ordinary Thais living in rural villages simply ignored the Monarchy and felt that it was irrelevant to their lives[5]. In the feudal *"Sakdina"* period, when the general population were subjected to enforced labour and forced to take part in brutal wars, the "Thai" population would have hated and feared all Kings and nobles. The Sakdina system was in place in the Ayuttaya and early Bangkok periods.

There are two reasons why many commentators fail to report the contradictory and changing attitudes towards the Monarchy throughout Thai history. Firstly there are those who are just too lazy to try to look beneath the surface appearance of an adoring population. But secondly, and very importantly, it is dangerous to write or speak about the truth.

---

4 Thak Chaloemtiarana (1979) *The politics of despotic paternalism.* Social Science Association of Thailand.

5 Katherine Bowie (1997) *Rituals of National Loyalty.* New York: University of Columbia Press.

2. Did King Bhumibol create stability and hold the country together?

It is common to hear foreign commentators say that King Bhumibol held the country together and created stability. The implication is that "after he goes, there will be chaos". Apart from the fact that there has been a deep political crisis and chaos since the royalist coup in 2006, we need to look at the historical facts and to question the meaning of "stability".

The kind of "stability" brought about by the presence of King Bhumibol was always the stability of the ruling elites to rule over a profoundly unequal and unjust society. Such stability is clearly not in the interests of the vast majority of citizens and luckily this stability of autocratic rule has often been challenged by mass movements. Never the less, this talk of how the King *symbolised* the stability of the reactionary elites, leads us to an important conclusion about the key ideological role of the King. This will be discussed in more detail later in the chapter.

Let us look at the historical facts about the King's interventions in political crises. The King has a very dubious track record. He allowed innocent people to be executed after they were falsely accused of killing his older brother. He allowed this event to be used as an excuse to exile radical Prime Minister Pridi Panomyong. He sided with corrupt and oppressive military dictators in the 1960s and 1970s and when society became extremely polarised as a result, he sat back and watched the army shoot pro-democracy demonstrators in 1973. Only after it became clear that the students and the people had beaten the dictators, did he appear on television and call for unity. Exactly the same thing happened in the mass uprising against military rule in 1992. His appearances on television were merely attempts by the elites to keep control of events, while sacrificing unpopular dictators.

Following the 1973 uprising, the King backed extreme right-wing groups which caused mayhem and murder and threatening Democracy. He was the patron of the violent gang that were called the "Village Scouts". He supported the blood bath at *Thammasart University* on 6th October 1976 because he felt that Thailand had had "too much Democracy"[6]. The 1976 blood bath threw Thai society into civil war between the elites and the Communist Party. His choice of Prime Minister after the 1976 coup was seen to be "too extreme" even by the right-wing generals who quickly replaced him after only one year in office.

Recently the King allowed the army to stage a coup in September 2006, using his name, without any word of criticism. Furthermore he allowed his name to be used by the army, the PAD protestors and the *Democrat Party*, in the continuing destruction of Democracy and chaos that followed the coup. This resulted in a deep political crisis. He remained quiet on his birthday in December 2008, refusing to make the usual annual speech. This might have been an occasion to call for genuine compromise and unity.

So how did the King created a stable society in Thailand?

3. Did the King try to promote Social Justice through his royal projects?

If we ignore the fact that many of these royal projects are riddled with corruption scandals and spend huge sums on the expenses of top officials engaged in the projects, it is clear that the royal projects merely scratch the surface and are dwarfed by Government poverty alleviation policies[7]. After all, the spectacular effectiveness of *Thai Rak Thai's* pro-poor policies was an important factor which turned the conservatives against the Taksin Government.

The King was always an advocate of economic views which revealed his opposition to state social welfare for the poor and income redistribution. He was on record as opposing a welfare state[8]. But what is worse, as one of the richest men in the world, the king had the arrogance

---

[6] In his December 1976 birthday speech he praised the coup for this reason.

[7] Paul Handley (2006) Already quoted.

[8] Kevin Hewison (1997) The Monarchy and democratization. In: K. Hewison (ed.) *Political Change in Thailand. Democracy and Participation*. Routledge.

to lecture the poor to be sufficient in their poverty through the notion of the "Sufficiency Economy". This was nothing more than a reactionary right-wing ideology that says that the poor must know their place.

According to *Forbes* magazine[9] in late 2009, forty of Thailand's wealthiest people, excluding the King, accounted for $25 billion. The King's total wealth, according to the same source[10], was $30 billion, *more* than the total combined wealth of Thailand's top capitalists and more than the wealth of any other monarch in the world. The figure for the King's $30 billion only includes wealth controlled by the Crown Property Bureau. There is more royal wealth than what is controlled by this organisation. In addition to this, the public subsidises the Monarchy from taxation. According to recent Budget Bureau figures, the Royal Household Bureau's draw on public funds has almost doubled from 1,136,536,600 baht in 2002 to 2,086,310,000 baht in 2008. Together with other costs, including 3.65 billion baht for four royal aircraft, total tax payer payments on the royals amounted to 6 billion baht in 2008. Spending on the Monarchy dramatically increased after the 2006 military coup. The conservative elites clearly felt that it was a wise investment.

On 11th December 2009, at Central Plaza, *Bin Kleaw* in Bangkok, one of the King's daughters showed off her pet dog, dressed in a Santa outfit with 150 million baht's worth of diamonds sewn into the cape. Was his daughter following the Sufficiency Economy advice from her father?

The Finance Minister, appointed by the military junta after the 2006 coup, explained that the King's Sufficiency Economics meant "not too much and not too little": in other words, getting it just right. No wonder Paul Handley described Sufficiency Economics as "pseudo-economics"[11]! With the help of academic Chris Baker, the UNDP report for Thailand was dominated by the Sufficiency Economy. Yet, Sufficiency Economics is a deadly serious conservative ideology, aimed at preventing redistribution of wealth and poverty alleviation. It is about trying to make people blame

[9] *Forbes* 23/09/2009.

[10] *Forbes* 17/06/2009.

[11] Paul Handley (2006), Already quoted, page 415.

themselves, accept their poverty and live within their means. Never the less, Chris Baker argued that there were some "very interesting and positive aspects to the Sufficiency Economy"[12].

4. How powerful is the King?

The elites have for decades ruled Thailand from behind the scenes as if it were their own personal fiefdom. A poisonous patron client network draws in new recruits to this "elite feeding trough" where fortunes are to be made at the expense of the hard-working poor[13]. This vast parasitic organism maintains its legitimacy by creating a false image that Thailand has an "Absolute Monarchy", where the King is an all-powerful god. Yet the King was always weak and had no "character" and his power was always a fiction. In addition, he was always lacking in any democratic principles. The Palace has been used to legitimise past and present dictatorships. The King never had the courage to defend Democracy or oppose military violence. The Queen is an extreme reactionary who backs any vicious right-wing movement. However the real people with power among the Thai elites are the army, high-ranking state officials and business leaders. Army generals, politicians, businessmen and privy councilors prostrate themselves on the ground and pay homage to the "powerful" king, while exercising the real power in the land and enriching themselves. This is an ideological play, acted out for the benefit of the public.

Over the years the King never showed any serious power in practice. As head of an institution that derived mutual benefit from all regimes, whether military dictatorships or elected Governments, he was happy to play his role. Under Taksin, the King even praised the Government's extra-judiciary killings in the war on drugs[14].

---

[12] Personal communication, February 2009.

[13] Duncan McCargo named this "Network Monarchy", although he implies that the King is more powerful than I believe to be the case. See Duncan McCargo (2005) Network monarchy and legitimacy crises in Thailand. *The Pacific Review* 18 (4) December, p. 499-519.

[14] King's speech on 4th December 2003. http://www.thaiveterans.mod.go.th/mas_page/about_king/speak_birth/4_12_46_1.htm

When the generals staged coups or intervened in politics, they were not following orders from Bhumibol. Bhumibol was always shy, timid, and weak-willed ever since he accidently came to the throne after his brother's death. Bhumibol never had any leadership qualities. He went with the flow. When Taksin was Prime Minister, he praised Taksin. When the soldiers staged a coup, he praised them. His rambling speeches used obscure language so that the elites could make their own interpretations to suit themselves and Bhumibol did not have to take any responsibility for anything. The speeches were reproduced by the elites like sacred texts, but they contained little of substance. He was happy that people crawled to him and he was happy accumulating his vast wealth.

When the generals decided to do anything, they staged an elaborate play in order to make us think that they were going to the palace to "take orders". In fact they were there to "tell" the King what they had already decided to do. Bhumibol would nod agreement or would be unavailable for an audience, depending on the advice he got from the Privy Council. The advice was not based on decisions made only by Prem, the Privy Council Chairman. It was based on the consensus of those in power in the army and conservative bureaucracy. That is the coordinating role of the Privy Council. After Bhumibol's nod of agreement, the generals would come out of the palace and announced to the public that they had "taken orders" from the King. That way they could build legitimacy for their actions and fear among those who wished to oppose them.

Since the military coup of 2006, Taksin and his close supporters have accused Prem of being the "devil master mind" behind his overthrow. Many believed this to be true and Taksin clearly thought that things might be different under the next king, with a reduced role for the Privy Council[15]. This demonisation of Prem was also partly a result of the lèse majesté law. While not being able to criticise the King, one could still criticise Prem. Many people talk about Prem when they mean the King. It is a kind of displacement activity born out of frustration with repression.

[15] Interview with *The Times* http://www.timesonline.co.uk/tol/news/world/asia/article6909258.ece 9/11/09.

The ruling class proposes that the Thai Monarchy is an ancient "Sakdina-Absolutist" institution, ignoring the historical and political differences between the feudal Sakdina kings of Ayuttaya and early Bangkok, and the capitalist Absolute Monarchy built under Chulalongkorn (Rama 5th). This elite view is drummed into us at school and through the media. We are strongly encouraged to believe that the King is all powerful and that we are mere serfs *(Prai)* under his rule. Royal language, the practice of crawling and the wild promotion of the Monarchy all play a part in this. While the ruling class wish to promote the idea of an ancient and powerful King, they introduce another contradiction, claiming that he is also a Constitutional Monarch. In this modern context, they say that we should not criticise the King "because he is above the dirt of day to day politics". And so you have the completion of an illogical circle which claims that the King is all powerful and yet does not engage in politics!

Obviously this view of the Monarchy is neither historically accurate nor scientifically logical. Yet that is not the point. Royalist ideology requires no scientific proof. We are made to accept this view in order to believe that there is no alternative but to swear total allegiance to the Monarch, since he is a semi-god who should be both loved and feared. But the important point is that by swearing such allegiance, we are really bowing down before the power of the army and entrenched conservative elites.

Any serious scholar will know from the works of Thongchai Winichakul[16] or Thak Chalermtiarana[17] and also that of Paul Handley[18] that the Thai Monarchy has evolved in a constantly changing environment full of political disputes. It can hardly be claimed that the institution remains the same as that which existed hundreds of years ago. But grovelling to a God-like King is promoted as an essential part of being "Thai". After the 2006 coup people like Anek Laothamatas suggested

[16] For example, Thongchai Winichakul (2005) *Stepping beyond the 14th October model of Democracy* (In Thai).

[17] Thak Chaloemtiarana (1979) Already quoted.

[18] Paul Handley (2006) Already quoted.

that the best political system for Thailand should be based on "tradition", where elected politicians share power with the Monarchy and the military[19]. In order to understand why this view benefits the modern Thai ruling class as a whole, it is useful to make a study of the role of modern monarchies in other countries, which appear on the surface to be quite different from the Thai case. In fact what all modern monarchies have in common is their ideological role in supporting the status quo. That is why they still exist in Western Europe.

There is no doubt that the mainstream image of the King is that of a very powerful institution and person. But the Marxist theory of alienation helps us to understand that widely held beliefs and appearances are often not the truth. The capitalist ruling class boosts its power by getting us to believe that the market, the family or the Monarchy are "natural institutions". This socialisation is helped by a feeling of lack of power among the general population. It is this feeling of fear and lack of status and confidence in Thai society, which is encouraged by the ruling class because it helps to make us believe that the Monarchy and King are all powerful. Yet it is an instrument to strengthen, not the Monarchy as an ancient institution, but the entire modern Thai capitalist class. This is why Taksin, the army, the civilian bureaucracy and the big corporations all support the Monarchy.

The lèse majesté law, which claims to protect the Monarchy from being critised or insulted, is a law designed to protect the entire conservative elites. It is used to criminalise pro-democracy activists and political opponents of the elite. Trials are held in secret and arguing that what was stated was "the truth" is no defense. The maximum sentence is 15 years in prison, but people can be found guilty of multiple instances of lèse majesté and sentenced to consecutive periods in prison. The computer crimes law can also be used in the same way.

In September 2009, the Bangkok criminal court convicted Daranee Chanchoengsilapakul ("Da Topedo") to 18 years in prison on three counts of lèse majesté arising from statements she made at a Red Shirt rally.

[19] Anek Laotamatas (2006) *Taksina Populism*. Matichon Press (In Thai).

In her speech, she connected the 2006 military takeover to the Palace, and drew parallels between events in Thailand and Nepal, where the Monarchy was abolished in 2008. The charges were brought against Darunee following a complaint from Sondhi Limthongkul. The judges made little pretence at conducting a fair trial. They denied Daranee bail three times, reportedly because they were worried that Darunee's release would affect public sensibilities, which is not a justifiable reason under the Criminal Procedure Code. They also closed the court to the public on grounds of national security and held the trial in secret.

Darunee joined Suwicha Thakor, who earlier had received ten years for posting "offensive images" on the Internet. At time of writing, others awaiting trial over similar alleged offenses include Chiranuch Premchaiporn, the webmaster of *Prachatai*, an important independent news site. Her alleged "crime" was not having removed sensitive comments from the website quickly enough. Lèse majesté charges can be filed by any citizen and the police are under pressure from the army to take up every case.

After Abhisit Vejjajiva and the *Democrats* came to power in late 2008, the military installed Government announced that pursuing lèse majesté cases would be the Government priority. This was at a time of world recession. *Democrat* Party Government Minister Satit Wongnongtoey and other Government MPs declared that they were keen to increase the maximum sentence for lèse majesté. They were supported by so-called "NGO senator" Rosana Tositrakul. This law more than any other makes Thailand resemble a Police State.

The dominant academic view that the King is all powerful

The dominant academic view which sees the King as all powerful, includes Paul Handley[20], Duncan McCargo[21], Same Sky *(Fa Deaw Kan)* Press[22],

[20] Paul Handley (2006) Already quoted.

[21] Duncan McCargo (2005) Already quoted.

[22] See Oct-Dec 2005 edition of the magazine (in Thai) and also the book *"The 19th Sept Coup"* published in Thai in 2006.

Kevin Hewison[23], Michael Connors[24] and Niti Eawsriwong[25]. There is a suggestion by these academics that Bhumibol organised the 2006 coup and has been manipulating politics since the 1970s.

Many of these intellectuals rely, consciously or unconsciously, on the old Maoist analysis, from the *Communist Party of Thailand* (CPT), that under-developed countries like Thailand have yet to complete their bourgeois revolutions and are therefore "semi-feudal". This analysis sees the major confrontation among the elites as being between the old semi-feudal order and the new rising capitalists. It is a mechanical application of the 1789 French Revolution to Thailand in the 21st century. In fact by 1848 the European capitalist class had more or less co-opted the remaining kings or feudal lords into their capitalist class and were no longer prepared to lead any more revolutions for fear of stirring up the masses. Set into the context of the 2006 coup, the belief is that the coup was the result of a conflict between the "feudal" Monarchy and the capitalist Taksin. This "Neo-Maoist" position has also been proposed in detail by Kasian Tejapira[26].

The Maoist (and Stalinist) analysis of under-developed countries characterised them as being "semi-feudal", since the "National Democratic Revolution" or bourgeois revolution had yet to be achieved. Unlike the analysis of Marx or Trotsky's theory of *Combined and Uneven Development*, Capitalism still needed to be established by a grand patriotic coalition of leftists and capitalists in order to fight the feudalists. This explains why many ex-communists supported Taksin. This school of thought ignores the fact that the ruling class networks which support the Monarchy also include the major bankers and industrialists and even Taksin. They also ignore the capitalist nature of the King's vast investments.

---

[23] Kevin Hewison (2008) A Book, the King and the 2006 Coup. *Journal of Contemporary Asia* 38 (1).

[24] M. K. Connors, M.K. (2003) *Democracy and National Identity in Thailand*. Routledge Curzon.

[25] Niti Eawsriwong (2008) Review of *The King Never Smiles*, made at the Thai Studies Conference that year. http://www.prachatai.com/ 17/1/2008.

[26] Kasian Tejapira (2007) "The dilemma of the Thai bourgeois revolution." http://www.prachatai.com/ 15/10/2007 (In Thai).

They therefore believe the Yellow Shirt accusation that Taksin and TRT are crypto-republicans. This is also the logic of Duncan McCargo's network conflict and the logic of those who believe in the 2006 "Royal coup". Yet Taksin has repeatedly vowed that he is a loyal subject of the King. His Government took part in the hysterical promotion of the King around the 60th anniversary of his reign and started the "Yellow Shirt Mania", where everyone was pressurised into wearing royal yellow shirts every Monday. Taksin's close supporters were also behind the grand petition to the King in 2009, asking for a royal pardon. All evidence points to the fact that Taksin is a royalist.

Another strand which is important in the mainstream academic view about the Monarchy, is the idea that Thai politics is really just about what the elites do, because the vast majority of the population are "passive" and "politically ignorant". The methods used by this school are to study the Monarchy and the elites by totally ignoring the Peoples Movement or struggles from below. Thai politics during the coup crisis of 2006 was therefore only about an inter-elite conflict. I call this a "neo-Riggsian" view point, since Fred Riggs was famous for putting forward this kind of analysis of Thai politics in the 1950s and 1960s[27].

In the case of Paul Handley, he insults the poor by saying that they are weak and stupid[28]. This patronising attitude fits with the excuses for the coup made by the Tank Liberals, although Handley isn't one of them. According to the Tank Liberals, the poor were bought by Taksin and did not really understand Democracy. That is why the majority vote could be dismissed so easily. In the case of Duncan McCargo[29], the elite view is clear when discussing the causes of the southern conflict. For him it is not primarily about oppression of the Muslim Malay population by Bangkok, but it is about a conflict between "network Monarchy" and "network Taksin"[30]. The elite-centred analysis is nothing less than a revival of

[27] Fred Riggs (1966) *Thailand. The Modernisation of a bureaucratic polity.* East West Press.

[28] Paul Handley (2006) Already quoted, pages 6,10,94,105.

[29] Duncan McCargo (2005) Already quoted.

[30] McCargo has cooperated closely in his work with the Thai academic Ukris Pathmanand. This view of network politics is shared by many Thai academics, including Niti Eawsriwong.

Fred Riggs' theory of the Bureaucratic Polity[31].

Never the less, the dominant analysis put forward by these mainstream academics has played an important and beneficial role in developing our understanding of the Thai Monarchy. This is because there was a tendency to totally avoid any discussion about the Monarchy by most academics in the past. It also raises the question about the King's power and the nature of this power. Handley seems to stress the King's individual power, but the benefits of his extremely valuable book are that it was carefully researched and contains a wealth of information which can be interpreted in different ways. There are many important occasions in the history of the King Bhumibol where Handley shows that the King was not heeded and he did not get his way. These include the overthrow of the Tanin Kraiwichien Government in 1977 and the popular uprising against Sujinda Kaprayoon's military junta in 1992. Both these regimes were favoured by the King.

McCargo points to a more collective, network power rather than individual power. Network politics is undoubtedly part of the Thai political scene but more questions remain to be answered. Is the King the most powerful person within "Network Monarchy"? Are there over-lapping and competing networks which all seek to support and use the Monarchy? Michael Connors suggests that the Monarchy is one Power Block in Thai politics[32]. Somsak Jeumtirasakul[33] argues that since 1992 the King has become the "head of the Thai ruling class". But in what way is this so? Is it as an all powerful head, or a symbolic Head of State?

There are other serious weaknesses with this mainstream analysis. The Neo-Riggsian model ignores the role played by the Peoples Movement in important events like the 14th October 1973, the rise of the Communist Party, the May 1992 uprising, and the role of trade unions and NGOs. Taksin's Populism was about buying social peace in response to

---

[31] Fred Riggs (1966) Already quoted.

[32] M. K. Connors (2003) Already quoted.

[33] Somsak Jeumtirasakul (2005) "After 14th Oct" In Fa Deaw Kan magazine, Oct-Dec 2005 (In Thai).

possible class struggle[34] and of course the mass protests of the PAD opened the door to the 2006 coup by calling on the King to solve the crisis. Without the struggles of the Peoples Movement would the democratic space have been opened up in the Seventies and Nineties? Would there have been a compromise with the Communists in the Eighties? Would the 1997 Constitution have come about? And without these struggles would the ruling elite need to constantly legitimise themselves in the eyes of the population by using the ideology of the Monarchy as a balance to Democracy?

What possible benefit could Taksin gain from reducing the power of the Monarchy? To show this, one needs to point to deep and serious economic and political differences in policy between the King and Taksin. Taksin's Populism might be cited as a difference in policy, yet it was not a burden on capitalist profits, including those of the Crown Property Bureau. Taksin also received support from all quarters, including the Monarchy, in his early years. Taksin and other modern capitalists have much more to lose by attacking the Monarchy and encouraging a general questioning of elite status and power.

A comparative study of the Monarchy

A good starting point is the English Revolution of 1640. This is useful because the English capitalist class brought back the Monarchy on a long-term basis after its overthrow, unlike the case of America 1776 or France 1789. Christopher Hill[35] shows that the return of the Monarchy after Cromwell's victory and the execution of Charles 1st was part of a need to crackdown on the radical movements of the poor, such as *The Levellers* and *Diggers*, who had been an important ally of the rising

[34] Kevin Hewison (2003) Crafting a new social contract: Domestic capitalist responses to the challenge of neoliberalism. In Ji Giles Ungpakorn (ed.) *Radicalising Thailand: new political perspectives*. Institute of Asian Studies, Chulalongkorn University.

[35] Christopher Hill (1959) *The English Revolution 1640. An Essay*. Lawrence & Wishart, London.

capitalists during the revolution[36]. The new Monarchy of Charles 2nd may have claimed to be appointed by God, but was in reality appointed by the new rising capitalist class. There was a need to "reinvent history"[37] to show that the power and privilege of this new capitalist ruling class was ancient and "God-given", interwoven with the Monarchy, and not really created by revolution from below against the feudal order.

It is the fear of revolution from below getting out of hand that made the capitalist class more and more reluctant to stir up revolution among the masses in order to overthrow the feudal order. It was also the weakening of such feudal forces and the growing strength of both the capitalist class and working class which tipped the balance. By 1848, as Marx explained with disappointment, the capitalists in Europe had come to an accommodation with the old order, but under the terms of the new capitalist class.

The English capitalists brought back the Monarchy in a different form, while claiming an ancient continuity, in order to use the Monarchy as a modern capitalist institution for enforcing conservative views against the rising working class. Today British and European ruling classes use their monarchies in order to promote conservative ideology. Yet, unlike Thailand, because of the strength of the working class, they are forced to frame such ideology in democratic terms. This is why the kings and queens of modern Europe are not promoted as sacred mythical beings.

In Thailand, the revolutionary transformation towards a capitalist state did not take the same form as the early Bourgeois Revolutions in England and France. Capitalist transformation occurred in a revolution from above by King Rama 5th of Bangkok, around the 1870s, in order to deal with the threat of Western Imperialism. In many respects the revolution of King Rama 5th was similar to the Meiji Restoration in Japan. Both were transformations to capitalist nation states in the face of imperialism. However the Thai transformation did not result in rapid economic development like in Japan. The ruling class in Bangkok decided to stall on

[36] Paul Foot (2005) *The Vote. How it was won and how it was undermined.* Penguin / Viking.

[37] Eric Hobsbawm (1995) Inventing Traditions. In: E. Hobsbawm & T. Ranger (eds) *The Invention of Tradition.* Cambridge University Press.

the process of land reform and economic development of production in order to stop valuable resources falling into the hands of foreign powers[38].

Neil Davidson explains that the definition of a Bourgeois Revolution, according to Marx, Engels, Deutscher, Tony Cliff and George Lukács is that it is *a revolutionary process which smoothes the way for the development of Capitalism*[39]. There are two main kinds of Bourgeois Revolutions: Revolution from Below, as in the case of England, America and France, and Revolution from Above, led by a section of the old feudal order itself, as in the case of Germany, Italy, Scotland and Japan. Revolutions from above to pave the way for Capitalism occurred in these late developing countries. Thailand's revolution can be counted among the latter. But the process did not end with King Rama 5th's revolutionary transformations in the 1870s. The Absolute Monarchy stage proved to be an unstable one[40], leading to the 1932 revolution and the establishment of a Constitutional Monarchy under capitalist class control.

Thak Chalermtiarana[41], Thongchai Winichakul[42], Kasian Tejapira[43] and Niti Eawsriwong[44] have all explained how royal political and social traditions, including the so-called "traditions" of the Constitutional Monarchy, have been invented. Therefore this is not really a disputed area among academics. What is open to debate, however, is the proposal that the Monarchy is an ideological tool of the modern Thai capitalist class, designed to stifle debate and any challenges to the authority of this modern class. By the "modern capitalist class" I mean both the private capitalists, like Taksin, the head of CP Corporation or the heads of the big banks, but also the Monarchy as a capitalist, and the top military and civilian

---

[38] Tomas Larsson (2008) Western Imperialism and Defensive Underdevelopment of Property Rights Institutions in Siam. *Journal of East Asian Studies* 8, 1-28.

[39] Neil Davidson (2004) The prophet, his biographer and the watchtower. *International Socialism Journal* No. 2:104, p.23.

[40] See Kullada (2004) Already quoted.

[41] Thak Chalermtiarana (1979) Already quoted.

[42] Thongchai Winichakul (2005) Already quoted.

[43] Kasian Tejapira (2005) Critique of Thainess. In Fa Deaw Kan magazine, Oct-Dec 2005 (In Thai).

[44] http://www.prachatai.com/ 14/3/2006 (In Thai).

bureaucrats as state-capitalists. All sections of this ruling class control the means of production via capitalist relations. The military and civilian bureaucrats have significant control over the state sectors, including the media.

The important ideological role of the Monarchy

The high profile and status of the King started from his systematic promotion by the military dictator Sarit Tanarat. This promotion of the Monarchy took place in the late 1950s at a time of heightening tensions in South East Asia during the Cold War. Sarit was supported in his pro-Monarchy policies by the US Government which saw his dictatorship and the Monarchy as useful in countering the spread of Communism[45]. In his book on the Sarit regime, Thak Chalermtiarana argued that Sarit promoted the King in order to gain legitimacy in the eyes of the population because he had no historical credentials from the 1932 revolution[46]. This may be true. Alternatively, Sarit's promotion of the Monarchy may have been designed to win legitimacy in the eyes of the Thai conservative elites and the US Government. Therefore the increasing importance of the Monarchy after 1932 was closely connected to the need have an ideology to counter Communism in order to protect the status quo.

The use of "Nation, Religion and King" as a conservative ideology, where the King symbolised the "heart of the nation", the head of religion and the embodiment of "all that is Thai", was central to combating Communism in the second half of the twentieth century. The importance of the King to the modern ruling elites in Thailand can be understood in this ideological role. The ruling elites, which are made up of the army, capitalists and high-ranking officials, are not some left over remains of a feudal system. They are the modern Thai ruling class: conservative, anti-democratic and barbaric. It is not the King who is in charge of this

---

[45] Katherine Bowie (1997) Already quoted.

[46] Thak Chalermtiarana (1979) Already quoted.

bunch of thugs. It is they who use the symbolic role of the King to protect their interests.

Because of the continuing class struggle for Democracy, which takes place on a global scale, and because of the increasing size of the Thai working class, it has become more difficult to claim legitimacy for military dictatorships. The Thai army can never convincingly claim democratic credentials. Capitalists and elite-based politicians can do this when it suits them, but the army relies totally of legitimising its actions by quoting the Monarchy and this legitimacy has to be cloaked in a myth that the King holds real power in society. The military then claim that they are merely obeying orders. This is so that the army is not seen to act in its self-interests, which it actually does all the time.

The fact that the military and the conservative elites are not committed to Democracy means that they have to use the symbol of the Monarchy in a more authoritarian manner compared to Western Europe. Not only is the Monarchy a representation of conservative ideology, but it is also dressed up in sacred robes, surrounded by mythology, and protected by harsh authoritarian laws. For those who want a Thai Monarchy along the lines of Western Europe, this means drastically reducing the power of the military, abolishing the lèse majesté law, scrapping royal language and also abolishing all the crawling and subservience to a so-called "sacred" King. There has to be open and free criticism of the Monarchy and the right to advocate a republic. Although some Red Shirt leaders have indicated that this is what they want, there is no evidence to suggest that this is the road that Taksin wishes to take when he hopes for a future reformed Monarchy. All evidence points to the fact that Taksin is still committed to a "sacred" King with a status above ordinary citizens.

After Bhumibol

The argument between Taksin and the coup supporters was never about reducing or increasing the power of the Monarchy because both sides have constantly claimed royal legitimacy in order to strengthen their rule over us. Both sides have also used the lèse majesté law against their opponents. The 2006 Coup was not a royalist coup against a republican Taksin, it was a conflict between two sections of the Thai ruling class, both of whom wish to use the Monarchy as an instrument of class rule. This conflict also had its roots in the strength of social movements and the need to win legitimacy from the electorate through elections.

Many Thais, whether they are royalist Yellow Shirts, or pro-democracy Red Shirts, are waiting for King Bhumibol to die. It may take years or he might be dead by the time you read this chapter.

Most Thais, both Yellow and Red, believe that Bhumibol has been the most powerful political actor. If it were the case that Bhumibol was all-powerful, like an absolute monarch, when he dies there would be a civil war between those who want to become the next king. The Princess' soldiers would fight the soldiers of the Crown Prince or those of the Queen. Prem's soldiers might place Prem on the throne! Is this likely? No.

There will be a power struggle and rivalries, but it will be a struggle among the elites, including Taksin, to see who can *use* the Monarchy for their own ends. After the 2006 coup Taksin lost this battle. Maybe he might return to the fight after Bhumibol's death.

When Bhumibol dies, my guess is that the army and the conservative elites will try to hold a gigantic and very expensive funeral for him. Resources which ought to go to building welfare and raising wages will be used for this. My guess is the funeral will be at least twice as long as the one recently organised for his sister, which lasted a whole year. Perhaps Bhumibol's funeral will last 5 years. Extensions of other King activities could take the whole thing to ten years! Pictures of the King will increase even more. The reason for this huge funeral will not be in order to satisfy "millions of Thais who will be heart-broken by Bhumibol's death". Many will be celebrating in private. No, the reason for a huge funeral will be in order to shift the propaganda machine into an even higher gear. The conservative elites will be desperately trying to promote and re-promote the ideology of the Monarchy. Anyone who opposes the army, or the authoritarian elites who are now in power, anyone who campaigns for Democracy, will be accused of lèse majesté and of trying to "overthrow Bhumibol". The fact that he is dead will be of little consequence. While all this is going on, the extremely unpopular and disrespected Crown Prince will be gradually shifted on to the Throne under the watchful eyes of the conservatives. His equally hated mother, the Queen, will be there too, but both will be under the larger than life picture of Bhumibol. We will never be able to forget Bhumibol and his so-called "wonderful works". We will see the Crown Prince, but the words "Bhumibol" will be blaring out from loud speakers.

If all this propaganda does not work, there will be the lèse majesté law, the contempt of court law, the computer law and the internal security law. If that does not work, the army can always shoot pro-democracy demonstrators.

After Bhumibol, the powerful army will still be there. The tanks and guns will not have disappeared. The raw and repressive power of the conservative elites rests with the army. But the generals will panic because their sole source of legitimacy will have died.

If the Crown Prince is hated and despised by Thais, why would the army promote him to be the next King? If Bhumibol is all powerful, why did he not appoint the Princess as his heir to the Throne? The answer lies in the need to use tradition as part of royal ideology. The army is reluctant to appoint the Princess over the Crown Prince because their false claim that the Monarchy is steeped in "ancient tradition" would collapse by such an appointment. Not only that, changing the succession, because the Prince was unsuitable, would mean that the Monarchy could always be changed and even be abolished. Its holy status would evaporate.

Do not think for one second that when Bhumibol dies, that Thailand will descend into chaos. It is and has been in chaos since 2006, despite Bhumibol.

When Bhumibol dies, the work of those who want a republic will not be easier. The King's death will provide opportunities and dangers. The royalist Yellow Shirts will be more desperate and dangerous. But the legitimacy of their actions can be attacked. Democracy does not fall from a branch like a ripe mango. We have to reach up and pick it and at the same time, reach up and pull down the conservative elites and their entire authoritarian system.

Chapter 4

An historical Perspective: from Pre-Capitalism to TRT

Capitalist transformation

Pre-Capitalism

Before the major transformation of the state into a centralised capitalist model in the 1870s, "Thailand" as a nation-state did not exist[1]. The back-projection of "Thailand's history" from the modern era to *Sukotai* (A.D.1270) and *Ayuttaya* (A.D.1350-1782) must therefore be seen as rewritings of history by people such as Luang Wichitwatakarn and Prince Damrong, to serve modern nationalistic ideology.

Before the 1870s the dominant economic and political system in the central and northern region can best be described as a "Mandala"[2], "Galactic Polity"[3] or "*Sakdina*"[4] state. This was a loose political entity based on clusters of powerful cities, such as *Sukotai, Ayuttaya, Chiang Mai* etc., whose political power changed over time and also decreased proportionately to the distance from each city. Not only was there no such

1 Thongchai Winichakul (1994) *Siam Mapped*. University of Hawaii Press.

2 O. W. Wolters (1968) "Ayudhaya and the Rearward Part of the World". *Journal of the Royal Asiatic Society* 3 / 4,166-178 & 173-176.

3 S. J. Tambiah (1977) "The Galactic Polity". *Annals of the New York Academy of Sciences*. 293, 69-97.

4 The term used in Thai to indicate the pre-capitalist political system.

thing as a centralised nation-state under an all-powerful king, but political power to control surplus production was also decentralised.

In this *Sakdina* system, control of surplus production, over and above self-sufficiency levels, was based on forced labour and the extraction of tribute. This was a system of direct control over humans, rather than the use of land ownership to control labour, and its importance was due to the low population level. One estimate puts the average population density in 1904 as 11 persons per square kilometre, compared to 73 in India[5]. The majority of common people *(Prai)* living near urban centres were forced to perform corvée labour for monthly periods. There were also debt slaves *(Taht)* and war slaves *(Chaleay Seuk)*. This direct control of labour was decentralised under various *Moon Nai* (bosses), nobles and local rulers *(Jao Hua Muang)*, who had powers to mobilise labour. The result was that under the Sakdina system both economic and political power was decentralised[6].

Trade played an important part in the economy. Control of river mouths as export centres, became more important as long distance trade increased. Local rulers sought a monopoly on this trade in cooperation with Chinese merchants who ran sailing junks as far as China and the Arab world. *Ayuttaya* was an important trading port, with ships from Europe, China, Java, Persia and Japan calling on a regular basis. The docks in *Ayuttaya* were run on an international basis. Official languages of trade included Malay and Chinese and one important port official was a Shia trader from Persia. He was the founder of the *Bunnarg* family.

War was also important. But war in the Sakdina period was not about controlling territory. It was about gaining war slaves, plundering neigbouring cities and proving power.

Since the *Sakdina* system was decentralised, it was not the only system of social organisation that existed in what is now Thailand. In areas

[5] Chattip Nartsupa (1985) *The economy of Thai villages in the past*. Sarng-San Press, Bangkok (In Thai).

[6] R.B. Cruikshank (1975) "Slavery in nineteenth century Siam". *Journal of the Siam Society*. 63(2), 315. Chatchai Panananon (1988) "Phrai, neither free nor bonded". *Asian Review* (Chulalongkorn University, Thailand) 2, 1.

far away from large towns and cities, people of varying ethnic composition also lived in semi-autonomous villages or small clusters of human habitation in various different ways. Apart from this, before the rise of *Ayuttaya*, there also existed a multitude of different states such the Khmer or Tawarawadi empires.

Imperialism and capitalist transformation

Although the increasing penetration of Capitalism and the world market into the region had already increased the importance of money and trade, especially in the early Bangkok period[7], it was direct pressure from Western Imperialism and internal class struggle that finally pushed and dragged the Bangkok rulers towards a capitalist political transformation. Evidence for this comes with looking at the effect of the British imposed Bowring Treaty of 1855. This treaty established free trade and the freedom for Western capital penetration into the area without the need for direct colonisation. While the monopoly over trade, enjoyed by the *Sakdina* rulers of Bangkok, was abolished, vast opportunities were created for the capitalist production and trade of rice, sugar, tin, rubber and teak. The King of Bangkok quickly adapted himself to gain from these opportunities and fought to centralise the state under his own power in the face of internal and external challenges. Thailand's Capitalist Revolution was not carried out by the bourgeoisie in the same style as the English or French revolutions. In Thailand's case, the ruler of Bangkok, King Rama 5th or *"King Chulalongkorn"* brought about a revolutionary transformation of the political and economic system in response to both pressure from an outside world which was already dominated by Capitalism and class struggle within.

Rama 5th's revolution was to create a centralised and unified nation-state under the rule of Thailand's first Absolute Monarchy[8]. This

[7] Niti Eawsriwong (1984) *"Pak-gai la Rua-bai"*. Collection of essays on literature and history in the early Bangkok period. Amarin Press, Bangkok. (In Thai).

[8] Chaiyan Rajchagool (1994) *The rise and fall of the absolute monarchy*. White Lotus, Bangkok. Kullada Kesboonchoo Mead (2004) *The rise and decline of Thai absolutism*. Routledge. Giles Ji Ungpakorn (1997) *The struggle for Democracy and Social Justice in Thailand*. Arom Pongpangan Foundation, Bangkok.

involved destroying the power of his *Sakdina* rivals, the *Moon Nai*, nobles and local *Jao Hua Muang*. Politically this was done by appointing a civil service bureaucracy to rule outer regions and economically, by abolishing their power to control forced labour and hence surplus value. Forced labour was also abolished in response to class struggle from below, since *Prai* had a habit of trying to escape corvée labour and both *Prai* and *Taht* would often deliberately work inefficiently. Forced labour was replaced by wage labour and private property rights in land ownership was introduced for the first time. Furthermore, investment in production of agricultural goods for the world market became more important than the simple use of surplus production for consumption and trade. This can clearly be seen in the various investments in irrigation canals for rice production in the *Rungsit* area of the central plains. These investments opened up the land for settlement and work by the peasantry, which had been freed from corvée labour. Thus a temporary class alliance was built between the Monarchy and the peasantry against the old *Sakdina* rulers and bosses, which served to support the new ruling class interests in the global rice trade.

The shortage of labour for capitalist accumulation was initially solved by recruiting labour from China in the early part of the twentieth century. Much later, beginning in the early 1960s, a large surge in "indigenous" wage labour occurred as a result of poor peasants being pulled off the land, often from the north-east, into more productive workshops and factories in urban areas, especially around Bangkok. Later still, Thai Capitalism started to depended on migrant labour from Burma and other neighbouring countries.

The capitalist transformation and the construction of the first Thai nation state, a product of continuous change, occurred at a time when similar transformations were taking place throughout colonised South-East Asia. In the neighbouring colonies belonging to Britain, France and The Netherlands, state centralisation and the development of a capitalist economy, based upon wage labour was also taking place. In fact we should view the process of Thai state formation as the "internal colonisation" of the north, south and north-east by the Chakri rulers of

Bangkok. Certainly the various north and north-eastern revolts against Bangkok indicate this to be true. The civil war today in the Muslim South also has its roots in this process. The main point to bear in mind is that the changes taking place in "un-colonised" Thailand were not very different from the rest of colonised South-East Asia.

Problems with the Stalinist/Maoist analysis of state formation

The Left in Thailand has shown considerable confusion about Thailand's capitalist transformation and this has influenced much intellectual analysis, way beyond the Left, to this day. This confusion results from applying a Marxist model in an extremely mechanical and a-historical manner, typical of the Stalinist and Maoist tradition. This is not surprising given that the only left-wing organisation of any significance, in terms of ideas and numbers of supporters, was the *Communist Party of Thailand* (CPT). A prime example of this mechanical analysis is Jit Pumisak's argument that land ownership was central to the extraction of surplus value in the Thai *Sakdina* system[9]. This is one of many attempts at trying to fit Thai history into a Western model. Marx never claimed that Asian history followed the same exact path as European historical processes. As an example of a different production system in Asia, he suggested that in certain areas there existed a society based on irrigation canals called the "Asiatic Mode of Production" (AMP)[10]. There is no archeological evidence that Marx's model of the AMP, with its complex irrigation system and centralised state, ever existed in "Thailand", although it might have existed in the Khmer empire, centred around Ankor. Yet, the mechanical Marxists have also tried to prove that pre-capitalist production in Thailand was a mixture of the *Sakdina* system and the Asiatic Mode of Production[11]. In doing so, they have been forced to transform the meaning

[9] Jit Pumisak (1995) *The nature of the Thai Sakdina system*. Nok Hook Press, Bangkok. (In Thai).

[10] Karl Marx (1992) "Articles on India and China". In: *Surveys from exile, Political Writings* volume 2. Penguin Books, London.

[11] Pakpat Tipayaprapai (1997) *The Asiatic Mode of Production as an explanation of Thai Villages*. The Office of Research Supporting Grants, Bangkok. (In Thai).

of the AMP to mean only a system of village production.

The mechanical approach by the Thai Left also betrays a total lack of understanding about the fundamental nature of Capitalism. Capitalism, for them, can only exist in the hands of private capitalists. They are unable to understand the concept of an absolute monarchy or military dictator being part of the capitalist class in much the same way that they are unable to understand the theory of State Capitalism in Russia which characterised the Stalinist regime as a form of Capitalism[12]. Maoist doctrine, which dominated the CPT, insisted that Thailand in the 1970s and 1980s was "semi-feudal, semi colonial"; a model copied directly from Mao's analysis of China. Even today many intellectuals try to explain the conflict between Taksin and the conservative royalists by saying that Thailand has yet to achieve its capitalist revolution.

Capitalism is a system whereby capital is invested in the production process with the aim of realising further capital accumulation. This process requires two things: firstly a significant population of waged workers who are separated from the means of production, in order that the small minority capitalist class can accumulate capital by the extraction of surplus value. Secondly, Capitalism needs the existence, in one form or another of market forces which lead to competition between different groups of capital. The important point about the capitalist class is not its outward form or title or the issue of personal ownership. The important point is the fact that the capitalist class controls the means of production and accumulation. Therefore it follows that the capitalist class, especially in under-developed countries can be made up of absolute monarchs, Government officials, communist party bureaucrats or private capitalists.

The first Thai capitalist state was controlled by the Absolute Monarchy, which was a key part of the indigenous capitalist class. Under this state, there were three main capitalist groupings in the Thai economy; the royal capitalists, the Chinese capitalist merchants and the "foreign" (Western and later Japanese) capitalists[13].

---

[12] Tony Cliff (1974) *State capitalism in Russia*. Pluto Press, London.

[13] Akira Suehiro (1989) *Capital accumulation in Thailand 1855-1985*. Centre for East Asian Cultural Studies, Tokyo.

From the 1932 revolution to the end of military rule in 1973

Thailand was well integrated into the world market by the 1930s and as a result of this, suffered the effects of the 1930s economic depression. The political fall-out from this was that a group of civilian and military state officials, under Pridi Panomyong's *Peoples Party*, staged a successful revolution against the Absolute Monarchy of Rama 7th in June 1932. The first declaration of the revolutionaries clearly identified the economic crisis as bringing things to a head, with mass unemployment, cuts in wages and increased taxation experienced by the mass of the population. The Royal Family was notably exempted from these tax increases!

The 1932 revolution was carried out on the back of widespread social discontent. Farmers in rural areas were becoming increasingly bold and strident in their written criticism of the Monarchy[14]. Working class activists were involved in the revolution itself, although they were not the main actors, and cheering crowds spontaneously lined *Rachadamnern Avenue* as the *Peoples Party* declaration was read out by various representatives stationed along the road. Nakarin Mektrairat details this wide movement of social forces which eventually led to the revolution. It is important to stress the role of different social groups in creating the conditions for the 1932 revolution, since the right-wing historians have claimed that it was the work of a "handful of foreign educated bureaucrats". In fact, there has been a consistent attempt by the Right, both inside and outside Thailand, to claim that ordinary Thai people have a culture of respecting authority and therefore show little interest in politics[15].

---

[14] Nakarin Mektrairat (1990) *Beliefs, knowledge and political power in the 1932 revolution.* Social Science Association of Thailand, Bangkok. (In Thai).

[15] Fred Riggs (1966) *Thailand. The modernisation of a Bureaucratic Polity.* East West Press. USA. David Morell & Chai-anan Samudavanija (1981) *Political conflict in Thailand: reform, reaction and revolution.* Oelgeschlager, Gunn & Hain. David Wilson (1962) *Politics in Thailand.* Cornell University Press. John Girling (1981) *Thailand. Society and politics.* Cornell University Press, USA.

The 1932 revolution had the effect of further modernising the capitalist state and expanding the base of the ruling class to include the top members of the civilian and military bureaucracy, especially the military. The reason why the military became so influential in Thai politics, finally resulting in 16 years of uninterrupted military dictatorship from 1957, was the fact that the *Peoples Party* lacked a solid mass base beyond the bureaucracy. In addition to this, the private capitalists and the working class were still weak in terms of social forces which could compete with the military.

The 1932 revolution meant that the role of the Monarchy was significantly changed for the second time in less than a century. In the 1870s King Rama 5th abolished *Sakdina* rule in favour of a centralised and modern Absolute Monarchy. Sixty years later, the 1932 revolution destroyed this Absolute Monarchy so that the King merely became one section of the Thai ruling class. It is important to understand this, because there has been a tendency by both the Left and the Right to exaggerate the importance and "long-lasting traditions" of the Thai Monarchy. Today's King may seem to have the trappings of "tradition", yet the influence of this institution has fluctuated over the last sixty years and in many cases its "sacredness" has been manufactured by military and civilian rulers to provide themselves with political legitimacy[16].

Many commentators argue that the "weakness" of Marxist or Communist ideology in Thailand was mainly due to the fact that there was no mass-mobilisation in the struggle for national liberation such as was seen in Indonesia, Burma or Vietnam[17]. It is not true that Communist ideology was weak in Thai society, especially in the 1940s, 1950s and mid 1970s, and mass-mobilisation for the purpose of nation-building did occur in the 1932 revolution. However, the fact that the CPT placed capitalist nation-building as its primary aim, in a similar vein to all other Stalinist-Maoist parties, did mean that the CPT had little to achieve, since

[16] See Chapter 3.

[17] Chai-anan Samudavanija (1989) "Thailand: a stable semi-democracy." In L. Diamond, J.J. Linz & S.M. Lipset (eds) *Democracy in developing countries*. Vol 3, Asia. Lynne Rienner & Adamantine Press.

the task of nation-building had already been started by King Chulalongkorn and was subsequently followed through by the 1932 revolution.

The rise of the private capitalists or bourgeoisie

Despite the fact that military dictatorships were overthrown by students and workers in 1973 and 1992, the main beneficiaries in terms of gaining political power, have been the private sector capitalists. Thailand's modern private bourgeoisie, including Taksin, have cleverly taken advantage of the struggle for Democracy waged from below in order to gain political power at the expense of the military state capitalists.

Although arising out of demands made by the May 1992 movement against the military, the drafting of the 1997 Constitution was, in fact, an important victory for the modern private bourgeoisie[18]. Liberalism was the main political influence among the drafting committee and the aim of this constitution, for the liberals, was to increase Government stability and reduce the more blatant forms of corruption. It was a charter for Thailand's modern capitalists.

The private capitalist class existed from the earliest period of Capitalism in Thailand. Initially they were businessmen of Chinese origin who cooperated with the royal state capitalists in the late 19th century, but after the royal family were removed from state power in the 1932 revolution, the royal capitalists joined the ranks of the private sector capitalist class. Today the King controls important interests in the Thai economy, including real estate, the Siam Commercial Bank and the Siam Cement company. He is a fabulously wealthy capitalist.

The importance of ethnic Chinese businesses, especially those associated with the big banks, increased during the Second World War when Western interests were temporarily excluded from Thailand[19]. Another two important sources leading to the development of major ethnic Chinese

[18] Michael Connors (1999) "Political reform and the state in Thailand". *Journal of Contemporary Asia* 29(2), 202-225.

[19] Hewison, Kevin (1989) *Power and politics in Thailand.* Journal of Contemporary Asia Publishers, Philippines.

businesses, were the joint venture import substitution industries, which relied on foreign capital, and the growth of agribusinesses such as the giant CP corporation[20].

Another important section of the private capitalist class grew from military and bureaucratic officials who used their state positions for personal enrichment or advantage during the periods of military domination. Early examples were the family dynasties of the various dictators such as Sarit, Tanom and Prapat, but also the Choonhawan family. However, in recent years other families have become prominent, some from provincial backgrounds.

The booming economy of the late 1980s and early 1990s also produced a new crop of Thai capitalists. Taksin is a good example. Although Taksin comes from a trading family from the north, his capitalist career started when he left the police force and started selling computers back to his old contacts in the police department. His IT business interests, however, really took-off after the partial liberalisation of the Thai telecommunication market. Initially Taksin entered parliamentary politics in the mid 1990s by helping to bank-roll the *Palang Tum Party*. He then set himself up as head of *Thai Rak Thai* (TRT).

Left to themselves, the private bourgeoisie would never struggle against military dictatorships, but once mass struggle by workers and students achieved Democracy, they were quick to take advantage of the new situation.

The 1970s: the Peoples Movement and the "October People"

In order to fully understand the Peoples Movement you need to look at what happened in the so-called "Sixties" wave of struggles. Internationally, the Sixties Movement was characterised by a general rise in the struggle of oppressed groups on a global scale. Central to this struggle was the role

[20] Akira Suehiro (1992) "Capitalist development in postwar Thailand: commercial bankers, industrial elite and agribusiness groups". In: *Southeast Asian Capitalists*. Ruth McVey (ed), Cornell University Press, USA.

of students and a new generation of activists in labour and peasant organisations. This took the form of movements against Racism, Sexual Oppression and especially Imperialism. Activists from this period are now to be found playing important roles in political systems throughout the world. However, their present day role is often in contradiction to their original beliefs during the Sixties. In Thailand the "Sixties" movement has helped to shape both the policies of TRT and the nature of the NGOs and the Peoples Movement.

It would be more accurate to talk of the "Seventies Movement" in Thailand, if we actually look at the decade when the struggle for Social Equality and Democracy reached its peak. But it is important to understand that it is not possible to separate this "Seventies Movement" in Thailand from the struggles of the "Sixties" internationally. This link between the Sixties and Seventies occurs in two ways. Firstly, the wave of student revolts and the activism among young people in Western Europe and the United States, the "1968 Movement", were an inspiration which ignited the left-wing struggles in the early 1970s in Thailand. Libertarian left-wing ideas from the Western movements entered Thai society by way of news reports, articles, books, music and the return of Thai students from the West, especially art students in the first instance. Secondly, the victory of Communist Parties in Indochina after the USA began to lose the war in Vietnam, had a massive impact in igniting struggles for a new society in Thailand. These Asian communist victories were also directly linked to the "Sixties" movement in the West in a dialectical manner. The radicals in the West were inspired by the local struggles against Imperialism and Injustice in South-East Asia and other areas of the globe. The anti-Vietnam War movement, which was an important part of the latter period of the "Western Sixties", helped to destroy the ability of the US to continue with the war[21].

What did the Thai "Seventies" look like? The first picture in one's mind should be half a million people, mainly young school and university students, but also ordinary working people, protesting around the

[21] Jonathan Neal (2001) *The American War: Vietnam 1960-1975*. London: Bookmarks.

Democracy Monument on 14th October 1973. This resulted in the overthrow of the military dictatorship. It was the first mass popular uprising in modern Thai history. The 14th October and the following struggles, victories, and defeats that make up the "Thai Seventies" have continued to shape the nature of politics and society to this day.

The 14th October uprising

The military domination of Thai politics, started soon after the 1932 revolution, but its consolidation of power came with the Sarit military coup in 1957. The economic development during the years of military dictatorship in the 1950s and 1960s took place in the context of a world economic boom and a localised economic boom created by the Korean and Vietnam wars. This economic growth had a profound impact on the nature of Thai society.

Naturally the size of the working class increased as factories and businesses were developed. However, under the dictatorship trade union rights were suppressed and wages and conditions of employment were tightly controlled. By early 1973 the minimum daily wage, fixed at around 10 baht since the early 1950s, remained unchanged while commodity prices had risen by 50%. Illegal strikes had already occurred throughout the period of dictatorship, but strikes increased rapidly due to general economic discontent. The first 9 months of 1973, before the 14th October, saw a total of 40 strikes, and a one month strike at the Thai Steel Company resulted in victory due to a high level of solidarity from other workers.

Economic development also resulted in a massive expansion of student numbers and an increased intake of students from working class backgrounds. The building of the *Ramkamhaeng Open University* in 1969 was a significant factor here. Student numbers in higher education increased from 15,000 in 1961 to 50,000 by 1972. The new generation of students, in the early 1970s, were influenced by the revolts and revolutions which occurred throughout the world in that period, May 1968 in Paris, being a prime example. Before that, in 1966 the radical journal, Social Science

Review, was established by progressive intellectuals. Students started to attend volunteer development camps in the countryside in order to learn about the problems of rural poverty. By 1971 3,500 students had attended a total of 64 camps. In 1972 a movement to boycott Japanese goods was organised as part of the struggle against foreign domination of the economy. Students also agitated against increases in Bangkok bus fares.

In June 1973 the rector of *Ramkamhaeng University* was forced to resign after attempting to expel a student for writing a pamphlet criticising the military dictatorship[22]. Four months later, the arrest of 11 academics and students for handing out leaflets demanding a democratic constitution, resulted in hundreds of thousands of students and workers taking to the streets of Bangkok. As troops with tanks fired on unarmed demonstrators, the people of Bangkok began to fight-back. Bus passengers spontaneously alighted from their vehicles to join the demonstrators. Government buildings were set on fire. The *"Yellow Tigers"*, a militant group of students, sent a jet of high-octane gasoline from a captured fire engine into the police station at *Parn-Fa* bridge, setting it on fire. Earlier they had been fired upon by the police.

The successful 14th October 1973 mass uprising against the military dictatorship shook the Thai ruling class to its foundations. For the next few days, there was a strange new atmosphere in Bangkok. Uniformed officers of the state disappeared from the streets and ordinary people organised themselves to clean up the city. Boy Scouts directed traffic. It was the first time that the *pu-noi* (little people) had actually started a revolution from below. It was not planned and those that took part had a multiplicity of ideals about what kind of Democracy and society they wanted. But the Thai ruling class could not shoot enough demonstrators to protect their regime. It was not just a student uprising to demand a democratic constitution. It involved thousands of ordinary working class people and occurred on the crest of a rising wave of workers' strikes.

---

[22] Much later, after the 19th September 2006 coup, most university rectors again collaborated with the military junta.

Success in over-throwing the military dictatorship bred increased confidence. Workers, peasants and students began to fight for more than just parliamentary Democracy. In the two months following the uprising, the new royal appointed civilian Government of Sanya Tammasak faced a total of 300 workers' strikes. A central trade union federation was formed. New radical student bodies sprang up. On the 1st May 1975 a quarter of a million workers rallied in Bangkok and a year later half a million workers took part in a general strike against price increases. In the countryside small farmers began to build organisations and they came to Bangkok to make their voices heard. Workers and peasants wanted Social Justice and an end to long-held privileges. A *Triple Alliance* between students, workers and small farmers was created. Some activists wanted an end to exploitation and Capitalism itself. The influence of the CPT increased rapidly, especially among activists in urban areas.

As part of the political reform process, in December 1973, the King presided over a hand-picked National Forum (often referred to as the *"horse track assembly"*, due to its location). This Forum, which had members chosen form various professions, was tasked with selecting a new parliament. Kukrit Pramote was chosen as the Chairman of the new parliament when it opened on the 28th December, while Sanya Tammasak remained Prime Minister. However, this parliament and the Sanya Government could not solve the increasing tensions in society between the conservatives and the Left or between the rich and the poor[23].

The first democratic elections, since the October 1973 uprising, were held in January 1975. Parliament had a Left colouring and Government policies reflected a need to deal with pressing social issues. Left-wing parties, such as the *New Force Party*, the *Socialist Party of Thailand* and the *Socialist Front Party* gained 37 seats (out of a total of 269) but did not join any coalition Governments. The first coalition Government, made up of the *Democrat Party* and the *Social Agriculture Party*, was established under Seni Pramote. This right-leaning Government announced that it would

[23] Charnwit Kasetsiri & Thamrongsak Petchlertanun (1998) From *14 to 6 October*. Bangkok: Social Science and Anthropology Book Foundation. (InThai).

follow "Social Democratic" policies. However, the Government lost a vote of no confidence in parliament in March 1975 and was replaced by a new coalition Government headed by Kukrit Pramote from the *Social Action Party*. The new Government introduced a number of pro-poor policies, including job creation schemes. This Government presided over a period of increasing social tensions. Strikes, demonstrations and political assassinations occurred on a regular basis. Eventually parliament was dissolved in January 1976 and elections held in April. The April elections resulted in a swing to the Right. This was due to a combination of factors, such as intimidation of the Left and a right-ward shift among the middle classes who were afraid of radicalism.

The student movement after 14th October 1973

It is important to remember that the 14th October 1973 was the peak of the anti-dictatorship struggle which then developed into a broader struggle for Social Justice and Socialism among students, workers and small farmers. It is interesting to consider the activities of newly radicalised young people who later became known as the October People *(Kon Duan Tula)*. It is this generation which has played an important leadership role in both the Peoples Movements and in sections of the establishment political parties in present day Thai society.

Student activism in society

In the period leading up to the overthrow of the military on the 14th October 1973, many student centres and coalitions were formed in various regions and different educational institutions. However, there were attempts to coordinate the actions of these different groups under a single umbrella: *The National Student Centre of Thailand*. This and other student centres became even more active in various social campaigns, often as part of the *Triple Alliance* with workers and peasants. Never the less, the movement was dogged by personal and political splits. Seksan Prasertkul, one of the 14th

October student leaders, formed the *Free Thammasart Group* and Tirayut Boonmi, another student leader from the 14th October uprising, formed the *People for Democracy Group*[24]. These so-called "independent groups" felt that the *National Student Centre* leadership was too conservative, often refusing to mobilise students on important issues like the successful protest against the return of the ousted dictator Field Marshal Tanom Kitikajorn in 1974. For this reason these various independent groups formed an alternative centre called the *"National Coalition Against Dictatorship"* with Sutam Saengpratoom as secretary[25].

One important area of activity for students was the struggle against US Imperialism and for so-called "Thai independence". The military dictatorship had been a close ally of the United States during the Cold War, sending token numbers of Thai troops to support the US in both Korea and Vietnam. In 1973 there were 12 US military bases in the country, with 550 war planes and thousands of troops stationed on Thai soil in order to help the US war effort in Indo-China. These bases were legally US territory, a point highlighted by the arrest and execution, by US military court, of a Thai citizen, Tep Kankla, for the murder of an American soldier in December 1973[26]. Apart from this, after the end of the Indo-China war, the US used *U-Tapao* naval base to attack Cambodia on 14th May 1975, without consulting the Thai Government.

The presence of such a large number of US forces, plus what was seen as the economic dominance of US companies in the local economy, seemed to confirm the Maoist analysis by the CPT that Thailand was a "semi-colony" of the USA. After 1973 there was therefore a growing campaign to kick out US bases. This campaign against US bases, which later received a boost from the defeat of the USA in Vietnam, and the

---

[24] Both Seksan Prasertkul and Tirayut Boonmi joined up with the *Communist Party of Thailand* for a period in 1976. They are now lecturers at Thammasat University.

[25] Sutam Saengpratoom was arrested in Bangkok on 6th October 1976. Much later he became a junior minister in the first *Thai Rak Thai* Government.

[26] *Sutachai Yimprasert (2001) 'How did the 6th October incident occur?'* In: Ji Ungpakorn & Sutachai Yimprasert (eds) *State Crime in a period of crisis and change*. Bangkok: The 6th October 1976 fact-finding and witness interviewing committee. (In Thai).

resulting new geo-political consequences, led to Prime Minister Kukrit's demand in March 1975 that the US withdraw. This was backed up by a massive anti-US base demonstration on 21st March 1976. The US finally withdrew its troops from Thailand shortly after this[27].

Another important area where the student movement was active was in the area of Human Rights and Democracy. Students campaigned to push for more democratic amendments to the 1974 constitution and they led struggles against state repression. On 24th January 1974 Government security forces attacked and burnt the village of *Na Sai* in the North-Eastern province of *Nong Kai*[28]. Three villagers were killed by Government forces. Initially the Government claimed that this atrocity was carried out by Communists, but Tirayut Boonmi, was able to prove in public that it was the work of the Government. Pressure from the student movement finally forced the Government to admit the crime and take steps to pay the villagers compensation. General Saiyut Kertpol, head of the *Communist Suppression Unit*, was also forced to admit that past Government policy had been "too harsh".

The *Na Sai* incident was followed by the exposure of another state crime in the Southern province of *Patalung*. It is estimated that between 1971 and 1973 Government forces had systematically arrested and interrogated villagers, resulting in over 3000 deaths. In what became known as the Red Drum *(Tang Daeng)* incident, villagers were killed and then burnt in petrol drums or pushed out of helicopters[29].

In addition to exposing state repression, student volunteers were also involved in the rather patronising state-sponsored campaign to "spread Democracy to the rural people" in the summer vacation of 1974[30].

[27] Since 9-11 the USA has sought to increase its military presence in South-East Asia under the banner of the War on Terror. However, the real reason behind US military expansion in the area may well be its rivalry with China. The Singapore military recently became the first foreign state to be allowed to station troops permanently on Thai soil since the 1970s US withdrawal.

[28] Sutachai (2001) Already quoted.

[29] Yos Juntornkiri (1975) 'Kicked down the mountain and burnt in Tang Daeng', in *Social Science Review* 13 (1), 41-71. Also *Prachachart* (1975) 21 February, 12. (In Thai).

[30] The Middle Classes have always regarded the poor as stupid and lacking in understanding of Democracy. This is seen clearly in the case of the 19th September 2006 coup.

However, this campaign did provide an opportunity for thousands of urban students to observe social problems in the villages at first hand, thus strengthening future cooperation between students and small farmers in the *Triple Alliance*. This helped to broaden the activities of students into areas of Social Justice and they became more left-wing.

On the cultural front, students campaigned for art and literature to be more in tune with the lives of ordinary people. Often this was influenced by narrow and mechanical ideas of Stalinist "socialist realism", which could be found in the writings of Jit Pumisak[31]. An exhibition titled "burning literature" condemned conservative books which served "feudal" interests. At the same time there was a flourishing of new "literature for the people", "theatre for the people" and the birth of the "songs for the people" movement, which sometimes added Thai words to tunes from Western protest songs from the same period. A campaign of criticism was also waged against the elitist and competitive education system. This campaign resulted in a Government committee being established in 1975 in order to reform education.

One important organisation which came out of these cultural activities was the *"Coalition of Thai Artists"*, which held a street exhibition of "Peoples Art" along *Rachadamnern Avenue* in October 1975. These artists and art students were also very important in producing agitational posters and banners used in campaigns against the influence of the military and in campaigns against US bases. In many ways the artist movement was more libertarian than many of the student organisations, being influenced by more radical ideas from the 1960s movements in the West, alongside the influence of the CPT[32]. After the 6th October 1976 bloodbath, many artists went to the jungle, but fought to maintain their free spirit amid the narrow Maoist ideology of the CPT.

---

[31] Jit Pumisak (1957) *Art for Life, Art for the People.* Tewawet Publishing Company. (In Thai).

[32] Ji Ungpakorn & Numnual Yapparat (2004) *Revival of the struggle. From the old Left to the new Left in Thailand.* Workers' Democracy Publishers, (In Thai).

Student politics within universities and colleges

An important consequence of the successful 14th October 1973 uprising against the dictatorship was the establishment of left-wing student political parties in universities and colleges. These contested elections for the student union. Some won immediate victories, while others gradually increased their influence at the expense of the right-wing. By mid-1976 most universities and colleges had Left student bodies, including *Kasetsart University*, which was previously believed to be a bastion of the Right. Once the victory of the Left parties was complete, the student body was able to unite once more around the *National Student Centre* with Kriangkamol Laohapairote[33] as secretary. One effect of the victory of the Left in universities and colleges was the temporary demise of the seniority (SOTUS) system[34], as students became more egalitarian and active in trying to change society. Student summer camps were organised in the countryside in order to share experiences with poor villagers and less emphasis was placed on inter-university football matches.

Despite the fact that the various left-wing student parties in various institutions were more or less autonomous in formal structure, they shared the same general ideology which was heavily influenced by the Maoism of the CPT. This can be seen by their concentration on countryside activity, although many groups also worked among urban workers[35]. One prominent labour organiser who was close to the CPT was Terdpum Jaidee. Thirty years later he became a supporter of the semi-fascist *Peoples Alliance for Democracy* (PAD) and an ardent royalist.

The student movement was basically a socialist movement which shared the CPT analysis of Thailand being a semi-feudal semi-colony of

---

[33] Kriangkamol Laohapairote later took up a position as a special advisor to the *Thai Rak Thai* Government.

[34] The SOTUS system returned with a vengeance after the 6th October 1976 crackdown. Today new first year students at *Chulalongkorn, Chiangmai and Kasetsart Universities* are subjected to systematic mental cruelty so that they conform to the seniority hierarchy and learn to be loyal to their institutions. But with the new green shoots of student activism today it may well be facing another left-wing challenge.

[35] Seksan Prasertkul was one of many student activist working with trade unions.

the USA. The armed struggle by the CPT in the countryside was seen as the key to building a better society. Many left-wing student groups also took the side of the CPT leadership in ideological disputes with people like ex-CPT leader Pin Bua-orn. Pin was against the CPT adopting armed struggle and wanted to continue the original Stalinist/Maoist cross-class alliance policy of working with the military dictators, which the CPT had advocated during the Pibun and early Sarit dictatorship period[36]. Student groups also became involved in taking the side of the CPT leadership over the faction fights taking place in China towards the end of the Cultural Revolution[37].

The influence of the CPT within the student movement was no secret conspiracy. It reflected the rise of left-wing ideas among many people in Thai society. In practice this CPT influence in the student body came from 3 main sources. Firstly, the CPT was the only left-wing political party which had a coherent analysis of Thai society and a clear plan of action. This naturally meant that many of those who were looking for answers would turn to the CPT, especially after the victory of various communist parties in neighbouring Indo-China. Secondly, some CPT youth members *(Yor)* and full members *(Sor)* were activists within the student movement. They had either been recruited while at secondary school or were recruited after they entered university. Recruitment was a long drawn out process, involving small secret study groups organised among contacts, but it helped to educate activists in CPT ideology. Thirdly, articles explaining CPT political strategy were printed in student newspapers such as *Atipat* and the CPT radio station, *The Voice of the People of Thailand*, was very popular among many people at the time.

---

[36] Stalinist and Maoist parties throughout the world advocated cross-class alliances with "progressive" leaders and capitalists, including Chiang Kai-shek in China, Sukarno in Indonesia and Nasser in Egypt. See Ian Birchall (1986) *Bailing out the system*. Bookmarks, London. Also Charlie Hore (1991) *The road to Tiananmen Square*. Bookmarks, London . In Thailand the CPT pushed for an alliance with the military dictators Pibun and Sarit. See Somsak Jeamteerasakul (1991) *The Communist Movement in Thailand*. PhD thesis, Department of Politics, Monash University, Australia.

[37] Sutachai (2001) Already quoted.

It would be quite wrong to assume that student leaders, even those who were party members, were receiving direct orders from the CPT Central Committee. For a start the party leaders were far away in the countryside and also the party never saw the urban struggle as being central to the overall Maoist revolutionary strategy. For this reason, it can be assumed that in the period between 1973 and 1976, student activists exhibited a high degree of self-leadership and organisation, while accepting the overall political analysis of the party. This is confirmed by many student activists from that period[38].

As already mentioned, between 1973 and 1976 left-wing student parties gradually won elections. At *Thammasart University* the *Palang Tum Party* (Moral Force Party) was established just before the October 1973 uprising and it won a number of subsequent elections, standing Pirapon Triyakasem as its candidate. At the *Ramkamhaeng Open University*, the *Saja-Tum Party* (Moral Truth Party) made gradual headway against a more middle of the road party, winning leadership of the student body by 1975. At *Chulalongkorn University* the *Chula Prachachon Party* (Chula Peoples Party) won elections in 1976 against a right-wing party and Anek Laotamatat[39] became student president. At *Mahidol* and *Sri-Nakarin* left-wing parties also won elections and at *Chiang Mai* Chaturon Chaisang[40] from the *Pracha Tum Party* (Peoples Morals Party) won the student union election in 1976.

The gradual shift towards left-wing politics among students throughout the period 1973-1976, until the Left became the main influence, reflected the polarisation between Left and Right that was

[38] Tongchai Winichakul and others confirmed this picture in interviews conducted by the author for the 6th October 1976 fact-finding and witness interviewing committee in 2000.

[39] Anek is known for his academic writings on the rise of the middle class and the political split between rural and urban Thailand. He went to the jungle to join with the CPT after 1976. Much later he became a party-list MP for the *Democrat Party* in 2001. Before the 2005 election he helped to establish the *Mahachon Party*, which was "bought" from a local gangster-politician using funds from the personal wealth of Sanan Kajornprasart. But the party only won two seats in the 2005 election. In 2006 Anek supported the military coup.

[40] He held cabinet positions in the *Thai Rak Thai* Government and became acting party leader after the 19th September 2006 coup.

taking place in wider society. From this we can see why the ruling class became determined to use whatever force necessary in order to destroy the left-wing student movement and their attempts came to fruition with the 6th October 1976 blood bath at *Thammasart University*.

The 6th October 1976 bloodbath

In the early hours of 6th October 1976, Thai uniformed police, stationed in the grounds of the National Museum, next door to *Thammasat University*, destroyed a peaceful gathering of students and working people on the university campus under a hail of relentless automatic fire[41]. At the same time a large gang of ultra-right-wing "informal forces", known as the *Village Scouts*[42], *Krating-Daeng* and *Nawapon*, indulged in an orgy of violence and brutality towards anyone near the front entrance of the university. Students and their supporters were dragged out of the university and hung from the trees around *Sanam Luang*; others were burnt alive in front of the Ministry of "Justice" while the mob danced round the flames. Women and men, dead or alive, were subjected to the utmost degrading and violent behaviour.

From before dawn that morning, students had been prevented from leaving the campus by police who were stationed at each gate. Inside the sealed university campus, violence was carried out by heavily armed police from the *Crime Suppression Division*, the *Border Patrol Police* and the *Special Forces Unit of the Metropolitan Police*[43]. Unarmed women and men students who had fled initial rounds of heavy gunfire to take refuge in the Commerce Faculty building were chased out at gun point and made to

[41] This account is compiled from witness statements given to 'The 6th October 1976 fact-finding and witness interviewing committee' in September 2000. The accounts have been published in Ji Ungpakorn & Sutachai Yimprasert (eds) (2001) *State Crime in a period of crisis and change*. The 6th October 1976 fact-finding and witness interviewing committee. (In Thai).

[42] See Katherine Bowie (1997) *Rituals of National Loyalty*. New York: University of Columbia Press.

[43] The police played a major role on 6th October 1976 because the military was divided and still recovering from its overthrow 3 years earlier.

lie face down on the grass of the football field, without shirts. Uniformed police fired heavy machine guns over their heads. The hot spent shells burnt the skin on their bare backs as they lay on the field. Other students who tried to escape from campus buildings via the rear entrance to the university, were hunted down and shot without mercy. State security methods on the 6th October 1976 bear an horrific similarity to methods used by the Taksin Government in the 2004 crackdown at *Takbai* in the South, where half a dozen unarmed protesters were shot and 87 prisoners later murdered in the backs of army lorries during transportation to an army camp.

The actions of the police and right-wing mobs on 6th October were the culmination of attempts by the ruling class to stop the further development of a socialist movement in Thailand. The events at *Thammasat University* were followed by a military coup which brought to power one of the most right-wing Governments Thailand has ever known. In the days that followed, offices and houses of organisations and individuals were raided. Trade unionists were arrested and trade union rights were curtailed. Centre-left and left-wing newspapers were closed and their offices ransacked. Political parties, student unions and farmer organisations were banned. The new military regime released a list of 204 banned books[44]. University libraries were searched and books were confiscated and publicly burnt. Over 100,000 books were burnt when Sulak Sivarak's book shop and warehouse was ransacked. Apart from obvious "communists" like Marx, Engels, Lenin, Mao or Jit Pumisak, authors such as Pridi Panomyong, Maxim Gorky, Julius Nyerere, Saneh Chamarik, Chai-anan Samudwanij, Charnvit Kasetsiri and Rangsan Tanapornpan appeared on the list of banned books.

The Thai ruling class' desire to destroy the further development of the socialist movement, especially in urban areas, can be understood by looking at the political climate at the time. Three years earlier, the 14th October 1973 mass movement had overthrown the military, which had been in power since 1957. However, the establishment of parliamentary

[44] Samak Suntarawej signed the order as Interior Minister.

Democracy on its own did not begin to solve deep-rooted social problems. Therefore the protests, strikes and factory occupations intensified. At the same time the USA was losing the war in Vietnam. By 1975 Communist Governments were in power in neighbouring Lao, Vietnam and Cambodia and in Thailand rural insurgency by the CPT was on the increase. The events of the 6th October and the subsequent coup were not a simple return to military rule. They were an attempt to crush the popular movement for Social Justice, to eradicate the Left and strengthen the position of the elite. It was not the first or last time that the Thai elite resorted to violence and military coups to protect their interests.

It would be wrong to think that there was a detailed and tightly coordinated plan, by the entire Thai ruling class, which led to the 6th October events. Conversely, it would also be wrong to suggest that only one or two individuals or groups were behind the crushing of the Left. What happened on the 6th October was a result of a consensus among the entire ruling class that an open democratic system was allowing "too much freedom" for the Left. However, it is likely that there were both areas of agreement and disagreement within ruling circles on exactly how to act and who should act. The general view that "extra-parliamentary methods" would have to be used, led to the uncoordinated establishment of various right-wing semi-fascist groups.

The role of the King in the 6th October events has been discussed by many writers. Most express the view that the King helped to pave the way for a coup, in a broad sense, by showing open support for the extreme right-wing[45]. What we know is that the Royal Family openly supported and encouraged the *Village Scout* movement. In addition, the King was close to the *Border Patrol Police* who established the *Village Scouts* and also played a central part in the killing at *Thammasat*. Finally the King and Queen supported the return of ex-dictator Tanom by paying him a visit soon after he arrived back in Thailand, just before the bloody events.

The general picture of the ruling class that emerges during 1976 is one of a degree of unity on the need to crush the Left, but disunity on how

[45] Katherine Bowie (1997) Already quoted.

to do so, and, much more importantly, who would rule the country. This had important consequences on the evolution of the dictatorship post-1976. The immediate impact of the bloodbath at *Thammasat* was that thousands of students went to the countryside to join the struggle against the Thai state led by the CPT. However, within one year the extreme right-wing Government of Tanin Kraiwichien was removed from power. Those gaining the upper hand within the ruling class were convinced, not only that the nature of the 6th October crackdown, but also the way the Tanin Government was conducting itself, was creating even greater divisions and instability within society and helping the CPT to grow. Not surprisingly, those army officers who advocated a more liberal line were those actually involved in front-line fighting against the CPT. They understood, like so many military personnel in this position, that the struggle against the Left must involve some kind of political settlement in addition to the use of force. As General Prem Tinsulanon, Prime Minister from 1980-1988, observed in an ITV programme in 1999: *"The students joined the Communists because they were brutally suppressed. The way to undermine the Communists was to establish justice in society"*.

Three years after 1976, the Government decreed an "amnesty" for those who had left to fight alongside the communists. This coincided with splits and arguments between the student activists and the conservative CPT leaders. By 1988 the student activists had all returned to the city as the CPT collapsed. Thailand returned to an almost full parliamentary Democracy, but with one special condition: it was a parliamentary Democracy without the Left or any political parties representing workers or small farmers. Previously, left-wing political parties, such as the *Socialist Party*, the *Socialist Front* and *Palang Mai* (New Force) had won 14.4% or 2.5 million votes in the 1975 General Election. These parties won many seats in the north and north-east of the country and outside the arena of legal politics, the CPT also used to have enormous influence. Now the organised Left was destroyed.

The problem with the CPT's Maoist strategy was that it more or less abandoned the city to the ruling class. The CPT argued that since the cities were the centre of ruling class power, a communist victory in Thailand would only come about by surrounding the cities with "liberated zones". The fact that the ruling class was planning some kind of urban crack-down against the Left before 6th October was not a secret. The CPT started to remove key activists out of Bangkok well before the crack-down actually occurred. Their Maoist strategy meant that they never at any time planned to resist a right-wing backlash in Bangkok. Not only did the CPT's politics fail to defend the Left in Bangkok in 1976, it also ensured massive demoralisation among the Left when international events began to undermine Stalinism and Maoism as a world current. On the 20th anniversary of the 6th October, a large gathering of former students and former communists came together at *Thammasat* for the first time since the massacre. Not one speaker from the platform at any of the meetings believed that there was still a future for Socialism. The present revival of the Thai Left today[46] has had to depend on an anti-Stalinist, Trotskyist, tradition which sees the various "communist" regimes which once existed as being the opposite to Socialism and Marxism[47].

The experience of students in the jungle with the CPT

There are many explanations for the exodus of the urban students from the CPT strong holds in the jungle in the early 1980s, which eventually contributed to the collapse of the party. CPT old-timers argue that the students were not "true revolutionaries", that they "had petty-bourgeois tendencies" and that they only went to the jungle to flee the crack down in the city. The Thai establishment argues something quite similar. It claims that the students were forced to flee the city and that most of them were not really communists (because presumably, no sane, educated person would be a communist). It also argues that the CPT was an "alien"

[46] *Turn Left* organisation.

[47] Since the formation of the Red Shirts, some ex-CPT activists have talked about reviving the CPT, but no concrete organisation has been built and the politics of these activists is indistinguishable from the pro-business TRT. The politics of the newly revived *Socialist Party* are also indistinguishable from TRT and its members are mostly pensioners.

organisation, dominated by "Chinese ideology". According to the mainstream explanation, the students only flirted with left-wing ideas in their misguided youth. This idea seems to be supported by student activists themselves, especially those who now hold important positions in society and wish to renounce their past. However, these explanations for the collapse of the CPT are very superficial.

Communist ideas from the CPT had a huge impact among young urban activists in the period 1973-1976. This is hardly surprising for two reasons. Firstly, the conservative ideology of "Nation, Religion and Monarchy" had been the mainstay of the military dictatorships for decades. It went hand in hand with corruption at the top and poverty at the bottom of society. Anyone wanting to build a better world would hardly be looking towards ruling class ideology for solutions. Secondly, the 1970s were a period when communist parties throughout the world were achieving victories against imperialism and it seemed that alternative societies were being built by communists in many countries. Therefore, despite later denials, the vast majority of students and young activists of the 1970s regard themselves as left-wing and they were dedicated to taking part in the socialist transformation of Thai society.

Thousands do not leave their homes and families to take up the armed struggle for justice in the countryside just for the excitement or as part of a fashion. Life in the jungle strong-holds of the CPT was tough. They had to fight the army, to grow their own food and to live in primitive conditions. In the rainy season, often their clothes would never dry, gradually growing mouldy. Food was monotonous[48] and fraternisation between the sexes was frowned upon[49]. For this reason it is fair to say that the students who joined the CPT ranks after 6th October 1976 were totally committed to the struggle for Socialism. Naturally, this meant different things to different people. Those who were less committed, or had pressing

[48] See Seksan Prasertkul's account in the film *The Moonhunter*.

[49] See Wipa Daomanee, writing under her nom de guerre 'Sung' (2003) 'Looking back to when I first wanted to be a Communist'. In Ji Giles Ungpakorn (ed.) *Radicalising Thailand. New Political Perspectives*. Bangkok: Institute of Asian Studies, Chulalongkorn University.

personal reasons, stayed behind in the cities. Despite the terrible events of 6th October 1976, it would have been possible for most students to just keep their heads down and cease to engage in politics. Many did precisely this and very few students were rounded-up and killed in Bangkok after 6th October.

The real reason for the exodus from the CPT camps a few years later was not a lack of commitment on the part of the students. It was the failure of the CPT to develop a credible strategy for the Thai Socialist Revolution and a failure to relate to the new generation of young activists who joined in the 1970s. This has everything to do with the Stalinist-Maoist politics of the party. Firstly the emphasis on rural armed struggle in Thailand did not fit reality. Since 1932 all significant social changes have taken place in the cities. Even rural movements come to the city to demonstrate. In addition to this, the struggle by small farmers was and still is important in terms of defending Social Justice for the poor, but it is fundamentally a defensive and conservative struggle to survive, not a struggle for a future society. Secondly, the authoritarian nature of Stalinist and Maoist parties meant that the CPT leadership were afraid to agitate among students in such a way as to let them lead their own struggles. The students were certainly capable of self-leadership. After all, they were key actors in overthrowing the military dictatorship in 1973. The main experience of student activists in the jungle with the CPT was a stifling of all original ideas and a lack of any freedom to debate[50]. This helped to destroy the momentum of the urban movement that went to the jungle after the initial honey-moon period following October 1976. Finally, the CPT's Maoism backfired when the Chinese Government turned its back on the party in order to build a relationship with the Thai ruling class. The resulting demoralisation among activists has helped to shape the

[50] Kasian Tejapira stated that the CPT leadership managed to ùdestroy intellectuals who went to the jungle'. See his article in 1996 published in *My University*. Somsak Jeamtirasakul and co (eds). Tammasat University Student Union. (In Thai). Even Udom Srisuwan from the CPT Central Committee, writing under the pen name Po Muangchompoo acknowledges that the CPT made mistakes in handling students. See Po Muangchompoo (2000) *To the battlefield of Pu-Parn*. Matichon Press. (In Thai).

politics of the October People and the Thai social movements today.

As the CPT collapsed and the October People returned to open society, the political regime in Thailand was gradually liberalised throughout the 1980s. Partly this was carried out from above under pressure from the revolts of the 1970s, but a mass uprising against a new military dictatorship in 1992 helped to hasten the process. The 1997 Economic Crisis was a further stimulus for change. Two important results of this change were the Constitution of 1997 and the rise of TRT.

The struggle carried out by all those urbanites who joined the CPT after 1976 and the massive polarisation of Thai society was not totally in vain. The ruling class was forced to acknowledge that it could not win the battle against the *pu-noi* by violence and coercion alone. By the early 1980s they were forced, by the level of resistance, to liberalise the political system. This occurred especially under the rule of Prime Minister Prem Tinsulanon. The ruling class came to a compromise with the urbanites who had fled to the hills and with the working class who stayed behind in Bangkok to fight the bosses. The result was a form of bourgeois parliamentary Democracy which did not challenge the interests of the elite. "Money politics" in parliament became more important to maintaining the interests of the bourgeoisie than military power as the economy expanded.

The "post-Communism" shift in ideology

The collapse of the CPT resulted in a shift in ideology within the Peoples Movement and the academic community towards Autonomism, Post-Modernism and Third Way Reformism[51]. This happened throughout the world, to a greater or lesser degree, after the collapse of the Berlin Wall and the end of the Cold War. Yet, very few people in the Thai Peoples Movement would admit to being Autonomists, Post-Modernists or Third Way Reformists. This is because the rejection of theory by these political currents encourages people to deny any political affiliation.

[51] Right-wing reformism which accepts that there is no alternative to the capitalist free-market. The ideas of Anthony Giddens.

Thai activists often articulate various international ideologies while believing that they are uniquely home grown.

Autonomism

Autonomism, as practiced in Thailand, is a form of "localist" Anarchism *(Chumchon-Niyom)*[52]. It is dominant among the leadership of the *Assembly of the Poor* and among other rural social movements. It is a political ideology that rejects the state, not by smashing it or overthrowing it, but by ignoring the state in the hope that it will become irrelevant. The aim is self-organisation at community level. Autonomists reject the building of political parties and place activity above political theory. It has many similarities with the ideas expressed by autonomists in other continents, such as John Holloway, Toni Negri and Michael Hardt[53].

The British Marxist Chris Harman explained that the strength of Autonomism is that it celebrates initiative and creativity from below and it seeks to reject compromise with the system[54]. This was seen very clearly in the fact that the *Assembly of the Poor* refused to support the *Peoples Alliance for Democracy* (PAD). The main reason was that they were worried about being dominated by conservative forces inside the PAD, while still being willing to oppose Taksin. They were also against the call by the PAD, in April 2006, for the King to appoint a new Government under section 7 of the 1997 Constitution. After the 19th September coup, the *Assembly of the Poor* also took a principled position against the junta.

On the negative side, autonomists rarely express their views theoretically and this is a weakness in fighting Neo-Liberalism and other ideologies of the ruling class. Again the *Assembly of the Poor* is a prime example. They warn against the use of theories because many of their

---

[52] One good example in the Thai literature is Chattip Nartsupa et al. (1998) *The Theory of Peasant Community Economics*. Witeetat 7.

[53] John Holloway (2002) Change the world without taking power. Pluto Press. Michael Hardt & Toni Negri (2000) Empire. Harvard University Press.

[54] Chris Harman (2004) Spontaneity, strategy and politics. International Socialism Journal # 104, U.K. p 8.

activists have had bad experiences with the CPT, which dictated the "ideological line" from above[55]. When autonomists do use theory, such as in the case of Michael Hardt, Toni Negri and John Holloway, they are often highly abstract or they claim their theories are uniquely local. The tendency to reject practical theory means that many autonomists capitulate to right-wing reformism, thus compromising with Neo-Liberalism and the market.

The capitulation of autonomists to Neo-Liberalism and right-wing reformism is due to its de-politicising effect. An important factor is the under estimation of the power of the state. The refusal to build a party of activists, with a united theory and programme, means that they turn their back on political agitation and debate within the movement. Nor is it deemed necessary to challenge the prevailing ideology of the ruling class, since each group merely acts autonomously in its own community. Without a serious Peoples Movement political challenge to TRT, the "Tank Liberal" argument that there was no alternative to the 19th September coup, appears more attractive to a wide audience in the movement.

Autonomist currents in the movement today support "Direct Democracy", such as self-organised local community action[56]. This is preferred to the failed "Representative Democracy" of the parliamentary process. Autonomists claim that "Direct Democracy" or "Direct Action" can pressurise the state without the need to go through parliamentary representatives or political parties[57]. They reject the building of political parties and reject the aim of seizing state power, preferring instead to organise

---

[55] Wanida Tantiwitayapitak, a founding member of the *Assembly of the Poor*, was in the CPT and experienced its authoritarianism. (Personal Communication).

[56] See Prapart Pintoptang (1998) *Street Politics: 99 days of the Assembly of the Poor*. Krerg University, Bangkok. (In Thai). Pitaya Wongkul (2002) Direct Democracy. Wititat Publications (In Thai). Also D. Morland & J. Carter (2004) Anarchism and Democracy. In: M.J. Todd & G. Taylor (eds) *Democracy and participation*. Merlin Press, U.K.

[57] See John Holloway in "Can we change the world without taking power?, a debate with Alex Callinicos at the 2005 World Social Forum. International Socialism Journal, 106, Spring 2005, p.114.since he supports a form of nationalism and the importance of using the state to counter the free market, p.83 & 211.

networks of autonomous single-issue movements which can turn their back on the state[58].

The problem is that by rejecting a more democratic model of exercising "Representative Peoples Power", autonomists are forced to accept the class power of the capitalist state in practice. The *Assembly of the Poor* advertises that it has no wish to take state power, being content to negotiate directly with the Government to solve villagers' problems and Prapart Pintoptang had a brief flirtation with the 2006 military junta. Autonomists also reject the model of "Participatory Democracy" built into the recallable representative systems invented by the international working class movement in times of struggle. The Paris Commune of 1871, the Russian Soviets before the rise of Stalin, or the various workers and community councils built through struggle in Poland, Iran and Latin America over the last 40 years are good examples.

In the early days of TRT, Wanida and the *Assembly of the Poor* had some illusions in Taksin's party, welcoming its election victory. Niti Eawsriwong[59] is one of many academics who rejects "Representative Democracy", or the present parliamentary system. Instead he favours "Direct Democracy". However, in January 2005 Niti argued for a vote for capitalist opposition parties against TRT[60]. The lesson is that "Direct Democracy" cannot be applied in practice without first dealing with the class power of the capitalist state. To do this we need political parties of workers and peasants. This has been a constant Marxist criticism of Anarchism or Autonomism.

By rejecting a formal political party in favour of loose networks, autonomists also fail to build internal democratic structures for their own organisations. The *Assembly of the Poor* is thus led by unelected NGO

---

[58] Seksan (2005) *The politics of the peoples movement in Thai Democracy*, Amarin Press, does not use the term "autonomist" to describe this kind of politics in the Thai movement. Instead he calls them part of a "Radical Democratic Movement", p.173. While seeming to agree with much of autonomist-community politics, Seksan is not an autonomist himself,

[59] Niti was one of the founders of the *Midnight University*.

[60] *Matichon Daily*. 31/1/2005. "Getting the dogs to bite each other".

activists rather than by poor farmers themselves[61]. The rejection of "Representative Democracy" is applied to the internal workings of the movement with dire consequences. Social movements in Thailand are dominated by unelected *Pi-liang* (NGO "nannies" or advisors) and *Pu-yai* (NGO "elders"). There is a real problem with the lack of self-leadership among activists and a lack of internal Democracy. Young people are expected to respect and listen to their elders in the movement and positions are never up for election. In addition to this, there is the problem of over funding by NGOs, which discourages the building of self-reliant movements which collect membership fees[62]. Individuals who hold the purse strings also dominate the movement by threatening to cut off funds. Many of the participants at the Thai Social Forum in 2006 received funds to attend[63].

Post-Modernism

Post-Modernism is still popular in Thai universities, despite its decline in other parts of the world. Post-Modernism rejects all "Grand Narratives" or ideologies and is therefore also de-politicising. For Post-Modernists, individual liberation comes about in the mind, at abstract levels. Post-Modernism is the academic sister of Autonomism, a theoretical expression of opposition to dictatorship, power and organisation.

Like Autonomism, the rise of Post-Modernism is a product of disillusionment with Stalinism plus a severe demoralisation about the possibilities of struggle, but it can only really exist among academics due to its highly abstract nature[64]. Post-Modernism claims to "liberate"

---

[61] See Bruce Missingham (2003) The Assembly of the Poor in Thailand. Silkworm Books. p.187 and Ji Giles Ungpakorn (2003) Challenges to the Thai NGO Movement from the dawn of a new opposition to global capital. In: Ji Giles Ungpakorn (ed) *Radicalising Thailand.* Already quoted.

[62] See Ji Giles Ungpakorn(2003) *Radicalising Thailand.* Already quoted, p.311.

[63] There is a dilemma here because rural activists are often extremely poor, but even the *Assembly of the Poor* has often managed to mobilise using villagers' own resources.

[64] See Alex Callinicos (1992) *Against Post-Modernism.* Polity Press.

humanity by the constant questioning and rejection of Grand Narratives or big political theories. They therefore reject a class analysis of society and reject Marxism, while also claiming to reject Neo-Liberalism and Capitalism. In practice, however, they often end up by accepting the dominant ideology of the market or remaining neutral and passive in the face of a neo-liberal onslaught on society.

However, like Autonomists, Post-Modernists have their plus sides. Rejection of authoritarianism and Grand Narratives by the *Midnight University* has meant that they rejected the PAD call for the King to appoint a Government under Section 7 and that they opposed the 19th September coup, just like the *Assembly of the Poor*. The *Midnight University* website was temporarily closed down by the junta because of this. Both the Assembly of the Poor and the Midnight University have also consistently opposed Thai state repression in the South. This is because they reject narrow-minded nationalism.

Autonomism and Postmodernism discourage a class analysis of society. Because of this, there is a great deal of misunderstanding and under-estimation of TRT "Populism" among the Peoples Movement. A class analysis of Populism explains that it arises, both from pressure from below, and from the needs of the capitalist class simultaneously. Many in the Peoples Movement saw TRT's populist measures, such as the 30 baht health care scheme and the various village funds, as a cruel hoax[65]. Many also claim that such policies led to a "patron-client" type of dependency by villagers upon the state. This is nothing more than the old neo-liberal criticism made against "nanny state" welfare projects made by the likes of Margaret Thatcher and others.

In short, the Peoples Movement criticism of TRT was made from the right-wing free-market position adopted by such neo-liberals as Ammar Siamwalla and Tirayut Boonmi, rather than from a left-wing pro-poor

---

[65] Statement by Wanida Tantiwittayapitak, advisor to the *Assembly of the Poor*, Peoples Assembly meeting 23/1/2005.

position[66]. This kind of analysis fails to grasp that TRT Populism actually delivers real benefits to the poor. Low-cost health care for all is a real concrete benefit for millions who were previously uninsured and who faced huge financial worries about sickness and ill health. Populism, carried out by a blatantly capitalist party like TRT could not work otherwise.

At a Peoples Movement Forum in Bangkok, the Post-Modernist academic Somchai Preechasilapakul, from the *Midnight University*, stated that the trade union fight against electricity privatisation was nothing to do with the interests of villagers. Yet villagers use electricity and suffer from neo-liberalism in other forms.

Another example of the acceptance of the free-market can be seen in publications by the *NGO-Coordinating Committee* which accepted that free trade could be beneficial[67]. Publications circulating at *Peoples Forums* also advocate separation of electricity generation and distribution in the interests of competition. Even worse was the illusion that an "independent" commercial television company could be genuinely independent of powerful interests. This was the dominant belief in the Peoples Movement in the mid 1990s when I.T.V. was established. These illusions were shattered when large capitalist corporations took over the television station.

Thai autonomists and post-modernists cannot put their theories into practice when confronted by the capitalist state and the capitalist free-market. When Autonomism and Post-Modernism prove to be powerless in defending the interests of the poor, in the face of attacks from the free-market and the state, autonomists and post-modernists fall back into pessimism and lose all faith in fighting for *any* reforms. Squeezing modest concessions out of the capitalist class becomes an "impossible dream". This is the same justification for right-wing Social Democracy adopting the "Third Way" or the capitulation to Neo-Liberalism.

---

[66] See Tirayut Boonmi "analysis of Thai society" 5/1/2003. Also Tirayut Boonmi and Ammar Siamwalla, Nation 4 page specials 9 May and 28 July 2003. Ammar Siamwalla was also an invited guest speaker at the 2nd Peoples Assembly held at *Thammasart University* in October 2003.

[67] NGO-COD (2002a) Thai Working Group on the People's Agenda for Sustainable Development, NGO Coordinating Committee on Development. Alternative Country Report. Thailand's Progress on Agenda 21 Proposals for Sustainable Development. p.25.

involved destroying the power of his *Sakdina* rivals, the *Moon Nai*, nobles and local *Jao Hua Muang*. Politically this was done by appointing a civil service bureaucracy to rule outer regions and economically, by abolishing their power to control forced labour and hence surplus value. Forced labour was also abolished in response to class struggle from below, since *Prai* had a habit of trying to escape corvée labour and both *Prai* and *Taht* would often deliberately work inefficiently. Forced labour was replaced by wage labour and private property rights in land ownership was introduced for the first time. Furthermore, investment in production of agricultural goods for the world market became more important than the simple use of surplus production for consumption and trade. This can clearly be seen in the various investments in irrigation canals for rice production in the *Rungsit* area of the central plains. These investments opened up the land for settlement and work by the peasantry, which had been freed from corvée labour. Thus a temporary class alliance was built between the Monarchy and the peasantry against the old *Sakdina* rulers and bosses, which served to support the new ruling class interests in the global rice trade.

The shortage of labour for capitalist accumulation was initially solved by recruiting labour from China in the early part of the twentieth century. Much later, beginning in the early 1960s, a large surge in "indigenous" wage labour occurred as a result of poor peasants being pulled off the land, often from the north-east, into more productive workshops and factories in urban areas, especially around Bangkok. Later still, Thai Capitalism started to depended on migrant labour from Burma and other neighbouring countries.

The capitalist transformation and the construction of the first Thai nation state, a product of continuous change, occurred at a time when similar transformations were taking place throughout colonised South-East Asia. In the neighbouring colonies belonging to Britain, France and The Netherlands, state centralisation and the development of a capitalist economy, based upon wage labour was also taking place. In fact we should view the process of Thai state formation as the "internal colonisation" of the north, south and north-east by the Chakri rulers of

Bangkok. Certainly the various north and north-eastern revolts against Bangkok indicate this to be true. The civil war today in the Muslim South also has its roots in this process. The main point to bear in mind is that the changes taking place in "un-colonised" Thailand were not very different from the rest of colonised South-East Asia.

Problems with the Stalinist/Maoist analysis of state formation

The Left in Thailand has shown considerable confusion about Thailand's capitalist transformation and this has influenced much intellectual analysis, way beyond the Left, to this day. This confusion results from applying a Marxist model in an extremely mechanical and a-historical manner, typical of the Stalinist and Maoist tradition. This is not surprising given that the only left-wing organisation of any significance, in terms of ideas and numbers of supporters, was the *Communist Party of Thailand* (CPT). A prime example of this mechanical analysis is Jit Pumisak's argument that land ownership was central to the extraction of surplus value in the Thai *Sakdina* system[9]. This is one of many attempts at trying to fit Thai history into a Western model. Marx never claimed that Asian history followed the same exact path as European historical processes. As an example of a different production system in Asia, he suggested that in certain areas there existed a society based on irrigation canals called the "Asiatic Mode of Production" (AMP)[10]. There is no archeological evidence that Marx's model of the AMP, with its complex irrigation system and centralised state, ever existed in "Thailand", although it might have existed in the Khmer empire, centred around Ankor. Yet, the mechanical Marxists have also tried to prove that pre-capitalist production in Thailand was a mixture of the *Sakdina* system and the Asiatic Mode of Production[11]. In doing so, they have been forced to transform the meaning

[9] Jit Pumisak (1995) *The nature of the Thai Sakdina system*. Nok Hook Press, Bangkok. (In Thai).

[10] Karl Marx (1992) "Articles on India and China". In: *Surveys from exile, Political Writings* volume 2. Penguin Books, London.

[11] Pakpat Tipayaprapai (1997) *The Asiatic Mode of Production as an explanation of Thai Villages*. The Office of Research Supporting Grants, Bangkok. (In Thai).

cover all issues together. The public hearings of the *Peoples Democracy Forum* were also organised in such a way as to encourage single issue discussions.

Third Way Reformism and Lobby Politics

Third Way Reformism is the dominant ideology of the Thai NGO movement. It is an acceptance of Neo-Liberalism and the free-market and the rejection of the state's ability to transform society for the benefit of the poor[72]. The reasoning behind this belief is, again, the collapse of "Communism" and the rapid development of Globalisation. Another related reason is the pessimistic view that open class struggle is doomed to failure. In fact it is a rejection of the possibilities of serious reforms by those who would like to reform society. Instead, NGO activists turn to "lobby politics", lobbying any Government, whether democratic or not, and even multinational companies.

Yet, during the TRT Government there were many examples of open class struggle. One of the most powerful challenges to Taksin's TRT Government occurred in 2004 when the Electricity Generating Authority Workers Union staged a long drawn out protest, including unofficial work stoppages of non-essential workers, at the EGAT headquarters just north of Bangkok. This protest was supported by other trade unions in the public sector and many activists from the Peoples Movement. It was unique in drawing together the rural movements and the State Enterprise Unions. The annual May Day march in 2004 was much more militant than previous years, with the majority of workers splitting away from the usual Government sponsored event to form a clear political protest. Apart from the issue of privatisation, other issues, such as opposition to the war in Iraq and demands for a woman's right to choose abortion were also raised, mainly by textile workers.

---

[72] Anthony Giddens (1998) *The Third Way. The Renewal of Social Democracy*. Polity Press, Cambridge.

Apart from the electricity workers, pressure from the *Assembly of the Poor* protests forced the TRT Government to open the sluice gates of the *Pak Moon* dam for limited periods of time. A massive anti-FTA protest in early 2006, involving thousands of well organised and highly motivated HIV+ activists, forced the negotiations between Thailand and the USA to be postponed. Finally, it should not be forgotten that many aspects of the TRT Government's populist programme reflected pressure from below from the Peoples Movement.

Maoism: its "de-politicising" effect and its defeat

Maoism is a de-politicising force. It discourages self organisation, political analysis and education. Members of the CPT were encouraged to read only a few texts written by Mao. Marxist works were ignored. The urban working class was also ignored as a force to change society. After the students went to the jungle, urban-based politics with its intellectual debate, open struggle and experimentation were exchanged for the mind-numbing politics of the most politically backward sections peasantry. Political though and analysis were the preserve of a handful of top cadres. Theory was therefore down-played. When the CPT collapsed, and later, when the authoritarian Thai state was liberalised, the Left was slow to recover. The booming Thai economy in the 1990s also played a part in keeping the Left weak. Until the economic crisis of 1997, things just seemed to be getting better all the time. The overall effect was that the more the Peoples Movement rejected theory, the more it came to rely on ruling class ideology. Acceptance of the market and nationalism are examples.

The 1997 economic crisis

The period leading up to the 1997 economic crisis was a period in which the Thai economy grew at a phenomenal rate. Average GDP growth rates reached 8% and on occasions the annual rate was in double figures.

The 1932 revolution had the effect of further modernising the capitalist state and expanding the base of the ruling class to include the top members of the civilian and military bureaucracy, especially the military. The reason why the military became so influential in Thai politics, finally resulting in 16 years of uninterrupted military dictatorship from 1957, was the fact that the *Peoples Party* lacked a solid mass base beyond the bureaucracy. In addition to this, the private capitalists and the working class were still weak in terms of social forces which could compete with the military.

The 1932 revolution meant that the role of the Monarchy was significantly changed for the second time in less than a century. In the 1870s King Rama 5th abolished *Sakdina* rule in favour of a centralised and modern Absolute Monarchy. Sixty years later, the 1932 revolution destroyed this Absolute Monarchy so that the King merely became one section of the Thai ruling class. It is important to understand this, because there has been a tendency by both the Left and the Right to exaggerate the importance and "long-lasting traditions" of the Thai Monarchy. Today's King may seem to have the trappings of "tradition", yet the influence of this institution has fluctuated over the last sixty years and in many cases its "sacredness" has been manufactured by military and civilian rulers to provide themselves with political legitimacy[16].

Many commentators argue that the "weakness" of Marxist or Communist ideology in Thailand was mainly due to the fact that there was no mass-mobilisation in the struggle for national liberation such as was seen in Indonesia, Burma or Vietnam[17]. It is not true that Communist ideology was weak in Thai society, especially in the 1940s, 1950s and mid 1970s, and mass-mobilisation for the purpose of nation-building did occur in the 1932 revolution. However, the fact that the CPT placed capitalist nation-building as its primary aim, in a similar vein to all other Stalinist-Maoist parties, did mean that the CPT had little to achieve, since

[16] See Chapter 3.

[17] Chai-anan Samudavanija (1989) "Thailand: a stable semi-democracy." In L. Diamond, J.J. Linz & S.M. Lipset (eds) *Democracy in developing countries*. Vol 3, Asia. Lynne Rienner & Adamantine Press.

the task of nation-building had already been started by King Chulalongkorn and was subsequently followed through by the 1932 revolution.

The rise of the private capitalists or bourgeoisie

Despite the fact that military dictatorships were overthrown by students and workers in 1973 and 1992, the main beneficiaries in terms of gaining political power, have been the private sector capitalists. Thailand's modern private bourgeoisie, including Taksin, have cleverly taken advantage of the struggle for Democracy waged from below in order to gain political power at the expense of the military state capitalists.

Although arising out of demands made by the May 1992 movement against the military, the drafting of the 1997 Constitution was, in fact, an important victory for the modern private bourgeoisie[18]. Liberalism was the main political influence among the drafting committee and the aim of this constitution, for the liberals, was to increase Government stability and reduce the more blatant forms of corruption. It was a charter for Thailand's modern capitalists.

The private capitalist class existed from the earliest period of Capitalism in Thailand. Initially they were businessmen of Chinese origin who cooperated with the royal state capitalists in the late 19th century, but after the royal family were removed from state power in the 1932 revolution, the royal capitalists joined the ranks of the private sector capitalist class. Today the King controls important interests in the Thai economy, including real estate, the Siam Commercial Bank and the Siam Cement company. He is a fabulously wealthy capitalist.

The importance of ethnic Chinese businesses, especially those associated with the big banks, increased during the Second World War when Western interests were temporarily excluded from Thailand[19]. Another two important sources leading to the development of major ethnic Chinese

[18] Michael Connors (1999) "Political reform and the state in Thailand". *Journal of Contemporary Asia* 29(2), 202-225.

[19] Hewison, Kevin (1989) *Power and politics in Thailand.* Journal of Contemporary Asia Publishers, Philippines.

financial sector was "overwhelmed by excess liquidity" which could not be shifted. Investing in the poverty alleviation has never been a profitable business.

The racist explanations of the Asian crisis which talked about Asian corruption, Asian Crony Capitalism and lack of good governance in Asia, are hardly worthy of serious consideration. This is because before the crisis, the same commentators were using such cultural explanations for the "miracle" Asian economic boom. More serious mainstream explanations for the crisis pin the blame on lack of proper controls over investment after economic liberalisation in the late 1980s[75]. Although it is true that the increased free movement of capital in and out of Thailand made the boom and the crisis more spectacular, these highly visible movements of money were more a symptom of what was happening in the real economy rather than the cause of the crisis. The implication of the neo-liberal explanation was also that if proper controls were established, then crises would never occur again. Clearly a review of Western economies shows this to be nonsense.

The Marxist theory of capitalist crisis identifies over-production and falling rates of profit as the key underlying factors causing a crisis. Both these factors result from the uncontrolled competition for profit found under Capitalism. The main cause of the general fall in the rate of profit is the increased investment in fixed capital as compared to the hiring of labour (from which surplus value is extracted). However, the falling rate of profit is only an overall tendency with many countervailing factors. Profit rates can be restored temporarily by increased labour efficiency, increased exploitation or the destruction of competitors[76].

---

[75] Siamwalla, Ammar (1997) "Trying to figure out how Thailand got into such a mess". *The Nation*, Bangkok, 12/11/1997. Jomo, K. S. (ed) (1998) *Tigers in Trouble. Financial Governance, Liberalisation and Crises in East Asia.* Hong Kong University Press, IPSR Books (Cape Town), University Press Dhaka, White Lotus (Bangkok) and Zed Books (London & New York). Rangsun Thanapornpun (1998) *Financial crisis and the financial sector in the Thai economy.* Kop Fai publishers, Bangkok. (In Thai).

[76] Chris Harman (2009) *Zombie Capitalism. Global Crisis and the Relevance of Marx.* Bookmarks, London.

In Thailand over-capacity and falling rates of return were not merely confined to the well-publicised real estate sector, which happened to be the initial trigger for the crisis[77]. Over-production should not merely be seen as a national problem, confined to the Thai economy. The declining rate of Thai exports, one important factor which lead to the run on the baht, was due to over-production of export products on a global scale.

Overproduction in an unplanned world market and the tendency for a decline in the rate of profit caused a shift in the direction of investment away from industry to real estate and share speculation. It is estimated that in 1996 about half of all investment was property related and this accounted for half of annual GDP growth[78].

The Russian revolutionary, Leon Trotsky, once explained during the 1930s that economic crises do not automatically lead to increased class struggle. The crisis can have contradictory effects. On the one hand many ordinary working people can become very angry about what is happening to their standards of living, especially when they feel that they themselves had no part to play in the creation of the crisis. However, on the other hand, the enormity of the scale of the crisis and the threat of losing their jobs understandably plants fear in the hearts of many workers, leading to passivity and a willingness to believe that current political rulers are the only people capable of solving the crisis.

This contradiction can be seen in the way the Thai working class reacted to the crisis. On the one hand, significant groups of workers were very angry when their annual bonus payments were cut. On one occasion, a Japanese-owned electronics factory was burnt to the ground. At many workers' protest gatherings after that, someone could be relied upon to scare the management with a cry of *"set fire to the bloody place!"* Most of the time it was just a bluff. On another occasion workers at Summit Auto Parts blocked a main highway in response to a bonus cut, but they were

---

[77] Jim Glassman (2003) Interpreting the economic crisis in Thailand: Lessons learned and lessons obscured. In: Ji Giles Ungpakorn (ed.) *Radicalising Thailand*. Already quoted.

[78] Kevin Hewison (1999) "Thailand's Capitalism: The impact of the economic crisis". *UNEAC Asia Papers* No. 1, University of New England, Armidale, Australia.

Democracy Monument on 14th October 1973. This resulted in the overthrow of the military dictatorship. It was the first mass popular uprising in modern Thai history. The 14th October and the following struggles, victories, and defeats that make up the "Thai Seventies" have continued to shape the nature of politics and society to this day.

The 14th October uprising

The military domination of Thai politics, started soon after the 1932 revolution, but its consolidation of power came with the Sarit military coup in 1957. The economic development during the years of military dictatorship in the 1950s and 1960s took place in the context of a world economic boom and a localised economic boom created by the Korean and Vietnam wars. This economic growth had a profound impact on the nature of Thai society.

Naturally the size of the working class increased as factories and businesses were developed. However, under the dictatorship trade union rights were suppressed and wages and conditions of employment were tightly controlled. By early 1973 the minimum daily wage, fixed at around 10 baht since the early 1950s, remained unchanged while commodity prices had risen by 50%. Illegal strikes had already occurred throughout the period of dictatorship, but strikes increased rapidly due to general economic discontent. The first 9 months of 1973, before the 14th October, saw a total of 40 strikes, and a one month strike at the Thai Steel Company resulted in victory due to a high level of solidarity from other workers.

Economic development also resulted in a massive expansion of student numbers and an increased intake of students from working class backgrounds. The building of the *Ramkamhaeng Open University* in 1969 was a significant factor here. Student numbers in higher education increased from 15,000 in 1961 to 50,000 by 1972. The new generation of students, in the early 1970s, were influenced by the revolts and revolutions which occurred throughout the world in that period, May 1968 in Paris, being a prime example. Before that, in 1966 the radical journal, Social Science

Review, was established by progressive intellectuals. Students started to attend volunteer development camps in the countryside in order to learn about the problems of rural poverty. By 1971 3,500 students had attended a total of 64 camps. In 1972 a movement to boycott Japanese goods was organised as part of the struggle against foreign domination of the economy. Students also agitated against increases in Bangkok bus fares.

In June 1973 the rector of *Ramkamhaeng University* was forced to resign after attempting to expel a student for writing a pamphlet criticising the military dictatorship[22]. Four months later, the arrest of 11 academics and students for handing out leaflets demanding a democratic constitution, resulted in hundreds of thousands of students and workers taking to the streets of Bangkok. As troops with tanks fired on unarmed demonstrators, the people of Bangkok began to fight-back. Bus passengers spontaneously alighted from their vehicles to join the demonstrators. Government buildings were set on fire. The *"Yellow Tigers"*, a militant group of students, sent a jet of high-octane gasoline from a captured fire engine into the police station at *Parn-Fa* bridge, setting it on fire. Earlier they had been fired upon by the police.

The successful 14th October 1973 mass uprising against the military dictatorship shook the Thai ruling class to its foundations. For the next few days, there was a strange new atmosphere in Bangkok. Uniformed officers of the state disappeared from the streets and ordinary people organised themselves to clean up the city. Boy Scouts directed traffic. It was the first time that the *pu-noi* (little people) had actually started a revolution from below. It was not planned and those that took part had a multiplicity of ideals about what kind of Democracy and society they wanted. But the Thai ruling class could not shoot enough demonstrators to protect their regime. It was not just a student uprising to demand a democratic constitution. It involved thousands of ordinary working class people and occurred on the crest of a rising wave of workers' strikes.

---

[22] Much later, after the 19th September 2006 coup, most university rectors again collaborated with the military junta.

the *Democrats*, which had totally ignored the plight of the rural and urban poor. TRT also made 3 important promises to the electorate. These were (1) a promise to introduce a Universal Heath Care Scheme for all citizens, (2) a promise to provide a 1 million baht loan to each village in order to stimulate economic activity and (3) a promise to introduce a debt moratorium for poor peasants.

The policies of TRT arose from a number of factors, mainly the 1997 economic crisis and the influence of both big-business and some ex-student activists from the 1970s within the party. When considering the "October People" today, it is necessary to divide them into two groups according to the trajectory of their political and social careers. On the one hand many activists became part of the Peoples Movement that we see today, leading social movements and NGOs which flourished from the 1980s onwards. These people ended up supporting the right-wing PAD and the 2006 coup. They also include people who became neo-liberal academics and politicians in the *Democrat Party*. On the other hand, sections of the ruling class also managed to co-opt a number of ex-activists into the political elite in order to help police the movement or in order to produce populist policies, which won the hearts and minds of the people. This process started with Prime Minister Chawalit Yongjaiyut and his *New Aspirations Party*, but later rose to a fine art under Taksin's TRT.

"October People" who entered the TRT Government

Before the first election victory of TRT, the party made very serious attempts to canvas a wide range of views in Thai society in order to come up with serious policies to modernise the country and deal with a number of social evils, such as poverty[83]. There was a growing sense of frustration and unease about the complacency of the *Democrat Party* Government to act in decisive and imaginative ways in order to pull the country out of the 1997 economic crisis. Ex-student and NGO activists, such as Pumtam

[83] Pasuk Phongpaichit & Chris Baker (2004) *Taksin. The business of politics in Thailand.* Silkworm Books.

Wejjayachai were recruited to TRT and became important links with the Peoples Movement. Dr Sanguan Nitayarumpong, who had for a long time been an advocate of a Universal Health Care policy, became an important designer of the new 30 baht health care scheme. October People encouraged the Prime Minister to meet with social movements like the *Assembly of the Poor* and they coordinated with movement and NGO leaders in order to solve disputes or dampen down protest actions against the Government[84].

Pumtam Wejjayachai was the director of the *Thai Volunteer Service*, which trained young people to become NGO workers. He became an important leader of TRT and held cabinet posts. He was very close to Taksin. "October People" like Pumtam used their previous involvement with social movements to the benefit of the Government. For example, in June 2005, he intervened to demobolise a protest by 5000 farmers who were angry about lack of debt relief. On the other hand, some NGO activists felt that by talking to him they had the ear of the Government.

Pumtam explained that Thailand needed a "Dual Track" development policy, where "Capitalism" and the "Peoples Economy" (community based activities) went hand in hand[85]. He believed that you could not use one single economic development or political theory and criticised many on the Left who he claimed were "unable to adapt their thinking to the modern world". He attacked the old Left for clinging to idealism, thinking, for example, that capitalists automatically exploited the poor. For such people he had a simple suggestion: go back and live in the jungle like in the old CPT days! Echoing the terminology of "Direct Democracy" used by the Peoples Movement, he argued that TRT was using a "Direct (Sales) Approach" to dealing with the problems of villagers, without having to pass through Middle Men: political or state

[84] In 2002, when leading NGO organisers found themselves under investigation by the Anti-Money Laundering Office on orders from the *Thai Rak Thai* Government, some NGO leaders complained that they had previously worked hard to dissolve demonstrations by farmers groups at the request of the Government and were now being attacked! (*Bangkok Post* 3/10/ 2002).

[85] See interview in *A Dayweekly* (2005) In Thai.

October student leaders, formed the *Free Thammasart Group* and Tirayut Boonmi, another student leader from the 14th October uprising, formed the *People for Democracy Group* [24]. These so-called "independent groups" felt that the *National Student Centre* leadership was too conservative, often refusing to mobilise students on important issues like the successful protest against the return of the ousted dictator Field Marshal Tanom Kitikajorn in 1974. For this reason these various independent groups formed an alternative centre called the *"National Coalition Against Dictatorship"* with Sutam Saengpratoom as secretary [25].

One important area of activity for students was the struggle against US Imperialism and for so-called "Thai independence". The military dictatorship had been a close ally of the United States during the Cold War, sending token numbers of Thai troops to support the US in both Korea and Vietnam. In 1973 there were 12 US military bases in the country, with 550 war planes and thousands of troops stationed on Thai soil in order to help the US war effort in Indo-China. These bases were legally US territory, a point highlighted by the arrest and execution, by US military court, of a Thai citizen, Tep Kankla, for the murder of an American soldier in December 1973 [26]. Apart from this, after the end of the Indo-China war, the US used *U-Tapao* naval base to attack Cambodia on 14th May 1975, without consulting the Thai Government.

The presence of such a large number of US forces, plus what was seen as the economic dominance of US companies in the local economy, seemed to confirm the Maoist analysis by the CPT that Thailand was a "semi-colony" of the USA. After 1973 there was therefore a growing campaign to kick out US bases. This campaign against US bases, which later received a boost from the defeat of the USA in Vietnam, and the

---

[24] Both Seksan Prasertkul and Tirayut Boonmi joined up with the *Communist Party of Thailand* for a period in 1976. They are now lecturers at Thammasat University.

[25] Sutam Saengpratoom was arrested in Bangkok on 6th October 1976. Much later he became a junior minister in the first *Thai Rak Thai* Government.

[26] *Sutachai Yimprasert (2001) 'How did the 6th October incident occur?'* In: Ji Ungpakorn & Sutachai Yimprasert (eds) *State Crime in a period of crisis and change*. Bangkok: The 6th October 1976 fact-finding and witness interviewing committee. (In Thai).

resulting new geo-political consequences, led to Prime Minister Kukrit's demand in March 1975 that the US withdraw. This was backed up by a massive anti-US base demonstration on 21st March 1976. The US finally withdrew its troops from Thailand shortly after this[27].

Another important area where the student movement was active was in the area of Human Rights and Democracy. Students campaigned to push for more democratic amendments to the 1974 constitution and they led struggles against state repression. On 24th January 1974 Government security forces attacked and burnt the village of *Na Sai* in the North-Eastern province of *Nong Kai*[28]. Three villagers were killed by Government forces. Initially the Government claimed that this atrocity was carried out by Communists, but Tirayut Boonmi, was able to prove in public that it was the work of the Government. Pressure from the student movement finally forced the Government to admit the crime and take steps to pay the villagers compensation. General Saiyut Kertpol, head of the *Communist Suppression Unit*, was also forced to admit that past Government policy had been "too harsh".

The *Na Sai* incident was followed by the exposure of another state crime in the Southern province of *Patalung*. It is estimated that between 1971 and 1973 Government forces had systematically arrested and interrogated villagers, resulting in over 3000 deaths. In what became known as the Red Drum *(Tang Daeng)* incident, villagers were killed and then burnt in petrol drums or pushed out of helicopters[29].

In addition to exposing state repression, student volunteers were also involved in the rather patronising state-sponsored campaign to "spread Democracy to the rural people" in the summer vacation of 1974[30].

[27] Since 9-11 the USA has sought to increase its military presence in South-East Asia under the banner of the War on Terror. However, the real reason behind US military expansion in the area may well be its rivalry with China. The Singapore military recently became the first foreign state to be allowed to station troops permanently on Thai soil since the 1970s US withdrawal.

[28] Sutachai (2001) Already quoted.

[29] Yos Juntornkiri (1975) 'Kicked down the mountain and burnt in Tang Daeng', in *Social Science Review* 13 (1), 41-71. Also *Prachachart* (1975) 21 February, 12. (In Thai).

[30] The Middle Classes have always regarded the poor as stupid and lacking in understanding of Democracy. This is seen clearly in the case of the 19th September 2006 coup.

Chapter 5
The War in Southern Thailand

Since the most recent eruption of violence in southern Thailand, various Governments, whether Taksin's *Thai Rak Thai Party* (TRT) Government, the military junta, or the military installed *Democrat Party* Government, have all failed to solve the crisis. It is becoming clear that the war has reached a stale-mate.

1. Most military commanders know that they cannot beat the insurgents[1]. The only strategy that they have is to try to contain the violent situation so that it does not get any worse. Meanwhile, ordinary soldiers, many of whom are recruited from the poor villages of the North-East, have no will to fight. They care nothing about "the protection of the nation" and try just to survive their tour of duty.
2. The insurgents have become more and more efficient and coordinated. They can hit multiple targets simultaneously and hit targets outside the deep South. Their bombs are larger and more sophisticated. More and more young people in the villages are drawn to support them because of the atrocities carried out by the

[1] Poldej Binprateep an under secretary at the Ministry of Social Development and Human Security in the junta's Government admitted this. http://www.prachatai.com/ 15/1/2007 (In Thai).

Thai State. Yet the rebels cannot beat the military either, because their mass base is too small.

3. Ordinary villagers of all ethnicity live in constant fear. The Thai state's arming of villagers only heightens the state of violence. Regular attacks occur against villagers, teachers, priests or Imams and they often cannot tell from which side these attacks originate. Villagers want an end to the violence and they want the troops and police to be withdrawn now.

Between January 2004 and late 2009, a total of 3,900 people had been killed in the southern civil war. Of this number, just over half were Muslims. The vast majority of people killed in this conflict were civilians[2]. Just after the 2006 coup the military launched a "surge" in the South which temporary reduced the number of insurgent attacks. However, by 2008, the effects of the surge were wearing off and violent incidents began to increase throughout 2009. This shows that the State's military option is not working despite having 60,000 soldiers in the region and spending up to 180 billion baht over 5 years[3]. Apart from the army, paramilitary rangers and police, there are 3,300 members of the Volunteer Defence Corps, 47,000 Village Defence Volunteers and 24,000 Village Protection Volunteers[4]. The Village Protection Volunteers are an exclusively Buddhist force, under the Queen's patronage.

In this situation, the response from within the ruling establishment, whether civilian or military, can be divided into the "hawks" and the "doves".

The hawks want to increase military and police pressure in the hope of stabilising the situation and containing the insurgency. Their emphasis is on increasing the "efficiency" and "better coordination" of the security forces and Government officials. They hope that the insurgents will surrender and

---

[2] http://www.deepsouthwatch.org/ (In Thai).

[3] Jom Petpradap, http://www.prachatai.com/ 11/06/2009 (In Thai).

[4] International Crisis Group (2009) *Southern Thailand: Moving Towards Political Solutions?* Asia Report No.181 - 8 December 2009. http://www.crisisgroup.org/library/documents/asia/south_east_asia/181_southern_thailand_moving_towards_political_solutions.pdf

that talks between the Thai and Malaysian Governments[5] and between the Thai Government and PULO "separatist leaders[6]" will help towards this stabilisation. Afterwards they want to attract business investment into the area. This policy is being pursued by top army generals and the *Democrat Party* and is little different from the policies of the Taksin administration before the 2006 coup. These hawks talk in an abstract manner about the need for a "political settlement", but because they refuse to consider the underlying root causes of the civil war, in practice they are only prepared to consider a military or security type solution.

General Sonti Boonyaratgalin, leader of the 2006 coup and *Matupum Party* leader, argued in November 2009 that "the pooling of resources and responsibilities of relevant agencies with a clear chain of command will create a breakthrough in the South"[7]. *Matupum Party* is also made up of Muslim politicians in the Wadah faction who were originally inside TRT, and before that, part of the Chawalit Yongjaiyut's *New Aspirations Party*. Despite being co-opted into the mainstream Thai polity by people like Prem Tinsulanon in the 1980s, they are now distant from the local population.

In October 2009, *Democrat Party* Prime Minister Abhisit Vejjajiva held talks with his Sri Lankan counterpart, Ratnasiri Wickramanayaka, on the Sri Lankan Government's success in putting down the Liberation Tigers of Tamil Eelam movement. Government spokesman Panitan Wattanayakorn said the Government was interested in the "negotiation approaches" used by Sri Lanka and its measures to squeeze the Tamil Tigers' sources of funding. Strengthening cooperation with neighbouring countries in keeping an eye on separatist movements outside the country was another interesting approach. Panitan also said that tough crackdowns were also key to Sri Lanka's success in its fight against the rebels, which should serve as a good lesson for Thailand[8]. Given that the Sri Lankan Government used indiscriminate violence against civilians in its war on the

---

[5] The Malaysian Prime Minister Najib Razak has suggested some sort of autonomy for the region, but this is not supported by the Thai Government.

[6] These are old generation leaders exiled abroad and out of touch with the present insurgency.

[7] *Bangkok Post* 19/11/2009.

[8] *Bangkok Post* 23/10/2009.

Tamils, this does not bode well for the residents of southern Thailand. There is already much evidence that the security forces in southern Thailand view the entire Muslim Malay population as potential "alien" enemies and indiscriminate violence against the population merely increases support for the insurgency.

On 29th November 2009, just before a visit by the Malaysian Prime Minister, Abhisit reaffirmed his commitment to a military and police solution to the unrest in the South in a speech in Songkla and claimed that there was already self-government in all areas of the country. According to Abhisit the Government only needed to concern itself with developing the economy in the South, while security matters should be in the hands of the military and police[9].

According to the International Crisis Group, the Abhisit Government has made no progress on solving the violence in the South and the huge Government budget directed to the region has created an "industry of insecurity" rife with corruption and acting as an obstruction to any resolution of the civil war. This is because the Government has not been using a policy of seeking a genuine political solution[10].

The hawks also include former TRT politicians like Chaturon Chaisang, although he is not as blood thirsty as Panitan and his *Democrat Party* bosses. Chaturon explained that paying more attention to a "political strategy" meant that when the Government launched a military operation it should take into consideration the political consequences[11].

The doves, who include some seasoned military men with experience of fighting the *Communist Party of Thailand* (CPT), understand that a military solution is not the answer. They believe that to end the civil war there will have to be some sort of autonomy and self-rule for the southern Muslim provinces. Yet they are not prepared to concede that the provinces have the right to separate completely from Thailand and they are not about to totally abandon the military solution either. However, they do

---

[9] http://www.prachatai.com/ 8/12/2009.

[10] International Crisis Group (2009) Already quoted.

[11] Seminar at Tammasart University to introduce his new book on the South, 15/01/2009. http://www.prachatai.com/ 15/01/2009 (In Thai).

see a political solution as a priority. This situation explains the remarks, later withdrawn under pressure from the military, made by former Prime Minister Samak Suntarawej and Interior Minister Chalerm Yubumrung in 2008, about the possibility of creating a weapons free zone and limited autonomy[12].

In 2009, in the same month that Abhisit was talking to the Sri Lankan leader, *Peua Thai Party* chief, retired General Chawalit Yongjaiyut, proposed some sort of local autonomy and self-Government for the Muslim South. He also helped to encourage the setting up a local southern committee to investigate political solutions to the conflict[13].

A long term solution to the civil war in the South requires that social movements must urgently push for the adoption of a political and non-military solution to the southern crisis. The problem is that the traditional movements got too close to the military and the ultra-nationalist PAD and many of the Red Shirts remain Taksin-style hawks. In order to push for a political solution, the social movements must shed any previous support for Thai Nationalism and any ideas that the borders are somehow sacred[14]. This would be a big step for the Red Shirts to make, but comments by people like Chawalit might help.

As a Marxist, I firmly believe that we have to side with all those who are oppressed by the Thai state. In practice, this means supporting the right of the insurgents to bear arms against the Thai state which has a long history of violent oppression in the South. Abstract calls for both sides to use "non-violence", often voiced by NGOs are not the solution. They merely end up by equating the Thai state's violence with that of the insurgents and fail to question the legitimacy of the state to govern Thailand's "colony" in the South. Never the less, as a Marxist, I also believe that armed struggle is not the solution. The answer is mass mobilisations of people against the state. This must be encouraged when ever it happens in the South.

---

[12] *Bangkok Post* 6,7,13/02/2008.

[13] http://www.prachatai.com/ 15/10/2009 (In Thai).

[14] Even organisations like the International Crisis Group, who advocate a political solution, still assume that the Thai unitary state is somehow sacred. International Crisis Group (2009) Already quoted.

The anti-war writer Arundhati Roy[15] once wrote that any Government's condemnation of "terrorism" is only justified if the Government can prove that it is responsive to non-violent dissent. The Thai Government has ignored the feelings of local people in the South for decades. It turns a deaf ear to their pleas that they want respect. It laughs in the face of those who advocate human rights when people are tortured. Under the emergency laws, no one in the south has the democratic space to hold political discussions. What choice do people have other than turning to violent resistance?

In another article, Roy explained that, we, in the social movements, cannot condemn terrorism if we do nothing to campaign against state terror ourselves. The Thai social movements have for far too long been engrossed in single issue campaigns. People's minds are made smaller by Thai Nationalism. It is time to support the oppressed in the South.

State crime at Takbai

On the 25th October 2004 Thai Government security forces broke up a demonstration at *Takbai* in the southern province of *Naratiwat*. Apart from using water cannon and tear gas, troops opened fire with live ammunition above the heads of protesters, but some fired directly into the crowd, killing 7 people and wounding many others, including a 14 year old boy. There were villagers of all ages and sexes in the crowd. After this, the troops moved in to capture young Muslim Malay men. While women and children huddled in one corner, the men were stripped to the waist and their hands were tied behind their backs. The prisoners were made to crawl along the ground while troops rained kicks down upon their heads and bodies and beat them with sticks. Many of the prisoners were roped together in a long line and made to lie face down on the ground. The local military commander of the 4th Area Army[16] told a reporter on television that this action should be a lesson to anyone who dared to defy the Government.

---

[15] Arundhati Roy (2004) *The ordinary Person's Guide to Empire*. Harper Perennial.

[16] Lt-General Pisarn Wattanawongkiri was the Fourth Army Region Commander at the time.

"We will do this again every time", he said. The whole event was captured on video, which only goes to show how arrogant and self-confident the security forces were[17].

Finally the bound prisoners were thrown into the backs of open-top army lorries, and made to lie, layer upon layer, on top of each other. Troops stood on top of their human cargo occasionally stamping on those who cried out for water or air and telling them that soon they would *"know what real hell was like"*. Many hours later the first lorry arrived at its destination, *Inkayut Army Camp*. A number of prisoners who had been at the bottom of this lorry were found to have died in transit, probably from suffocation and kidney damage. Six hours later the last lorry arrived with almost all those on the bottom layers found to be dead. During those six hours between the arrival of the first lorry and the last one, no attempt was made by the authorities to change the methods of transporting prisoners. In total nearly 80 prisoners died. We must agree with a senate report[18] on the incident which concluded that this amounted to "deliberate criminal actions likely to cause deaths" by the security forces. Prime Minister Taksin's first response to the incident was to praise the security forces for their "good work". Later the Government claimed that the deaths of over 80 demonstrators were a regretful "accident". Four years later on 9th February 2008 Prime Minister Samak Suntarawej told *Al Jazeera* television that the men who died at *Takbai "just fell on top of each other" "what was wrong with that?"* Later in the same interview he lied about the 6th October 1976 massacre, saying that *"Only one guy died"*[19].

From 6th October to *Takbai*. The Thai state's culture of violent crimes.

The lies told by Samak about Takbai and the 6th of October are clearly connected. Anyone watching the Takbai incident would be reminded of

[17] See the video http://www.youtube.com/watch?v=seSIT8nfPg0

[18] Thai Senate Committee on Social Development and Human Security December 2004.

[19] See Chapter 4.

the 6th October 1976 massacre of students in Thammasart University[20]. In 1976, after attacking a peaceful gathering of students with automatic weapons, men and women were stripped to the waist and made by the police to crawl along the ground under a hail of kicks and beatings. Some students were dragged out of the campus and hung from trees, others were burn alive in make-shift bonfires, mainly by right-wing thugs, some of whom were members of the ultra right-wing Village Scout Movement[21].

After both *Takbai* 2004 and the 6th October 1976, Government spokespersons told deliberate lies. One lie was that the security forces were "forced to act as the situation was getting out of hand". In fact this was never the case. At *Takbai*, senator Chermsak Pintong reported that the security forces admitted to a team of investigating senators that they broke up the demonstration in order to arrest 100 ring-leaders, the names and photographs of whom were on a Government black-list. Under the 1997 Constitution, Thai citizens were supposed to have the right to peaceful protest and were supposed to be innocent before trial. The actions of the police and army at *Takbai* show that they did not regard the villagers as citizens. The demonstration was more or less peaceful until it was broken up violently by security forces. In the minds of the troops and their commanders, the *Takbai* prisoners were captured prisoners of war, "nasty foreigners" or "enemies of the state" who needed to be punished. So were the students at *Thammasart* in 1976 ....

After the 6th October 1976 and *Takbai* 2004, Government spokespeople also claimed that the trouble- makers were foreigners and couldn't speak Thai. In 1976 they were supposed to be Vietnamese[22]. In 2004 the state claimed that they were Arabs or Malays. All prisoners killed or captured in 1976, and at *Takbai* in 2004, were Thai speaking Thai

---

[20] See the video http://www.youtube.com/watch?v=jWaZExPSmKk and http://www.youtube.com/user/Giles53#p/u/5/cZn3qJ5MMGQ

[21] Katherine Bowie (1997) *Rituals of National Loyalty. An Anthropology of the State and Village Scout Movement in Thailand.* Columbia University Press. Giles Ji Ungpakorn ed. (2003) *Radicalising Thailand: New Political Perspectives.* Institute of Asian Studies, Chulalongkorn University.

[22] A claim made by Samak Suntarawej and others.

citizens. Government spokespeople also told lies that the students in 1976 and the demonstrators at *Takbai* in 2004 were well-armed and posed a threat to security forces. There is no evidence to support this. No Weapons of Mass Destruction were found at either site. At *Takbai* a rusty rifle, which had been lying in the river for years, was paraded as "evidence".

After *Takbai*, the Queen spoke of her concern for Thai Buddhists in the South. No mention was made of our Muslim brothers or sisters. No mention was made of *Takbai* and worse still, the Queen called on the *Village Scout Movement* to mobilise once again to save the country[23]. Luckily most *Village Scouts* are middle-aged and unlikely to commit violent acts anymore.

After the military coup of 19th September 2006, the junta's Prime Minister travelled down to the South to "apologise" for what the Taksin Government had done[24]. He announced that charges *against some demonstrators* would be lifted. Yet, his Government, and the previous Taksin Government, did not prosecute a single member of the security forces for the *Takbai* incident. No holder of political office has been punished either. In 2007 the junta continued to emphasise the military "solution" in the South with a troop surge. In January 2007 the junta renewed the Taksin Government's southern emergency decree, which gives all security forces sweeping powers and immunity from prosecution. Late in 2007, just before the elections, the junta passed a new Security Law which enshrined the undemocratic role of the army in Thai society.

Takbai was not the only violent incident to capture the news headlines. In April 2004, about a hundred youths, wearing "magical" Islamic headbands, attacked police stations in various locations. But they were only armed with swords and rusty knives. They were shot down with automatic fire. Discontent was being articulated through a religious self-sacrifice. In one of the worst incidents that day, the army attacked the

---

[23] *Post Today* 17/11/2004 (In Thai).

[24] Prime Minister Surayud needs to apologise for what he did in the May 1992 crack-down on unarmed pro-democracy demonstrators!

ancient *Krue-Sa* mosque with heavy weapons after the youths fled into the building. Ex-senator Kraisak Choonhawan maintained that apart from the excessive force shown by the Government, some prisoners in this event were bound and then executed in cold blood. He was referring to a group of youths from a local football team who were shot at point blank range at *Saba Yoi*. The army officer in charge of the blood bath at *Krue-Sa* was General Punlop Pinmanee. In 2002 he told a local newspaper that in the old days the army simply used to shoot rural dissidents and Communists. Now they send people round to intimidate their wives[25]. No state official has been punished for the events at *Krue-Sa*.

Torture and detention without trial

The military push in the South under the junta's Government, which started in June 2007, resulted in 1000 detentions without trial in the first two months. The military spokesman for the "joint civilian, military and police command" in the South, General Uk Tiproj, claimed that those detained were people with *"misguided beliefs who needed to be re-educated"* [26].

The *"Southern Lawyers' Centre"* reported that between July 2007 and February 2008 there were 59 documented cases of torture by the security forces. In two incidents the torture resulted in death. In late January 2008 seven activist students from *Yala* were arrested and tortured[27]. Torture methods included beatings, being imprisoned, wet, in cold air conditioned rooms and the use of electric shocks[28]. According to the Lawyers' Centre, most of the torture occurred in the first 3 days of detention, when prisoners were not allowed any visitors. The places where torture occurred were the *Yala* Special Unit 11section of the *Yala* Army Rangers camp and the *Inkayut Army Camp* in *Pattani*. Needless to say, no one has been punished for killing and torturing detainees.

[25] See Pasuk Phongpaichit & Chris Baker (2004) *Thaksin. The business of politics in Thailand.* Silkworm. Page 19.

[26] http://www.prachatai.com/ 9/10/2007 (In Thai).

[27] http://www.prachatai.com/ 18/2/2008 (In Thai).

[28] *Turn Left* March 2008. www.pcpthai.org/ (In Thai).

The creation of the Thai nation state is the start of the violence

The root cause of today's violence can be traced back to the creation of "Thailand" as a Nation State in the 19th Century. But the historical causes alone are not enough to explain the present civil war. Continuous repressive policies towards the local inhabitants by the Thai state over the years have refuelled resentment. Duncan McCargo points out that the southern conflict is not a religious conflict between Muslims and Buddhists and that the Thai state has a tradition of murder, massacre and mayhem in the region.

McCargo shows that the Thai State has used a "dual track" policy of repression and co-opting local religious leaders and politicians in order to control the area, the latter especially in the period when Prem Tinsulanon was Prime Minister in the early 1980s[29]. By 1988 Thailand had become much more democratic with a fully elected Prime Minister and Government. Local Muslim politicians were encouraged to join mainstream political parties, especially retired General Chawalit Yongjaiyut's *New Aspirations Party*, where they formed a group known as the *Wadah Faction*[30].

By the late 1990s Prem's policy of co-opting local leaders was beginning to fall apart because it did little to solve the marginalisation of the majority of the Muslim Malay population and resulted in a gap opening up between grass roots people and their official leaders or representatives. Those who wish to pin the blame for the violence on the Taksin Government alone claim that he meddled in the security structures which were controlling the peace in the region. This is both unhistorical and

[29] Duncan McCargo (2008) "What's Really Happening in Southern Thailand?" ISEAS Regional Forum, Singapore, 8 January 2008. Duncan McCargo (2009) "Thai Buddhism, Thai southern conflict". Journal of Southeast Asian Studies 40(1): 1-10. Duncan McCargo (2009) "The Politics of Buddhist identity in Thailand's deep south: The Demise of civil religion?". Journal of Southeast Asian Studies 40(1): 11-32.

[30] Carlyle A. Thayer (2007) *Insurgency in Southern Thailand: Literature Review.* http://www.scribd.com/doc/17965033/Thayer-Insurgency-in-Southern-Thailand

completely ignores the fact that the unrest has been going on in various forms for over a century and that "peace deals" made by the Thai state in the mid 1980s with local elites, were failing to address real grievances. Never the less, the *Takbai* and *Krue-Sa* massacres under the Taksin Government had a big impact on the rise of the insurgency.

History of Thai state repression in the South[31]

The nation state of "Thailand" was created by Bangkok's colonisation of the North, North-East and South. However, what was special about the South was that the *Pattani* ruling class was never co-opted or assimilated into the Thai ruling elite and the Muslim Malay population have never been respected or seen as fellow citizens since then. Bangkok and London destroyed and divided up the *Pattani Sultanate* between them and Bangkok has ruled the area like a colony ever since.

1890s King Chulalongkorn (Rama 5) seized half of the *Pattani Sultanate*. The Sultanate was divided between London and Bangkok.

1921 Enforced "Siamification" via primary education. Locals forced to pay tax to Bangkok.

1923 *Belukar Semak* rebellion forced King Rama 6 to make concessions to local culture.

1938 More enforced "Siamification" under the ultra Nationalism of the dictator Pibun.

1946 Pridi Panomyong promoted local culture, but he was soon driven from power by a coup.
Haji Sulong proposed an autonomous state for the Malay southern provinces within Siam.

1948 Haji Sulong arrested.

[31] Nik Anuar Nik Mahmud (2006) *The Malays of Patani. The search for security and independence*. School of History, Politics and Strategic Studies, University Kebangsaan, Malaysia.

April 1948 police massacre innocent villagers at *Dusun Nyior, Naratiwat.*

1954 Haji Sulong killed by police under orders from police strongman Pao Siyanond .

When considering the violence in the South, we need to listen to what local people are saying. Local Muslim people do not generally hate their Buddhist neighbours. The civil war never started as "communal violence" between people of differing religions. This is still the case now, despite the counter-productive efforts by Thai Governments in saturating the region with arms, including the arming of local villagers. Some Buddhist monks have been brutally killed and in June 2009 armed Buddhists gunned down praying Muslims at the *Al Furqan Mosque*. It is thought that they were led by an ex-military ranger. Apart from soldiers and rebels, local traders, rubber tappers, priests, Imams, ordinary villagers, school teachers and Government officials have all been victims of violence. Most of those killed may have died at the hands of the security forces.

In the late 1990s most local people were not really demanding a separate state, despite the fact that Thai Government violence may now have pushed people towards supporting separation. The southern border provinces have been neglected economically and when there has been development it has not been the majority of local Malay Muslims who have benefited. There is a high level of unemployment in the area and many people seek work in neighbouring Malaysia. Never the less, economic development alone cannot solve the violence.

What local people are saying more than anything is that they want respect. Their religion, language and culture are not respected by the Thai state. The state education system emphasises Thai, Buddhist, and Bangkok history and culture. This is why schools are often burnt. In the past 60 years successive Thai Governments have arrested religious leaders, banned the teaching of *yawee* (the local dialect of Malay spoken in the area), closed religious schools, forced students to learn the Thai language, forced students to wear Thai style clothes, encouraged people to change their names to "Thai" names and forcibly changed the names of local districts to "Thai-sounding" names. All this has been carried out by Bangkok Governments which maintain an occupying army in the southern border provinces[32].

In the 1960s the military dictatorship settled some Buddhist north-easterners in the area in order to "strengthen" the occupation[33]. It reminds one of the British policy in Northern Ireland or Palestine. Buddhist temples were built in predominantly Muslim areas. In this period there were times when Muslims were made to bow down before Buddha images. Even now they are made to bow down before pictures of the King, which is an offence to their religion. There are house-searches by troops using dogs. Again this is an insult to Muslims. Recently soldiers were conscripted to become monks in southern temples and the temples have army guards. This represents the militarisation of religion.

The occupying army and the police are feared and hated. The army likes to claim that the locals hate the police and love the army. It is simply not true. Local people know that their sons, brothers and fathers have been taken away at night, then tortured and killed by the Thai army and police, often in plain clothes[34]. In 2004, the defence lawyer Somchai Nilapaichit, who was a key human rights activist on this issue of torture, was kidnapped in Bangkok and killed by police from different units. He was trying to expose police tactics in torturing suspects into confessions about stealing guns from an army camp in early 2004. The involvement of police from different units in his murder indicates a green light from above: from Prime Minister Taksin and others in his Government. To date, no one has been charged with Somchai's murder and his body has not been found. This is

---

[32] Ahmad Somboon Bualuang (2006) Malay, the basic culture. In *The situation on the Southern border. The views of Civil Society*. Published by the Coordinating Committee of the Peoples Sector for the Southern Border Provinces. (In Thai).

[33] There have been some Buddhists living in the region for centuries.

[34] Akerin Tuansiri (2006) student activities in the violent areas of the Southern border provinces. In *The situation on the Southern border. The views of Civil Society*. Already quoted (In Thai).

despite the fact that the *Democrat Party* Government claimed to be "different" from TRT.

It isn't hard to find green lights, right at the top, for Thai state violence. No one has been punished for the 1976 bloodbath at *Thammasart*, the May 1992 massacre, or for the killings at *Takbai* or *Krue-Sa* in 2004. The Taksin Government also sanctioned the extra-judiciary murder of over 3000 "drug suspects" in its war on drugs. Many were killed in the South, others killed were among northern ethnic minorities. The King approved of the War on Drugs and the 6th October massacre. Since 2008, the military installed *Democrat Party* Government has contributed to the collapse in the rule of law and has sanctioned the shooting of civilians in Bangkok. The courts have always protected those in power and offer no justice.

After the February 2005 election TRT lost almost all seats in the South because of its policies, especially the *Takbai* incident. But it gained a huge overall majority nationally. The Government established the *National Reconciliation Commission* under ex-Prime Minister Anand Panyarachun. He had served as a civilian PM under the military junta in 1991. Most people in the South doubted whether this commission would solve their problems. Anand was quoted in the press as saying that self-rule and autonomy were "out of the question" and that people should "forget" the Takbai massacre[35].

Despite Anand's remarks, the report of the *National Reconciliation Commission* came up with some progressive statements and suggestions[36]. Firstly, it stated that the problems in the South stemmed from the fact that there was a lack of justice and respect and that various Governments had not pursued a peaceful solution. It went on to describe how the TRT Government had systematically abused human rights and was engaged in extrajudicial killings. The Commission suggested that local communities in the South be empowered to control their own natural resources, that Civil Society play a central part in creating justice and that the local

[35] *Bangkok Post* 10/8/2005 and 9/5/2005.

[36] *National Reconciliation Commission*, 16/5/2006 (In Thai).

Yawee language be used as a working language, alongside Thai, in all Government departments. The latter suggestion on language is vital if local people are not to be discriminated against, especially by Government bodies[37]. Yet it was quickly rejected by both Taksin and Privy Council Chairman General Prem Tinsulanon[38].

Unhelpful explanations about the violence in the South

There are a number of irrelevant or unhelpful explanations for the violence in the South. They all share a common thread which ignores and dismisses the oppression of the Muslim Malays by the Thai state. They also share the belief that the locals are somehow "incapable" of conducting a home-grown insurgency without outside instigation and support. As with most "elite theories", history and conflict are confined to actions of the ruling elites while the general population is regarded as mainly ignorant passive spectators. Those who promote such theories wish to ignore the political and social causes of the civil war and concentrate on using military and diplomatic solutions to end the conflict.

One theory claims that the violence was created by disgruntled army officers, afraid of losing a share of the lucrative cross-border black-market trade. According to the theory, these soldiers sponsored the violence in order to "prove" that the army was still needed. It is true that the military is involved in illegal cross-border trading and that if they were withdrawn from the area they would lose this lucrative activity. But this theory begs the important question about why soldiers occupy the South as a colony in the first place, unlike the situation in the North or the North-East. It is also quite clear that there has been an insurgent movement throughout recent history and it enjoys support from important sections of the local population for real reasons.

---

[37] This proposal was supported by the Malaysian politician Anwar Ibrahim. http://www. prachatai.com/ 5/5/2009 (In Thai).

[38] *Bangkok Post* 26 and 27/6/2006.

Another theory claims that it is just the work of "foreign Islamic fanatics", who have managed to brain-wash some local youths into supporting a separatist movement. This is what Thai Governments claim. George Bush and Tony Blair's encouragement of Islamophobia to support their invasions of Afghanistan and Iraq, stirred-up such views and allowed human rights abuses against Muslims world-wide. But why would local youths just allow themselves to be brain-washed if there was not just cause? There is every indication that the insurgency is home grown for good reasons: there has been a history of state repression. Never the less, local insurgents and separatist movements have built links with sympathetic foreign Governments and organisations[39]. This does not, however, indicate that the civil war is somehow instigated from abroad by "international Muslim extremists".

Yet another theory comes from those who need an excuse to say that ex-Prime Minister Taksin "wasn't all that bad".... They are old supporters of the CPT, now siding with Taksin. They believe that the southern violence was planned by the CIA in order to increase US Government involvement in the region. These conspiracy theorists also believed that the CIA planned the September 11 attacks in New York. The fact that the CIA used to support Bin Laden seems to make this plausible. But what is overlooked is the Cold War context of supporting Islamic fighters in Afghanistan against Russia soldiers.

Some academics have maintained that the violence started as a "patch war" between The Palace, with the support of the army, and the Taksin Government. Duncan McCargo[40] suggests that the southern violence can be explained as conflict between "Network Monarchy" and "Network Taksin". This is similar to the attempts to explain the 19th September coup as a conflict between "Feudalism" and "Capitalism". It is true that the Taksin Government wanted to reduce the role of the military in controlling the South and transfer many powers to the police. But this is

---

[39] Carlyle A. Thayer (2007) Already quoted.

[40] Duncan McCargo (2005) Network monarchy and legitimacy crises in Thailand. _The Pacific Review_ 18 (4) December, 499-519.

more about his attempts to "regularise" governance in the region and also to stamp out the black market, a policy pursued in other parts of the country. This undoubtedly caused resentment among the army, but it does not explain the main underlying causes of the civil war.

Who are the insurgents?

Back in the 1970s a clear separatist movement existed, cooperating in its struggle against the Thai state with the Communist Parties of Thailand and Malaysia. The *Barisan Revolusi Nasional* (BRN) was established in 1963 and the *Pattani United Liberation Organisation* (PULO) was founded in 1968. PULO are not in a position to control much of what is happening on the ground today. One PULO activists admitted to the BBC that *"Right now there is a group which has a lot of young blood. They're quick and fast and they don't worry what will happen after they do something. They don't care because they want the Government to have a big reaction, which will cause more problems"* [41].

By 1984 the BRN had split into three. One organisation which originated from the BRN, is the *Barisan Revolusi Nasional-Koordinasi* (BRN-C). By 2005 the *Runda Kumpulan Kecil* (RKK or Pattani State Restoration Unit) was becoming more prominent in the insurgency. It is believed to be a loose grouping of people from the BRN-C who trained in Indonesia. There seem to be many organisations operating today. They do not claim responsibility for their actions because by deliberately not claiming responsibility they make it extremely hard for the Thai Intelligence services to understand who is who and which of the various organisations is taking what action [42].

The southern insurgency follows the patterns of many middle-eastern struggles against Western Imperialism and local despotic ruling classes. In the 1960s and 1970s they were secular movements allied to

---

[41] Interview with the B.B.C.'s Kate McGeown 7/8/2006. http://www.bbc.co.uk/worldservice/

[42] Zachary Abuza. Terrorism Monitor 8/9/2006 James Town Foundation http://www.jamestown.org/terrorism/news/article.php?articleid=2370

communist parties. But with the decline of the communist parties, partly as a result of their collaboration with local despots, especially in the middle-east, rebels and insurgents turned to new forms of ideology, mainly radical Islam[43]. This explains why radical Islam is the banner under which the present day insurgents fight. It is not the rise of radical Islam which has caused the violence. The brutal actions of Thai Governments and the failure of the CPT have pushed radicals into adopting Islam.

Mass political action is the answer

The resistance is not just about planting bombs and shooting state officials. Communities act in a united way to protect themselves from the security forces who constantly abduct and kill people. Women and children block the roads and stop soldiers or police from entering villagers. On 4th September 2005 they blocked the entrance to *Ban Lahan* in *Naratiwat* and told the Provincial Governor that he and his soldiers were not welcome in their village[44]. Two weeks later villagers blocked the road to *Tanyong Limo*. Earlier two marines had been captured by villagers and then killed by unknown militants. Villagers suspect that the marines were members of a death squad sent in to kill local people[45]. The villagers held up posters aimed at the authorities, saying: *"You are the real terrorists"*. In November 2006, six weeks after the coup, villagers protested at a school in *Yala*, demanding that troops leave the area. One of their posters read: *"All you wicked soldiers.. .get out of our village. You come here and destroy our village by killing innocent people. Get out!"* [46]

Many slogans against the military are painted on roads. In August 2007 'Darika'[47] made a note of some:

> *"Peace will come when there are no soldiers."*

---

[43] Chris Harman (1994) "The Profit and the Proletariat". International Socialism Journal 64.

[44] *Bangkok Post* 5/9/2005.

[45] *Bangkok Post* 22/9/2005.

[46] *The Nation* 6/11/2006.

[47] Darika (2008) Records from Kollo Balay village. A Village in the Red Zone. South See 5, Social Research Centre, Chulalongkorn University. (In Thai).

"We don't want the soldiers in our village. We are afraid."
"Without the soldiers, the people will be happy."
"The curfew is unjust. They are killing innocents."

Such protests in villages continue to occur today after various incidents involving the security forces.

On 31st May 2007 the *"Student Network to Defend the People"* organised a mass rally of 3,000 at the *Pattani Central Mosque*. The rally started because of 4 murders and 1 rape carried out by Army Rangers at a village in *Yala*. The demands of this peaceful protest were for a total review of Government policy in the South and a withdrawal of soldiers from the area[48].

Assistant Professor Dr Srisompop Jitpiromsri from *Songkla University* reported that between 2005 and 2008 there were a total of 26 mass demonstrations in the South. Thirteen of them were to demand the release of detainees and another 5 demanded that troops and police leave the area. These mass actions by villagers and students are the real hope for freedom and peace in the South. Yet the Thai state and the mainstream media brand these mobilisations as "violent". They make no distinction between peaceful social movements and the armed insurgency. The arrest and torture of 7 *Yala* student activists in 2008 confirms this point[49]. This will only drive more young people into the arms of the insurgents.

If the mass action of these social movements is to succeed, we must give them every encouragement and support.

Peace can only be achieved in the South by:

1. The abolition of martial law and all security laws.
2. An end to human rights abuses, detention without trial, torture and extra-judicial murders by the Thai state.
3. A withdrawal of troops and police from the area in order to build a weapons free zone. Disarming all civilian village militias.

[48] http://www.prachatai.com/ 4/6/2007 and http://www.prachatai.com/ 17/6/2007. (In Thai)
[49] http://www.prachatai.com/ 2/2/2008 (In Thai).

4. Serious political discussions by local people should be officially encouraged in order that they can decide their own future. No pre-conditions should apply to these discussions and all forms of autonomy, including full independence, should be discussed.
5. Social movements must campaign against Thai Nationalism.
6. The Thai state should admit previous State Crimes in order to build new standards of human rights.
7. Thai society should respect all ethnicities, religions, languages and cultures. Religious festivals, other than Buddhist festivals, should be decreed as national public holidays. Different languages should be officially recognised alongside Thai and taught in schools in all parts of the country.

Left to themselves, mainstream politicians, the military and Government officials will not put any of these demands into practice. Only a genuine "peace movement" from below, which campaigns for total respect for the Muslim Malays, can push for a solution to the civil war. Such a movement must also be part of the movement for Democracy in the rest of Thai society.

Chapter 6
A Personal Note

lèse majesté

"Look! There's a police summons for you on charges of lèse majesté!" That was my wife Num's first reaction while going through our accumulated post. We had just spent Christmas 2008 in Oxford. It had snowed. It was the first time my son and my wife had seen snow. My son Jun lay down in the snow and raised his arms, making an "angel" shape. I was glad to have been there when he experienced his first snow. For the last two years we had lived thousands of miles apart, communicating by Skype. When the PAD closed down the international airports in December 2008, I nearly did not make it to visit him.

When we got back to balmy Bangkok, to the *Soi Aree* house where I was born, the *Ratri* fragrant flowers were at their best. So were the Bougainvilleas which I had replanted. I loved that house. It was an oasis among the high rise buildings and hot noisy streets of Bangkok. It was where I learnt to love nature as a boy. It was where Jun had also learnt about animals and plants and my daughter Louise had painted a wonderful picture of leaves and flowers.

When I first wrote the book *"A Coup for the Rich"*, criticising the 2006 military coup and discussing the relationship between the army, the PAD, the NGOs, academics and the Monarchy, I had thought that they would never dare charge me with lèse majesté. I thought that since I had been careful to write about well-known facts, that the elites wouldn't want to be exposed in a high profile court case. But after the book came out in early 2007, it became more and more obvious that there was no rule of law in Thailand. The courts were mere political tools of the conservative elites, the media was totally neutered and cowardly and the majority of Thai academics and NGO activists supported the royalists and the destruction of Democracy.

Suwicha Takor had already been arrested and held without bail under lèse majesté. His trial was going to be held in secret. Mine would be too. Clearly I would receive no justice from the courts. My only defence was to go on the attack and publicise my case on an international basis. My fight would be an open fight on the basis of democratic and academic freedom. I launched a petition calling for the scrapping of the law. Over one thousand seven hundred people, all over the world and in Thailand, signed the petition.

I called a press conference to condemn the lèse majesté law as a gross infringement of democratic rights. Only the foreign press came and reported my statement. There were some Thai journalists present, but they dared not report what I had said, such was the destruction of press freedom in Thailand.

My Oxford friends, Tamsin and Chris, and my SWP comrades, especially Alex Callinicos, swung into action to help build my international defense campaign. English PEN, the writers organisation, put a lot of work into supporting me and I am extremely grateful to all those who gave me solidarity. The warmest solidarity I received from within Thailand was from Red Shirts and from a group of progressive students and staff at *Chulalongkorn University* who came to the police station with me when I went to hear the details of the lèse majesté charges.

On January 31st I was honoured to be invited on to the platform of a mass Red Shirt rally at *Sanam Luang*. It was the first time I ever addressed a crowd of over a hundred thousand people and I shall always remember that moment. It was Jakrapop Pencare who invited me on to the stage and gave me a warm hug. My friend Jaran Didtapichai was also there. Below, among the crowd, my comrades from *Turn Left* were selling our socialist newspapers and pamphlets. They always sold like hot cakes at Red Shirt rallies. People were hungry for reading material and ideas. Beside our stall, there were dozens of other stalls, set up by local Red Shirt groups from various provinces.

A few days later, I travelled to the North-East city of *Ubon Rajatanee*. I had been invited by progressive academics at this "Red Shirt" university to give a talk about lèse majesté. I met a few of my ex-students there who were now lecturers. The lecture hall was packed. There must have been around 500 people. Half were university students and staff and the other half were Red Shirt villagers from the area around Ubon. I had contacted a local Red Shirt community radio "DJ"[1] from the *Chack Tong Rop* group and invited the local Red Shirts along. The *Chack Tong Rop* shirt they gave me was one of my prize processions which I packed in my single suitcase when I left Thailand. At first, the staff at the university were rather worried by the influx of villagers, but they soon saw that these were peaceful pro-democracy activists. Some of these middle aged Red Shirt women told me how they wrestled with computer and internet technology in order to access uncensored news. Others said that they just left it to their younger relatives to download information for them to read.

In this period I got abuse from Yellow Shirts. Dr Niran Pitakwatchara, ex-senator, PAD supporter and later, Human Rights Commissioner, tried to get *Ubon Rajatanee University* to cancel my lecture. At the airport, yellow-shirted travellers were abusive about me and my wife and we received death threats by telephone.

However, what was most disappointing was the attitude of NGO and Human Rights activists. My locally elected senator, Rosana Tositrakul, just laughed when I suggested that she take up the issue of human rights

1 Community radio stations started to play an important role in alternative media and news sources for the Red Shirts and the people running the programmes were called "DJs". They were also local organisers of Red Shirt groups.

abuses arising from lèse majesté. She could not understand why she should listen to the views of one of her constituents who had voted for her. The concept of accountability to the electorate never occurred to her. The head of the *National Human Rights Commission*, Prof. Sanay Jamarik, refused to help and put the phone down on me. Prominent academics like Pasuk Phongpaichit or Charnwit Kasetsiri never replied to the requests to sign the petition. The *NGO-Coordinating Committee* remained silent. *Amnesty International* refused to act.

Among those people who I know were personally opposed to the use of the lèse majesté law, like my brother Jon or some Thai academics, such as Thongchai Winichakul, they felt that my public political campaign was not the way to go about things. Thongchai felt that I was only interested in boosting my ego. I remain perplexed to this day as to his reasoning. I have always respected Thongchai as a historian. My brother Jon certainly did not want his younger brother to go to jail and was not a supporter of the lèse majesté law either. But after I launched my political campaign, he text messaged me to say that *"no one can help you now"*. I believe that he had hoped to have words with people in high places to get the charges against me dropped. He was on familiar terms with people like Satit Wongnongtoey, a *Democrat Party* MP who became government censorship boss in 2009. Jon's solution would probably have involved me begging for forgiveness at some point in a messy compromise. Not only was I never going to beg to be forgiven for a crime that I did not commit, but all experience indicated that such begging did not prevent people going to jail. Suwichai Takor was tricked by police into pleading guilty. He still received a very stiff prison sentence.

At time of writing, over a year after the PAD violence at Government House and at the international airports, no one has been punished for these crimes. Also no "PAD guard" has been punished for shooting my friend Chainarin in the leg outside his taxi driver's community radio station in Bangkok.

During that January I forced myself to visit a number of foreign ambassadors. The Canadian Ambassador was most sympathetic. He talked about the worrying lack of human rights in the country. The French Ambassador invited me into the beautiful embassy building by the river. He was polite, but suggested that my campaign should be focussed on people inside Thailand. He suggested I visit Anan Panyarachun, ex-Prime Minister under the military junta of 1991. This I reluctantly did, but when I showed Anan the passages in my book[2], he told me that I had insulted the King and that I had a "very bad image" in Thailand. He was probably right if you only count the views of the conservative elites as being relevant. He also said that he knew the King very well and that the King was a "true democrat" and "was not at all rich".

The British Government were pressurised into doing something by the campaign inside the UK, but they were very wary because I hold dual Thai-British nationality. The British Ambassador at the time was also a fan of military-backed Prime Minister Abhisit and had publically praised him. Never the less, the British Government did eventually grant political asylum to my wife after many months of trauma and worry.

My experiences in that hectic few weeks in January 2009, convinced me that I would never receive a fair trial in Thailand. Jakrapop Pencare was also of the same opinion. If I got banged up in some dreadful Thai prison, where twenty people sleep in one cell, chained together at night, I would not be able to do much for the struggle for Democracy. If I waited until the police forwarded my case to the public prosecutor, they would take my passport away and only release me on a hefty bail. It was time to leave. Num and I hired a car and spent a day in the ancient city of Ayuttaya. We went to my favourite ruin by the river, Wat Chaiwatanaram, and I lay on the grass, resting and smoking a cigar. It was a way of saying goodbye. I made arrangements to mark my students' final essays by e-mail and I gave my surprised comrades in *Turn Left* some big hugs. Nothing was said about leaving, but some may have guessed.

Music has always been important to me and those weeks before we left Thailand are remembered in Albinoni's Oboe Concerto No.2, Op.9

[2] See the appendix following this chapter.

Adagio. It was playing in the car on our way back from Ayuttaya as we passed food stalls advertising fried Cobras and field rats.

On February 6th Num and I boarded a direct flight to London with only one suitcase each. There were some tense moments at the airport, going through immigration, but we made it on to the plane and into the air. Jon had agreed to be on hand if I was detained, although he was not aware that I would not be returning. It was on the plane that I wrote my "Red Siam Manifesto"[3], which I e-mailed to hundreds of people in Thailand a few days after arriving in Oxford. I also placed it on my blogs. Needless to say, my blogs were soon blocked to Thai readers by the Abhisit Government.

Oxford

Our plans to leave Thailand had been kept secret. Only 3 people knew. My son Jun did not and he was very surprised and pleased to see me on the snowy evening when I turned up to collect him from a friend's house. Our Oxford friends looked after us from the beginning until we could find our own accommodation.

In early March that year, military appointed Prime Minister Abhisit paid a visit to his old college in Oxford University to make a speech about Democracy. Outside St John's College a large group of Thai Red Shirts held a protest and we later formed the *UK Red Shirt Group*. Abhisit's talk about Democracy was full of lies, excuses and half-truths and the Vice Chancellor of Oxford University and the President of St John's College, like a couple of bumbling fools, praised Abhisit's "commitment to Democracy".

Abhisit claimed that he had been "democratically elected" and that he was a "guardian of Thai Democracy". Yet, he fully supported the destruction of Democracy since 2006 and only became Prime Minister through bribery and military manoeuvrings. He also supported using lèse majesté to prosecute me for writing an academic book which criticised

[3] See at the English version at the end of this chapter.

the 2006 coup. However, he claimed that he could not remember in which part of the book I had actually "insulted the King". He lied that the lèse majesté charges against Chotisak Oonsung had been "dropped" and that the arrest of *Prachatai website* manager was a "police mistake". He claimed that he had "cleared the matter" with a phone call to the *Prachatai* manager. He stated that the PAD leaders who seized the airports would "definitely be charged" and that the generals responsible for the *Takbai* massacre "would also be charged". He denied that his Foreign Minister was a PAD supporter who took over the airports. Despite accusing me of "running away from Thailand", he was not brave enough to take up my challenge of a live public debate on Thai TV.

The Thai embassy in London was extremely worried about my presence at the meeting in Oxford and many attempts were made to bar me. They were unsuccessful because Oxford University insisted that I had the right to attend. Around the same time, I did a speaking tour of a number of British Universities, such as SOAS, Oxford, Cambridge and Leeds. They were well attended and clips of my SOAS talk on U Tube caused a stir inside Thailand. The Thai embassy organised some Yellow Shirt students to go and argue with me at some of these meetings, which was fine with me.

The government and their PAD allies accused me of being part of a "Taksin plot to overthrow the Monarchy". I have never denied being in favour of a republic, but Taksin was being libelled. The crazy Yellow Shirt media also accused me of being responsible for the Thai stock market crash in late 2009 by supposedly circulating "false rumours" about the King's health. At the time the King had been in hospital for over a month. The irony is that previously I told foreign news agencies that although the King was clearly seriously ill, he could live for another few years. The foreign news agencies were convinced he was on his death bed. Because of the high level of censorship, many Thais believed at the time that the King was already dead and that the government was telling lies. The authorities later showed him attending a function in a wheel chair. Yellow Shirt senators also tried to get me charged again with lèse majesté for articles written about the Monarchy while living in the U.K.!! These incidents would be laughable if it was not for the fact that 4 people were arrested in Thailand for "spreading false rumours".

My father, Puey Ungpakorn, 1917-1999

The phone dropped from my hand and I crumpled into a heap in the public phone box somewhere in Durham. I had feinted after hearing from my brother Peter that my father, Puey Ungpakorn, had just had a very serious stroke. The year was 1977 and I was studying Ecology for a Master's degree at Durham University in the north of England. My father's stroke marked the end of my childhood relationship with the man who had been my father, the man who had got me a butterfly net, the man who took me in the sea at *Hua Hin* and *Songkla*, the man who taught me to eat fried fish heads and tails, the man who had the bravery to stand up to military dictators.

My father was a man who brought back exotic coins and stamps from his work trips abroad. He always sent me postcards. Towards the end of this period, I had a glimpse of what an adult relationship with him might have been like. He came into my room one day and asked me to recommend a couple of good books on Green Politics. At the time, I was an environmentalist. After his stroke, he no longer spoke or wrote. His vast knowledge of Thai political history would be forever locked inside his brain. This was something I came to very much regret later. As a boy and a young man I had not taken the time to talk to him about Thai politics or his close relationship with Pridi Panomyong. All I knew was that Pridi sent him marron glacé from France every Christmas and we all enjoyed them.

My father was a very gentle man, although he could get angry too. He joined the *Free Thai Force 136* as part of the British Army during the Second World War. Thailand was under Japanese occupation, with the dictator Pibun collaborating with the Japanese. When I was growing up in our house at *Soi Aree* in Bangkok, he had a bayonet and leather club from his army days hidden above his wardrobe. I used to sneak a look, but he didn't like me playing with them. I doubt if he could have shot anyone, but you can never tell. Luckily he didn't have to. He was arrested after parachuting into Thailand during the war. It was in this period when he met Pridi Panomyong for the first time[4]. Pridi was the leader of the *Free Thai* inside Thailand. Pridi was also a socialist and one of the leaders of the 1932 revolution against the Absolute Monarchy. When my father wasn't acting as a government official by being Governor of the Bank of Thailand, he was more of a Social Democrat than a Socialist. He published a manifesto for a Thai welfare state in 1973, the year that students and workers overthrew the military dictatorship in Bangkok.

It was while I was studying in Durham that I heard about the 6th October 1976 massacre at *Thammasart University*, where my dad was Vice Chancellor. I was walking past the traditional butcher's shop in Framwell Gate Moor, where I lived, when I saw the headline from the *Northern Echo* displayed outside the newsagents. This local paper had a picture from Sanam Luang on its front page. It was a picture of a student being hung from a Tamarind tree and being beaten with a folding chair by right-wing thugs. It was strange to walk past the bowls of tripe and beef in the window of the butcher's shop and have the events in Bangkok suddenly brought to my attention. Many years later I managed to get a plaque to Wichitchai Amornkul placed on the wall of the Faculty of Political Science, *Chulalongkorn University* where he had been a student. It was Wichitchai who had been hung and beaten and whose picture was beamed across the world. His plaque joined other plaques on the same wall. The others were all ex-students who had become government officials and died in the war against the communists.

I suppose we had all expected something bad for some months in 1976. My brother Jon had left Thailand and come to Britain just before. He was in the *Communist Party of Thailand* (CPT) and they had all been warned to get out. My brother Peter was studying at the London School of

---

[4] See Puey Ungphakorn (1981) *A Siamese for all seasons*. Komol Keemthong Foundation, Bangkok.

Economics. Only my father was still in Thailand. Very soon we got news that he was waiting in Frankfurt to catch a plane to London. He had got the earliest flight available out of Bangkok after the massacre on the 6th October. He had been followed to the airport by a gang of *Village Scouts*. They were looking for him and would have killed him if they had found him. Some said that they didn't even know what he looked like! While checking in and getting his ticket sorted, my father was assaulted by a policeman named Salang Bunnag. This policeman had taken part in the massacre earlier that day. Later in the 1990s he went on to make a name for himself by shooting alleged drug dealers in cold blood while they were handcuffed. He was also involved in some scam to sell a "cure for AIDS". Apart from the policeman, a couple of fascist academics from *Thammasart* were at the airport to abuse my father.

My father got away. He arrived in Frankfurt without an overcoat that October and spent a few hours walking the freezing streets. As soon as he arrived in London he went with all of us to the BBC World Service to give a radio interview. That was the start of his campaign against the brutality of the conservative elites. I remember that while giving his interview he often stopped to think, making "err" noises on many occasions. I was naively amazed that they managed to edit all the pauses and "errs" out for the actual broadcast. Much later, when I arrived in Britain in 2009, after being charged with lèse majesté, my mother said: *"It all sounds familiar"*.

My father survived his serious stroke in 1977 and lived for another 22 years in a disabled state. The fact that he could walk, watch TV and just about feed and dress himself was no consolation. His intellectual life was destroyed. He couldn't talk, write or concentrate enough to read a book. In the early days this torture reduced him to tears. Later, he came to quietly accept his state of affairs. At the time when he suffered his stroke he was reading a French book. He was fluent in 3 languages, but not his father's Chinese.

I remember travelling back to Thailand with my father in1987. It was the first time he and I had been back since 1976. Thousands of people came to meet him at receptions at the Bank of Thailand and *Thammasart University*. Among those thousands were his genuine supporters, mainly ex-students from the 1970s and some personal friends. But there were also hundreds of insincere opportunists, who claimed to respect Puey. I remember very well that in 1976, when my father was hounded out of Thailand and hundreds of people were slaughtered by the government and the right-wing, only three groups of people spoke up and supported Puey. These were the students and a handful of academics, people in Sulak Sivarak's organisation, and the Communist Party. Puey was not a communist. He was an anti-communist social democrat. But the government, army, and right-wing, branded him as one.

One of the things that my father was known for was his refusal to engage in corruption and various means to accumulate wealth. He had a reasonably simple life-style, but it was a far better standard than the ordinary Thai citizen. I was very much amused when we boarded the plane in Bangkok to return to London in 1987. We were flying Bangladesh Airways because I and my family could not afford the more expensive airlines. After their initial shock that my dad was flying by a cheap airline, they could not believe that he was flying economy class as well. These people were not interested in Puey's personal values. They just wanted to be associated with a celebrity.

I don't remember when exactly in July 1999 that my dad died. But I remember the fuss made by all sorts of opportunists around his funeral. The sad thing was that often his genuine supporters and friends were edged out and not given respect by "more important" people. I remember the "little people" who quietly and sincerely came to the funeral events and nodded to me. I remember a local Chinese shopkeeper who quietly stroked my arm, without saying anything, while I was buying water from his shop. I remember my cousin who played his saxophone "for my father, for the last time". Our relatives were very supportive. One organised the sprinkling of his ashes in the sea from a naval ship. It was the first and last time I have ever been saluted by soldiers! I remember planting a white Lantom tree in our garden at *Soi Aree*, next to the house where he and my mother lived after the Second World War. I and my brother Peter were born in that house. Puey loved fragrant flowers, especially *Lantom, Mali* and *Jumpa*.

I remember the nonsense around my father's funeral. By chance, I had to take my father's ashes to *Thammasart University* for a ceremony. He had been cremated by my mother in England and Jon had brought them back to Thailand. I drove up to the university gates in my battered fifteen year old Nissan Sunny, which my brother Peter had given me. The guards took one look at the car and wouldn't let me in! Those who professed to respect Puey's simple life had expected me to arrive in a chauffer driven BMW or Mercedes Benz. One daily tabloid criticised me for wearing a red shirt, claiming falsely that I was trying to make my father's funeral into a socialist event. In fact the shirt was dark red and made of traditional Thai silk. It was the smartest shirt I could find. I have been very careful never to use my father to justify or legitimise my beliefs and actions. I have always said that Puey was never a Marxist and that he had his beliefs which were different from mine.

Just after my father died, I received a phone call from the King's office. They wanted me to return my dad's royal decorations. All royal decorations are only given on loan because the King is supposed to own everything, even your life. When I explained that Puey had left Thailand "in a hurry" on 6th October 1976 and that those things were lost, the Palace official threatened to fine me the equivalent of two to three months wages. Such is the attitude of the Palace. The incident only ended because one of my high-ranking relatives intervened. Some years later, when I became an Associate Professor I was awarded the usual royal decoration which went with the position. I told the Vice Chancellor of *Chulalongkorn University* that I was refusing it. No one listened and an unlucky porter was asked to come and hand it to me in person. She entered my "Introduction to Marxism" class and I was able to formally refuse the royal decoration in front of all my students.

The house in *Soi Aree* is a beautiful wooden house, surrounded by a wild garden. It used to have owls, turtles, fish, bats, colourful birds, squirrels and snakes. I grew up there and became interested in natural history as a result. In the 1960s middle class people regarded the house as rather old fashioned and "poor-looking". The dictator Field Marshall Sarit offered to buy my father a bigger, more modern house. My father refused, like he refused the crate of whiskey and the huge colour TV which I saw arriving at our house as potential bribes. My mother's unwavering principles helped to give my father a strong backbone against all forms of corruption. She is a principled feminist and pacifist and does not tolerate any bowing and scraping. She is also an atheist and regards superstition with contempt. Our house at *Soi Aree* was probably the only house without a Land God's shrine.

The opportunism surrounding the memory of Puey today, reminds me of what Lenin wrote in the opening passages of his book *The State and Revolution*. Lenin wrote that *"During the lifetime of great revolutionaries, the oppressing classes meted out to them constant persecution, received their teachings with the most savage malice, the most furious hatred and the most unscrupulous campaigns of lies and slander. After their death, attempts are made to convert them to harmless icons, to canonise them, so to say, and to surround their names with a certain halo for consolation of the oppressed classes and in order to dupe the latter, while at the same time emasculating the content of the revolutionary teaching, blunting its revolutionary edge and vulgarising it."* Puey was never a revolutionary, but he was accused by the conservative elites of being a dangerous communist because he believed in Democracy and a welfare state funded by taxation of the rich.

If I were to sum up what Puey stood for, it would be an uncompromising opposition to military coups and dictatorships, opposition to corruption and the need for serious distribution of wealth by building a welfare state. His passionate belief in redistribution of wealth is in complete opposition to the King's "Sufficiency Economy" ideology.

Some claim that he collaborated with dictatorships in the Sarit and Tanom eras. This is not true. My father worked as a government official in the Ministry of Finance, Bank of Thailand and Budget Bureau, because he was educated in Britain on a government scholarship. This scholarship, according to him, was paid for by the taxes on the peasants and the poor. He believed that he had an obligation to repay the citizens of Thailand. He never accepted any political or ministerial positions under the military dictatorship[5], and refused to draw more than one salary, despite being eligible to amass wealth by this method. When he retired from the Bank of Thailand, he dedicated himself to university teaching and a volunteer programme for rural development.

I am confident about my father's beliefs because our family dinner table at *Soi Aree* was an arena for political discussions. The army's dictatorship and corruption were regularly criticised. I remember seeing the piles of water pipes lying by the side of Rama 6 Road as my mother drove me home from school. The pipes were there because the contract to lay them was riddled with corruption. The road was one-way at the time, but army jeeps regularly drove down the wrong way with impunity, much to my parent's disgust. I remember also how my father was criticised for not being a true patriot because he married an English woman, such is the narrow-minded racism of Thai society. I myself experienced that racism every day when I was a university lecturer in Bangkok. Every single day, people would say that I looked foreign and that although I spoke Thai, I spoke it with an "accent". In fact the "accent" was a figment of their imagination, since I speak English with the same kind of voice.

Today there is a statue of Puey at the *Rungsit* campus of *Thammasart University*. People come to pray in front of it for good exam results. My dad hated superstition just like my mum. Inside the "Puey Ungpakorn" library on the same campus, there is a painting of my father in his office with a picture of the King on the wall. To the best of my knowledge, my father never hung such a picture. I know for sure that he refused to hang out flags at our house on the King's birthday, spoke English instead of having to use royal language when he had the misfortune of being in the company

[5] Some people wrongly compare him to Anan Panyarachun, who accepted position of Prime Minister after the 1991 military coup. Anan is a conservative royalist who believes in neo-liberal policies.

of royals, and viewed the King as a contemptible person, hand in glove with the military, and lacking in character! The *Thammsart University* establishment, who have "canonised" Puey, and also Pridi, supported the 19th September 2006 military coup and are royalist Yellow Shirts who see the need to curtail Democracy because the electorate "do not understand Democracy". They are also neo-liberals who are opposed to state welfare.

After the 6th October 1976 blood bath, Puey wrote a passionate condemnation of the events. It is one of his most powerful pieces of writing. He stated that the conservative elites: soldiers, business people and land owners, staged the bloody coup because they felt that Democracy was threatening their interests. He said that all the protests by students, trade unionists and farmers, however disruptive, were part of the process towards Social Justice and that the bloody coup had given the students no choice but the take up arms alongside the CPT.

Today there are many PAD Yellow Shirts who claim to follow in Puey's footsteps. People like Banjong Nasa or Pipop Tongchai are among these opportunist liars. They work hand in glove with some conservative elites who were responsible for the 6th October 1976. Others in the PAD who want to whip up extreme nationalism over *Preah Vihear*, have criticised me for opposing nationalism, saying that they respect Puey, but have contempt for his youngest son. At home, back in the early 1960s, when the World Court ruled that the temple belonged to Cambodia, the family consensus at Soi Aree was that it was a good decision and that the Thai government's objection was nonsense.

I don't expect people in Thai society to agree or to respect Puey. That is their own personal choice, but if anyone claims to do so, they ought to be honest.

My best childhood memories of my father are about summer holidays in Thailand. He organised the best holidays; often travelling by sleeper train, taking me in the sea or introducing me to wonderful foods. I tried to do the same for my daughters Louise and Rosa when they visited Thailand. Rosa especially liked Thai food. I also took them both to my grandfather's village in southern China so that they would remember my father's Chinese roots.

Becoming a Marxist

The massacre at *Thammasart* in 1976 was an important turning point for me and for thousands of other Thais of my age. We later became known as the "October People". Most of them joined the Maoist CPT and took up the armed struggle against the government. I looked for the *Communist Party of Great Britain* in Durham, but found only an old man giving out leaflets to students. A little way beyond him were a bunch of young students selling *Socialist Worker*, the newspaper of the Trotskyist *International Socialists* (IS). I joined them instead. Apart from the 6th October , one other reason why I joined the IS in 1977 was that they took a principled stand against racism, calling the racist politician Enoch Powell an "inciter to murder". It was a refreshing change to meet people who were uncompromisingly anti-racist and not afraid to make honest statements.

Even before 1976, I was becoming interested in socialist politics. In 1970-71, while I was studying at Hammersmith College of Further Education in London, I occasionally read the *Morning Star* newspaper, which was produced by the British Communists. It was there that I met my first wife Rebecca. My Chemistry teacher claimed to be a "Communist", but he was a racist! I was an enthusiastic supporter of the Allende government in Chile, believing it to be a great example of the parliamentary road to Socialism. When the government was overthrown by a brutal coup in 1973, I began to realise that to achieve Socialism, we would need a revolution. In my first year at Sussex University, where I studied Biochemistry, I bought a copy of the *Militant* newspaper. But I was never active in politics, despite there being a miners' strike and a student occupation.

When I joined the IS in 1977 in Durham, I was a Maoist! At the time I was very much influenced by the CPT and by my eldest brother Jon, who I later found out, had joined the CPT. To be fair to him, he did tell me that if he had been in my situation he would probably have joined the IS too. But my mother was appalled. She is a supporter of Old Labour. She was a "conscientious objector" in London during the Second World War, when she met my father at the London School of Economics. My mother accused me of joining a "violent revolutionary organisation".

I used to have endless arguments with the IS comrades in the *Coal Pits* pub, where we had regular meetings. I defended the Maoist peasant revolution. They emphasised the importance of the working class. The person who finally convinced me of the futility of the peasant armed struggle in Thailand was Nigel Harris. He talked to me about Thailand and I read his book on China: *"The Mandate of Heaven"*. The internationalism of the IS was amazing. They had people who took an interest in every part of the world. Not long after I joined the IS, they changed their name to the *Socialist Workers Party* (SWP). We had a public meeting in Durham about the new party. Paul Foot came to speak and I remember him telling us that when we joined the revolutionary party, *"you won't be given a gun"*. It was about building the party rooted in the trade union movement. That summer, I was able to witness the annual Durham Miners' Gala and I was proud to be able to sell a copy of *Socialist Worker* to Arthur Scargill, the militant miners' leader! I had a lot of respect for him even then. He led the miners in support of the Asian women on strike at the photo processing firm "Grunwicks".

The time when we sold most copies of *Socialist Worker* in Durham was when we hit the streets with the anti-Monarchist headline "Stuff the Jubilee!" This was in 1977. Lots of people liked the headline, but a little old lady came up to me and said disapprovingly: *"I could box your ears young man!"*

I had to be a little careful about political activities at the time because I was applying for British citizenship. Being born in Thailand of a Thai father and British mother, I only qualified for Thai citizenship. But after the 6th October massacre, I burnt my Thai identity card and military service papers, which caused me some inconvenience 20 years later when I returned to work in Bangkok!

As a science graduate, I never studied Marxism or Socialism at university. I learnt my Marxist politics and economics as a member of the SWP. They held educational meetings and conferences and encouraged us to read. To begin with, I found it hard to read political books, but as time went on, I found it essential. Apart from Marxist politics and economics, I also learnt about the trade union movement and how to be a shop steward, although I never managed to lead a single strike when I eventually became one. I was edged out of two jobs, one at Blackwells Scientific Publications, and the other as a laboratory technician in the Department of Pharmacology, Oxford University, as a result of union activities. In the mid 1980s I began to systematically study South-East Asian politics, mainly by reading the *Far Eastern Economic Review* in my spare time.

The 1992 mass uprising against the military dictatorship in Bangkok, propelled me into taking Thai politics much more seriously. I had turned my back on Thailand since the late 1970s. I began to brush up on my rusty written Thai and attended political meetings organised by Thai students in Britain. I then had an opportunity to study for an MA in South-East Asian politics and economics at the London School of Oriental and African Studies. This allowed me to obtain a post as a politics lecturer at *Chulalongkorn University* in Bangkok in 1996. I arrived in Thailand with Tamsin just as the Asian economic crisis struck and the international value of our entire savings was halved! Luckily we spent our savings in Thailand due to my low salary as a lecturer.

As soon as I arrived in Bangkok, I went to trade union and political meetings and announced that I was a socialist. My surname ensured that not everyone in those meetings regarded me as a complete nutcase. Soon I began to be invited to meetings of fellow socialists, some of whom were ex-CPT activists. There had been one single attempt by a lone academic to introduce Trotskyism to Thailand in the late 1980s, but this had come to nothing. I set about trying to revive Marxism in a climate when the Maoist CPT had collapsed and most people believed that Marxism was dead. I started to write Marxist pamphlets and books in Thai and I learnt to type in Thai. We had a friendly left-wing printer who would print all our materials at cost price. I opened a Marxism course at the university. People liked to say that I was "the last Marxist in Thailand". I would answer that I was "the first of a new generation". Together with other activists, we built an organisation called "Workers Democracy". The name was a way of calling ourselves Socialist. The anti-Communist act was still on the statute books, but had not been used in practice for many years.

From Workers' Democracy to *Turn Left*

Workers' Democracy started out with 30 members. We had a monthly newspaper of the same name which we photocopied. Some months we might sell up to 300 copies. I ended up writing half the articles, but did manage to get others to write too. We called ourselves Marxist and I managed to get the comrades to agree to a Trotskyist programme. But nearly all the members were not really convinced. There were Maoists, nationalists and trade union bureaucrats in our membership. At first, we were mainly workers and intellectuals. One prominent member was Somsak Kosaisuk, leader of the railway workers union, who later became a leader of the semi-fascist PAD. After a couple of years in *Workers' Democracy*, Somsak and some of his comrades split with us over the issue of nationalism. They believed that the best way to oppose privatisation of state enterprises was to use nationalism. I believed that we had to oppose the free market and promote internationalism. Somsak was known to try to justify keeping enterprises in the public sector by quoting King Rama 5th who founded the railways.

Other members left our organisation because they were NGO activists and weren't committed to building a Marxist party. They didn't see the benefits of weekly meetings and political education, despite being good activists in their own fields. I used to pay yearly visits to Tony Cliff and Alex Callinicos in London, where Cliff would try to give helpful suggestions. I remember his criticism of our initial policy to have monthly meetings. He said *"it isn't a Marxist organisation if you only meet once a month"*. He was right. It was in this period that we turned to student work, partly as a result of prodding by our Australian socialist comrades.

Emphasising student work was very important to us because we recruited many young intellectuals who became Marxist activists. Our membership became younger and more vibrant and we started to build links with Korean, Malaysian and Australian socialists. We went to the World Social Forum in Mumbai, India in 2004 and came home enthusiastic. In Thailand we were an important part of the small movement against the British and American war in Iraq.

We always argued for the building of a socialist party. However, we misjudged the mood in Thai society about party building. There was much talk at the time about the need to build such a socialist party. Some NGO and labour activists were holding discussions. But we later realised that they were just saying the same old things that they had been saying 10 years ago and would continue to say, without acting in a concrete manner. We launched an appeal for a *"Peoples Coalition Party"*, with an anti-imperialist, anti-neoliberal platform. This forced us to be much more outward looking and to work with NGO activists and student groups. We campaigned with others on a whole number of issues such as human rights in the south or neo-liberalism. We worked with a number of NGOs to organise the Thai Social Forum in October 2006. Our new paper, *Turn Left*, was successful in expanding the number of pages and contributors. We also sold more papers. But the party itself was a failure because it was not a "coalition" of radical activists. It was just us and our new young recruits. We eventually abandoned the project and revived ourselves as a Marxist organisation called *"Turn Left"*. This was after the 19th September 2006 coup.

During the Taksin government, we were never *Thai Rak Thai* supporters. We argued against TRT's neo-liberal policies and condemned the government's human rights violations. But we saw TRT's Universal Health Care Scheme and pro-poor policies as a progressive step forward. When the NGOs joined with Sonti Limtongkul in the anti-government PAD, we kept the PAD at arms length because of its reactionary politics.

When the army staged a coup in 2006 we joined with a small group of young activists in the *"19th September Network against the Coup"*. Initially we also kept the small band of Taksin supporters who opposed the coup at arms length too. But two years later when the Red Shirts became a mass movement of the poor for Democracy, we joined them, while retaining our criticisms of Taksin.

"Red Siam" Manifesto 9th February 2009

"The enemies of the Thai people and Democracy may have their army, courts and prisons. They may have seized and rigged parliament and established the government through crimes like the blockading of the airports and other undemocratic actions by the PAD. Yet those that love Democracy, the Red Shirts, have strength in numbers and are waking up to political realities. Disorganised and scattered, this movement of ours will be weak, but a party that is organised and self-led can create a democratic fist to smash the dictatorship.

While world leaders such as Obama struggle to solve the serious economic crisis, the Democrat Government in Thailand is allowing thousands of workers to lose their jobs. The government sees its priority only in cracking down on opposition using lèse majesté. It has even created a web-site where citizens can inform on each other. Troops have been sent into communities and villages to stifle dissent.

The enemies of Democracy have guns, an army and shadowy bosses in high places. But their weakness is that they are united around an absurd and un-scientific ideology: the ideology of the Monarchy. This ideology seeks to make Thais into grovelling serfs. They want us to believe that an ordinary human being, just because of an accident of birth, can be transformed into a God, when the true abilities of the King are no different from millions of ordinary engineers, artists, farmers or skilled workers.

The conservative elites want us to believe that the King loves and takes care of the people. But the Thai population are quite capable of looking after themselves. All that is beautiful and honourable about Thai society has been created by working people.

This King:

grew in stature under the corrupt military dictators: Sarit, Tanom and Prapass.

allowed innocent people to be executed after they were falsely accused of killing his older brother.

supported the blood bath at *Thammasart University* on 6th October 1976 because he felt that Thailand had "too much Democracy". He was also the patron of the violent gang that were called the *"village scouts"*.

allowed the army to stage a coup in September 2006. Furthermore he allowed his name to be used by the army, the PAD protestors and the *Democrat Party*, in the destruction of Democracy.

has been an advocateof economic views which reveal his opposition to state social welfare for the poor. But what is worse, as one of the richest men in the world, the King has the arrogance to lecture the poor to be sufficient in their poverty (through the notion of the *Sufficiency Economy*).

Finally, this King allows his supporters to proclaim that he is "the father of the nation," and yet his own son is not respected by anyone in Thai society!

The elites in Thailand, who claim legitimacy from the King, are exploiters and blood-suckers. They are not the real owners of society. They should remember that their wealth and status is as a result of the hard work of those ordinary citizens whom they despise.

For the millions of Thais who know all this to be true, it is only fear and intimidation that stops us all from speaking this truth out loud.

If we are alone, we will be frightened. If we are together we will have courage. It is time to bring into the open courage and reason in order to destroy the fear in Thai society and to bring light back to our country. We must all ask questions about the present regime, which after all is nothing other than a dictatorship which shrouds us in darkness. When we all stand up and ask questions, they cannot jail us all.

So long as we crawl before the ideology of the Monarchy, we shall remain no better than animals. We must stand up and be humans, citizens in a modern world.

The red, white and blue Thai flag was copied from the West in order to indoctrinate us to be loyal to "Nation Religion and King", the same slogan which was recently used by the PAD protestors who blocked the airports. Yet during the French Revolution, the red white and blue meant "Liberty Equality and Fraternity". This is the slogan we must use to free Thailand from the "New Order" which the PAD and the army have installed.

How can we organise?

Stop dreaming that ex-PM Taksin will lead the struggle to free society. We cannot rely on the politicians of Peua Thai, either. They will only fight within the confines of present structures of society while thousands of citizens wish to go further. Fighting outside the confines of present day Thai society does not mean taking up arms. It means arming ourselves and the masses of pro-democracy people with ideas that can lead to freedom. We must set up political education groups and form ourselves into a party. This party must be led from below by people in all communities, workplaces and educational institutions. Yet we must be coordinated. We must be firm and confident that all of us can be empowered take a lead and determine our policies. This will be our strength. Our weapons will be mass demonstrations, strikes and spreading ideas to all sections of society, including the lower ranks of the army.

As a movement for genuine Democracy, our party must act openly. But in the face of repression through violence and legal means such as lèse majesté, we shall also have to organise secretly. They must not be able to destroy our movement by arresting top leaders. This is another reason why we want self-leadership from below.

What should our common platform look like?

It is not for one person to determine the common platform, which must of necessity be a collective decision. But as a staring point I offer the following ideas, the ideas of one red-shirted citizen.

1. We must have freedom of expression and the freedom to choose our own government without repression and fear.
2. We must have equality. We have to abolish the mentality of "big people-little people". We must abolish the practice of crawling to the royal family. Politicians must be accountable to the electorate, not to shadowy conniving figures beyond popular control. We need to build a culture where citizens respect each other. We must have freedom and equality of the sexes and among different ethnicities. We must respect women, gays and lesbians. We must respect Burmese, Laotians, Cambodians and the Muslim Malay people in the south. Women must have the right to chose safe abortions. Refugees should be treated with friendship and dignity as any civilised society would do.
3. Our country must be a welfare state. Taxes must be levied on the rich. The poor are not a burden, but are partners in developing the country. People should have dignity. The present exploitative society stifles individuals and destroys personal creativity.
4. In our country the King should honour his constitutional role and stop intervening in politics. But the ruling class in Thailand gain much from using the Monarchy and they will not easily stop doing this. Therefore the best way to solve this problem is to build a Republic where all public positions are elected and accountable.

5. For too long Thai society has been under the iron heels of the generals. We must cut the military budget and abolish the influence of the army in society ensuring that it can no long be an obstacle to Democracy.
6. We must have justice. The judges should not claim power from the Crown in order to stop people criticising their decisions. We must change the way that the "contempt of court" law is used to prevent accountability. We need to reform the justice system root and branch. We need a jury system. The police must serve the population, not extract bribes from the poor.
7. Citizens in towns and communities must take part in the management of all public institutions such as state enterprises, the media, schools and hospitals.
8. Our country must modernise. We need to develop the education system, transport and housing. We should create energy from wind and solar power to protect the environment.
9. Our country must be peace-loving, not start disputes with neighbouring countries or support wars.

The dinosaurs of Thai society, the Yellow Shirted royalists, will froth at the mouth in anger at this manifesto, but that is merely the symptoms of people who carry superstitious beliefs from the past, seeking to cling to their privileges at all costs. Their time is finished. We, the pro-democracy Red Shirts will move forward to build a new society.

The elites have no right to rob the people of their dignity in order to prop up their own statuses. This sacrifice of the poor for the benefit of the elites must stop.

Those that say that Thailand is "a special case because we have a King", are merely confirming that the special status of Thailand, which they want to protect, is barbarism and dictatorship. Statements about "National Security" are only about the security for those who exploit and oppress the rest of us. It is not about peace and security for citizens.

This manifesto is just a proposal for a joint platform among Red Shirts. My own view is that our country should move even further to a socialist society, democratic and without class exploitation. But that is a long term goal.

The ruling class only appears powerful because we are crawling on our knees. What we need to do is to stand up, think and act for ourselves. Then we will see how weak and pathetic they really are!

In the past, whether it was during the 1932 revolution or the 1970s struggles against dictatorship, people dreamt of freedom, Democracy and social justice. It is time to turn this dream into reality."

Appendix

Details of lèse majesté charges against Giles Ji Ungpakorn

On the 20th January 2009 the police informed me that I had been charged with lèse majesté because of 8 paragraphs in Chapter 1 of my book *"A Coup for the Rich"*. The paragraphs are reproduced below. Normally, in most lèse majesté cases, it is illegal to publicise or report on the details of charges. It is deemed to be lèse majesté if such details are reported. This ensures a total lack of transparency and a regime of injustice.

According to the official police charge sheet, my lèse majesté charges arose from the fact that the Director of *Chulalongkorn University* Bookshop decided to inform Special Branch that my book "insulted the Monarchy". The bookshop is managed by the academic management of the university.

Paragraphs deemed to have "insulted the Monarchy"

(1) The major forces behind the 19th September coup were anti-democratic groups in the military and civilian elite, disgruntled business leaders and neo-liberal intellectuals and politicians. The coup was also supported by the Monarchy. What all these groups have in common is contempt and hatred for the poor. For them, "too much Democracy"

gives "too much" power to the poor electorate and encourages governments to "over-spend" on welfare. For them, Thailand is divided between the "enlightened middle-classes who understand Democracy" and the "ignorant rural and urban poor". In fact, the reverse is the case. It is the poor who understand and are committed to Democracy while the so-called middle classes are determined to hang on to their privileges by any means possible.

(2) The junta claimed that they had appointed a "civilian" Prime Minister. Commentators rushed to suck up to the new Prime Minister, General Surayud, by saying that he was a "good and moral man". In fact, Surayud, while he was serving in the armed forces in 1992, was partly responsible for the blood bath against unarmed pro-democracy demonstrators. He personally led a group of 16 soldiers into the Royal Hotel which was a temporary field hospital. Here, his soldiers beat and kicked people. News reports from the BBC and CNN at the time show soldiers walking on top of those who were made to lie on the floor. Three months after the 2006 coup, on the 4th December, the King praised Prime Minister Surayud in his annual birthday speech.

(3) The members of the military appointed parliament received monthly salaries and benefits of almost 140,000 baht while workers on the minimum wage receive under 5000 baht per month and many poor farmers in villages live on even less. These parliamentarians often drew on multiple salaries. The government claimed to be following the King's philosophy of "Sufficiency" and the importance of not being greedy. Apparently everyone must be content with their own level of Sufficiency, but as Orwell might have put it, some are more "Sufficient" than others. For the Palace, "Sufficiency" means owning a string of palaces and large capitalist conglomerates like the Siam Commercial Bank. For the military junta it means receiving multiple fat cat salaries and for a poor farmer it means scratching a living without modern investment in agriculture. The Finance Minister explained that Sufficiency Economics meant "not too much and not

too little": in other words, getting it just right. No wonder Paul Handley described Sufficiency Economics as "pseudo-economics"! In addition to this, the junta closed the Taksin government's Poverty Reduction Centre, transferring it to the office of the Internal Security Operations Command and transforming it into a rural development agency using Sufficiency Economics.

(4) It should not be taken for granted that the anti-Taksin military-bureaucratic network is a network led by or under the control of the Monarchy, despite any Royal connections that it might have. Paul Handley argues that the Monarchy is all powerful in Thai society and that its aim is to be a just (*Thammaracha*) and Absolute Monarch. For Handley, Taksin was challenging the Monarchy and seeking to establish himself as "President". There is little evidence to support the suggestion that Taksin is a republican. There is also ample evidence in Handley's own book that there are limitations to the Monarchy's power. Never the less, Handley's suggestion that the 19th September coup was a Royal Coup, reflects a substantial body of opinion in Thai society.

(5) The Monarchy over the last 150 years has shown itself to be remarkably adaptable to all circumstances and able to gain in stature by making alliances with all sorts of groups, whether they be military dictatorships or elected governments. The Monarchy may have made mild criticisms of the Taksin government, but this did not stop the Siam Commercial Bank, which is the Royal bank, from providing funds for the sale of Taksin's Shin Corporation to Temasek holdings. Nor should it be assumed that Taksin and *Thai Rak Thai* were somehow "anti-royalist". For over 300 years the capitalist classes in many countries have learnt that conservative Constitutional Monarchies help protect the status quo under capitalism and hence their class interests. However, it is also clear that the Thai King is more comfortable with military dictatorships than with elected governments. This explains why the Monarchy backed the 19th September coup.

(6) In April 2006 the present Thai Monarch stated on the issue of the use of Section 7 that: *"I wish to reaffirm that section 7 does not mean giving unlimited power to the Monarch to do as he wishes... Section 7 does not state that the Monarch can make decisions on everything... if that was done people would say that the Monarch had exceeded his duties. I have never asked for this nor exceeded my duties. If this was done it would not be Democracy."* However, by September and certainly by December, the King publicly supported the coup.

(7) For this reason there is a very important question to ask about the 19th September 2006 coup. Did the Thai Head of State try to defend Democracy from the military coup which destroyed the 1997 Constitution on the 19th September? Was the Head of State forced to support the military junta? Did he willingly support those who staged the coup? Did he even plan it himself, as some believe? These are important questions because the military junta who staged the coup and destroyed Democracy have constantly claimed legitimacy from the Head of State. Starting in the early days of the coup they showed pictures of the Monarchy on TV, they tied yellow Royalist ribbons on their guns and uniforms and asked the Head of State to send his representative to open their military appointed parliament. Later in his annual birthday speech in December, the King praised the military Prime Minister. We need the truth in order to have transparency and in order that Civil Society can make all public institutions accountable. What we must never forget is that any institution or organisation which refuses to build transparency can only have conflicts of interest which it wishes to hide.

(8) In the early part of his reign the Monarch was young and unprepared for the job. He only became King because of an accident which happened to his elder brother. More than that, the Thai government at the time was headed by General Pibun who was an anti-royalist. Therefore the Monarchy faced many problems in performing its duties as Head of State. This helps perhaps to explain why the Monarchy

supported the military dictatorship of Field Marshall Sarit. It is Sarit who was partly responsible for promoting and increasing respect for the Monarchy. But many years have passed. The status and experience of the Thai Head of State have changed. The Monarch has much political experience, more than any politician, due to the length of time on the Throne. Therefore the Monarch today exhibits the confidence of one who has now gained much experience. For example, he chastised elected governments, like that of Prime Minister Taksin. The important question for today therefore is: if the Monarch can chastise the Taksin government over the human rights abuses in the War on Drugs, why cannot the Monarch chastise the military for staging a coup and abusing all democratic rights?

Glossary

1. People

Abhisit Vejjajiva Democrat Party Prime Minister installed by the military in 2008

Anan Panyarachun Business executive and former Prime Minister installed after the 1991 military coup

Boonyuen Prasertying lèse majesté prisoner

Chamlong Simuang PAD leader and conservative, anti-abortion Buddhist

Chartchai Choonhawan *Chart Thai Party* Prime Minister in the 1980s, overthrown by military coup in 1991

Chattip Nartsupa Radical political economist, Community Anarchist in his later years

Chaturon Chaisang Former TRT Government Minister

Chawalit Yongjaiyut Former army general and head of *Peua Thai Party* in 2009

Chermsak Pintong Broadcaster and former elected Senator, Yellow Shirt

Chiranut Premchaiyaporn Web manager for Prachatai

Chotisak Oonsung Student accused of lèse majesté for refusing to stand for the King's song in the cinema

Chuan Leekpai Former *Democrat Party* Prime Minister

"Da Torpedo" or Daranee Charnchoengsilpakul lèse majesté prisoner

Jakrapop Pencare Former TRT Government Minister and Red Shirt leader

Jatuporn Prompan Red Shirt leader, one of the *Kwam Jing Wan Nee* team

Jit Pumisak CPT intellectual, killed in a gun battle with the government

Jom Petpradap Outspoken TV journalist

Korn Chatikavanij *Democrat Party* Finance Minister, businessman and supporter of the 2006 coup

Kraisak Choonhawan Former elected Senator, son of Chartchai

Kularp Saipradit Socialist writer in the 1930s and 1940s

Natawut Saikua Red Shirt leader, one of the *Kwam Jing Wan Nee* team

Newin Chitchorp Former TRT politician who switched sides to support the military and the *Democrats*

Niran Pitakwatchara Former elected Senator, supporter of the PAD and National Human Rights Committee member

Pairote Ponpet Chairperson of the NGO-Coordinating Committee

Pao Siyanon Notorious police chief in the 1950s dictatorship

Pibun Songkram *(Plaek Pibun Songkram)* Dictator, army Field Marshall and one of the leaders of the 1932 Revolution

Pipop Tongchai PAD leader and NGO elder

Prapart Jarusatien Corrupt military Field Marshall and close associate of dictator Tanom kitikajorn, overthrown in 1973

Prawase Wasi Conservative royalist doctor, link between the state and the NGOs

Prem Tinsulanon Head of the Privy Council and former military Prime Minister

Pridi Panomyong Leader of the Peoples Party, socialist and one of the leaders of the 1932 Revolution, exiled abroad for many years

Pumtam Wechayachai Former NGO leader who became Taksin's right hand man

Rosana Tositrakul Elected NGO Senator and supporter of the PAD

Samak Sundaravej Former PPP Prime Minister in 2009, extreme right-wing politician

Sanguan Nitayarumpong Medical doctor who campaigned for a Universal Health Care System

Sarit Tanarat Corrupt military dictator who came to power through military coups in 1957/58

Satit Wongnongtoey Censorship boss in Abhisit's *Democrat Party* Government

Seksan Prasertkul Former student leader from the 1970s, now a university lecturer

Somchai Nilapaichit Defence Lawyer murdered by police during the Taksin Government

Somkiat Pongpaiboon PAD leader and *Democrat Party* MP

Somsak Kosaisuk PAD leader and retired Railway Workers Union boss

Sonti Boonyaratgalin Army general who led the 2006 coup

Sonti Limtongkul Media tycoon and head of the PAD and *New Politics Party*

Sujinda Kaprayoon Army general who staged a coup in 1991 and gunned down pro-democracy demonstrators in 1992

Sulak Sivarak Eccentric royalist who criticises the King and acts as a social critic

Surachai Sae-Darn Former CPT activist, now a Red Shirt

Surayud Chulanon Military Prime Minister after the 2006 coup, Privy Councillor and butcher of 1992 alongside Sujinda Kaprayoon

Suriyasai Katasila Former student activist and PAD spokesman

Sutam Saengpratoom Former student activist from 1976 and TRT MP

Sutep Teuksuban *Democrat Party* big shot and thug in the Abhisit Government

Suwicha Takor lèse majesté prisoner

Taksin Shinawat Former elected TRT Prime Minister overthrown by the 2006 coup, rich businessman

Tanin Kraiwichien Extreme right-wing Prime Minister installed after the 1976 coup

Tanom kitikajorn Military dictator and Prime Minister after Sarit died, overthrown in 1973

Terdpum Jaidee Former trade union activist and CPT member, now in the PAD

Teptai Senpong Abhisit Government spokesperson

Wanida Tantiwitayapitak NGO Leader of the Assembly of the Poor, former CPT member

Watana Asawahame Gangster politician from *Samut Prakarn*

Wira Musikapong Red Shirt Leader, key member of the *Kwam Jing Wan Nee* team

Wira Somkwamkit PAD activist who tried to start a war with Cambodia

Pro-coup academics

Ammar Siamwalla Neo-Liberal economist, founder of TDRI Research Institute

Anek Laotamatat Academic and politician

Chai-anan Samudwanij Conservative and royalist academic

Chaiyan Chaiyaporn Post-modernist at *Chulalongkorn University*

Kotom Ariya "Human Rights" activist

Panitan Wattanayakorn *Democrat Party* Spokesman

Pratumporn Wucharasatien Retired *Chulalongkorn University* academic

Sopon Supapong Nationalist and former CEO of Bang-Jarg Oil Company

Sujit Boonbongkarn Right-wing political scientist

Sungsit Piriyarungsan Former CPT activist and economist

Surapong Jaiyarnarm Former diplomat

Surat Horakul Political Scientist at *Chulalongkorn University*

Surichai Wankeaw "NGO academic" at *Chulalongkorn University*

Tirayut Boonmi Former student leader from the 1970s and university lecturer

Yuk Si-Araya (***Tienchai Wongchaisuwan***) Former CPT activist and nationalist

Pro-democracy academics

Mahawitayalai Tiangkeun (Midnight University) group Radical academics organised around a website based in Chiang Mai
Chaiyan Rajakool History lecturer at *Chiang Mai University*
Niti Eawsriwong Retired history lecturer, founder of the *Midnight University* but left after a personal dispute
Pichit Likitkitsomboon Ex-Marxist turned Neo-liberal at *Thammasart University*
Somchai Pataratananun Former CPT activist, lecturer at *Mahasarakarm University*
Surachart Bumrungsuk Former student leader from 1976, expert in military matters and lecturer at *Chulalongkorn University*
Sutachai Yimprasert Left-wing history lecturer at *Chulalongkorn University*
Tanet Choroenmuang Red Shirt Lecturer at *Chiang Mai University*
Wipa Daomanee Socialist, former CPT activist and lecturer at *Thammasart University*

2. Places

Ayuttaya Ancient city, powerful between 1350-1782
Chiang Mai Major city in the North
Inkayut Army Camp Notorious army camp in the South where prisoners are tortured
Khon Kan Major city in the North-East
Krue-sa Sacred ancient mosque in the South where people were shot down by the military in 2004
Naratiwat One of the three Muslim Malay provinces in the South
Nong Kai Major city in the North-East
Pattani Centre of the ancient Pattani Sultanate and one of the three Muslim Malay provinces in the South

Prawiharn (Preah Vihear) Temple Khmer temple belonging to Cambodia, on the Thai-Cambodian border

Rachadamnern Avenue Large avenue in the centre of Bangkok, site of many demonstrations and the Democracy Monument

Sanam Luang Large open grounds in front of *Thammasart University* and the Temple of the Emerald Buddha, site of many political rallies

Sukotai Ancient 13th Century city

Takbai Village in Naratiwat, site of protest in 2004 where civilians were murdered by security forces

Ubon Rajatanee Major city in the North-East

Yala One of the three Muslim Malay provinces in the South

3. Organisations

Assembly of the Poor Mass movement of poor farmers

Barisan Revolusi Nasional-Koordinasi (BRN-C) Key insurgent group in the South

Blue Shirts Unofficial paramilitary gang used by the *Democrat Party* Government

Chart Thai Party or ***Thai Nation Party*** Right-wing political party with a history of collaboration with the military

***Communist Party of Thailand* (CPT)** Maoist mass party established in the 1930s, collapsed in the mid 1980s

***Council for National Security* (CNS)** Military junta in 2006

Democrat Party Long standing conservative and royalist party

Krating-Daeng Right-wing gang made up of technical college students in the 1970s

***Kwam Jing Wan Nee* (Truth Today) Programme** Red Shirt TV Programme, founding organisation for the Red Shirts run by Wira Musikapong

Manager Group & ASTV Extreme right-wing media company run by PAD leader Sonti Limtongkul

Matupum Party **(Motherland Party)** Political Party set up by gangster politician Watana Asawahame and headed by General Sonti Boonyaratgalin, 2006 coup leader

NGO-COD National NGO Coordinating Committee

National Reconciliation Commission Commission set up by the Taksin Government to solve the southern violence

Nawapon right-wing gang in 1976

New Aspirations Party or ***Kwam Wangmai Party*** Populist party headed by retired General Chawalit Yongjaiyut before they joined TRT

Palang Prachachon Party or **Peoples Power Party (PPP)** Party set up by former TRT politicians after TRT was disbanded

Palang Tum Party Former political party set up by Chamlong Simuang, now of the PAD. Also included Taksin Shinawat

Pattani United Liberation Organisation Separatist movement in the South in the 1960s

Peoples Alliance for Democracy **(PAD) Pantamit Prachachon Peua Prachatipatai** Right-wing semi-fascist or ganisation that welcomed the coup in 2006 and used violence and the seizure of the airports to help overthrow the elected PPP Government in 2008

Peua Thai Party or **For Thais Party (PTP)** Party set up by former TRT politicians after PPP was disbanded

Prachatai Independent website newspaper

Privy Council King's advisors

Pumjaitai Party or **Proud to be Thai Party** Party set up by former TRT politician Newin Chitchorp

Ramkamhaeng Open University Thailand's first open university in Bangkok

Runda Kumpulan Kecil **(RKK or Pattani State Restoration Unit)** Major insurgent group in the South

Student Network to Defend the People Southern student group

Thai Rak Thai Party or **Thais Love Thais Party (TRT)** Populist party set up by Taksin Shinawat, the first party to win a landslide majority in parliament

Village Scouts Right-wing, mainly rural based, gang used to counter the Left in the 1970s
Wadah Faction Faction of southern Muslim politicians
19th September Network against the Coup Small network that mounted the first anti-coup protest in 2006

4. Concepts, laws, systems

Chumchon-Niyom Community Anarchism
lèse majesté "to insult the Monarchy", a draconian law used to punish political opponents of the conservative elites
October People *(Kon Duan Tula)* The generation who became politicised as students in the 1970s
Sakdina The pre-capitalist system
Sufficiency Economy Right-wing ideology espoused by the King to argue against redistribution of wealth